Contents at a Glance

Contents

Building WebObjects 5 Applications

About the Author

Jesse Feiler is the author of several Mac OS X books including *Mac OS X: The Complete Reference*, *Mac OS X Developer's Guide*, and *Java Programming on Mac OS X*. He is also the author of *WebObjects 5 Developer's Guide*, as well as many books on the Web-based enterprise (such as *Database-Driven Web Sites* and *Managing the Web-Based Enterprise*), the Y2K problem, home offices, databases, and FileMaker. His books on OpenDoc, Cyberdog, Apple Guide, and Rhapsody are now collector's items.

He has worked as a developer and manager for companies such as the Federal Reserve Bank of New York (monetary policy and bank supervision), Prodigy (early Web browser), Apple Computer (information systems), New York State Department of Health (rabies and lead poisoning), The Johnson Company (office management), and Young & Rubicam (media planning and new product development).

His interest in new forms of technical training have led him to MediaSchool (http://www.mediaschool.com), for which he has authored several Mac OS X courses available over the Internet, as well as to Geek Cruises' Mac Mania cruise to Alaska. He is also the first author of a technical book to be published both on paper and on an e-book.

Active in his community, he is President of the Mid-Hudson Library System, Chair of the Philmont Comprehensive Plan Board, founder of the Philmont Main Street Committee, and Treasurer of the HB Playwrights Foundation.

He lives 100 miles north of New York City in the village of Philmont with a rescued greyhound and a cat. His research into iMovie, iDVD, and Image Capture has earned him the sobriquet "The Digital Scourge of Philmont."

Building WebObjects 5 Applications

Jesse Feiler

McGraw-Hill/Osborne

New York   Chicago   San Francisco
Lisbon   London   Madrid   Mexico City
Milan   New Delhi   San Juan
Seoul   Singapore   Sydney   Toronto

270188

JUL 03 2002

McGraw-Hill/Osborne
2600 Tenth Street
Berkeley, California 94710
U.S.A.

To arrange bulk purchase discounts for sales promotions, premiums, or fund-raisers, please contact **McGraw-Hill**/Osborne at the above address. For information on translations or book distributors outside the U.S.A., please see the International Contact Information page immediately following the index of this book.

Building WebObjects 5 Applications

1234567890 CUS CUS 01987654322

ISBN 0-07-213088-1

Publisher	Brandon A. Nordin
Vice President & Associate Publisher	Scott Rogers
Senior Acquisitions Editor	Jane Brownlow
Senior Project Editor	Carolyn Welch
Acquisitions Coordinators	Emma Acker, Ross Doll
Technical Editor	Scott Keith
Copy Editors	Chrisa Hotchkiss, Bob Campbell
Proofreader	Stefany Otis
Indexer	Jack Lewis
Computer Designers	Tabitha M. Cagan, Lucie Ericksen
Illustrators	Michael Mueller, Lyssa Wald
Series Design	Roberta Steele
Cover Series Designer	Greg Scott
Cover Illustrator	Eliot Bergman

This book was composed with Corel VENTURA™ Publisher.

Part IV   **Creating Dynamic Web Sites with WebObjects**

Chapter 13   **WebObjects at Work** **193**

Chapter 14   **Using WebObjects Builder** **215**

Chapter 15   **Using Project Builder** **229**

Acknowledgments

Many people have contributed to the development and production of this book. In more or less chronological order, they are listed here.

To begin with, Carole McClendon at Waterside Productions worked her usual magic with the initial proposal and contract. At McGraw-Hill/Osborne, Jane Brownlow and her assistants Emma Acker and Ross Doll helped move the project along. Senior project editors Carolyn Welch and Lisa Theobald provided excellent assistance in making the book look like it does. Copy editors Bob Campbell and Chrisa Hotchkiss helped to make the text clearer and consistent. Finally, Lydia Griffey and Sherry Bonelli helped see the book through its debut into the world.

In addition, Scott Keith of OpenBase International was a great source of information not only about OpenBase but also about WebObjects. His technical review of the book is a significant contribution.

Notwithstanding the help of so many people, any errors are the sole handiwork of the author.

Preface

The history of the computer age has been of large, complicated devices and technologies becoming smaller and easier to use. This is as true of computers themselves as of the software that runs on them.

When WebObjects was created, it was a tool for the largest corporations to use. Their support staffs included people who were experts in database administration, telecommunications, and programming. Today, WebObjects is a tool for use in small to medium size businesses as well as in enterprises of global scale. That change has come about in large part because of the rapidly increasing demands of small to medium size businesses for dynamic Web sites, sophisticated data management, and transaction processing. The level of sophistication of users has dramatically increased—both Web site developers who use WebObjects to build their sites and end users who use the WebObjects applications.

WebObjects may be the easiest application development tool for the complex applications expected today in all but the most trivial Web sites. Its Direct to Web and Direct to Java Client tools are unsurpassed for building applications and even ad hoc projects for single user, one-time use.

However, WebObjects does pose a problem for many people. Since it brings together so many disciplines and technologies, the learning curve can be steep. This book attempts to address that issue. It provides the background of the various technologies involved, and it shows you how to work with them to achieve your goals. The focus is on real-world problems. You will find actual code sprinkled throughout the book, and you will find the code repeated in several sections.

As one example, the concept of WebObjects display groups is covered twice. Display groups let you specify data to be retrieved from a database and then to display it using the typical Web format of batches of records. If you want, you can add links to each of the entries so that people can explore further (or add items to a shopping cart). You will find display groups discussed in Part III, which focuses on the database side of things with Enterprise Objects Framework. Then, you will find it addressed again in Part IV, which focuses on WebObjects itself.

WebObjects applications almost always use relational databases for their data management. A variety of such databases are used. In this book, OpenBase is used to demonstrate database issues. You can download a free evaluation copy of OpenBase from their Web site (http://www.openbase.com). OpenBase works particularly well with WebObjects, but you will find that any relational database can be integrated with WebObjects. Furthermore, the tools that OpenBase provides are similar to those provided with other databases. The lingua franca of modern relational databases, SQL, is what makes it all work.

How This Book Is Organized

There are six parts to this book.

Welcome to WebObjects and OpenBase

The first part of the book gets you started with the basic concepts behind WebObjects including application servers, object-oriented programming, and modern database technology. If you are experienced with programming, you may be familiar with some of these concepts. Pay particular attention to Chapter 2, The World of Application Servers. This is the fundamental architecture of WebObjects, and everything that follows relies on these principles.

Building a Database with OpenBase

Almost all WebObjects applications use relational databases, and this part of the book introduces you to the concepts and shows you how to use OpenBase to create and manage databases. (Other databases work in much the same way, so this section is applicable to them, too.)

If you are used to desktop databases or to single-user applications, some of the concepts here may be new to you. In particular, whereas personal productivity tools and databases combine interface and database, database managers such as OpenBase separate the two.

Interacting with Databases Using Enterprise Objects Framework

Enterprise Objects Framework converts the relational database you use into objects that can be used in the object-oriented world of WebObjects. This is actually one of the most exciting aspects of WebObjects; it addresses an issue that developers have long struggled with: the question of how to convert database data to objects. The sophistication of Enterprise Objects Framework is justly appreciated by those who use it.

Creating Dynamic Web Sites with WebObjects

Having dealt with the database itself and the object-oriented representation provided by Enterprise Objects Framework, you are ready to actually build a WebObjects application. This section provides the meat of WebObjects itself.

Jump-Starting WebObjects

This part of the book focuses on some of the newer features of WebObjects. In particular, the Direct to Web and the Java Client technologies that let you produce customizable applications quickly. The notion of WebObjects as a big tool for big projects in big enterprises is debunked by some of these jump-start technologies. WebObjects is great for ad hoc data analysis by power users who use these technologies.

Deployment Issues

Finally, the last part of the book addresses some of the deployment issues for databases and for WebObjects. These include performance and the critically important issue of security.

More Information

More information is available on Apple's Web site at http://www.apple.com/webobjects. Information on OpenBase is available at http://www.openbase.com. You can also find updates and other information on the author's Web site at http://www.philmontmill.com.

Welcome to WebObjects

OBJECTIVES

▶ Get to know the big picture of WebObjects

▶ Application servers: See how WebObjects fits into the world of the Web

▶ Object-oriented programming: Find out about the programming environment for WebObjects

▶ Databases: Fit WebObjects into an organization's data structure

WebObjects and OpenBase

IN THIS CHAPTER:

ccording to Apple, WebObjects 5 for Java is "the flexible, scalable way to develop and deploy high-performance network applications." If that sounds a little murky, that's because WebObjects is many things:

▶   It's an application server—software that runs Web sites and mediates between users' browsers and databases or legacy applications.

▶   It's a rapid application development (RAD) environment geared specifically to developing Web-based solutions.

▶   It's a tool for dynamically creating Web pages and for managing complex media (such as video).

This chapter provides an overview of WebObjects and a roadmap to the book.

WebObjects History

Here is how this book began prior to May 2000: This book provides a complete overview of WebObjects and its related technologies. WebObjects is a back-of-the-shop tool—an application server—that integrates databases and legacy applications with dynamic Web pages. It features a rapid application development environment that makes even the development of traditional, static Web pages remarkably easy. It is a tool for Web site developers and managers.

In bringing together the Web and databases, WebObjects allows for the rapid deployment of e-commerce solutions. The WebObjects user base is an impressive collection of some of the world's major corporations: Standard & Poor's, Toyota, AT&T, the BBC, Fleet Bank, and more (including the Apple Store). As a critical component of these companies' Web presence, WebObjects runs on a variety of platforms, including Windows 2000, Mac OS X Server, HP-UX, and Solaris; in addition, it interacts directly with databases such as Oracle, Sybase, and Informix. It is frequently deployed in complex environments with multiple copies of the software running to manage a heavy load of transactions.

As is the case with such high-end products geared to the corporate market, pricing is determined on a sliding scale based on usage: the number of processors at a given site on which it runs, for example. The price of WebObjects ranges from just over $1,000 to $50,000.

Apple changed the rules in May 2000—not just for WebObjects, but for the entire application server market segment. Apple stopped pricing WebObjects on a sliding scale; a uniform price of $699 was set. (Yes, $50,000 marked down to $699.) Apple also announced the next version of WebObjects—WebObjects 5 for Java. Instead of maintaining separate code for the various platforms, WebObjects now runs as a Java application on any platform that supports Java.

The price change was significant because it signaled a major shift in the use of WebObjects. None of the features changed and no functionality was dropped, but the substantially lower price meant the following:

► E-commerce functionality and dynamic Web pages were accessible to individuals and small businesses as well as to large corporations. They could be implemented *the same way* they were on the largest sites.

► The modern development techniques that are part of WebObjects (object-oriented programming and the rapid application development tools) let everyone develop for the Web in the same way. No longer are there two types of development environments: the corporate information technology world with large development budgets and the make-do world of CGI scripts, Perl, and hand-written Hypertext Markup Language (HTML).

► The WebObjects deployment tools enable sites to be managed on high-speed connections from home offices and small business.

The last time large-scale corporate technology was made available to individual users, small offices, and home offices, a revolution swept through the world. Desktop publishing was made possible by the relatively low-priced laser printers, What You See Is What You Get (WYSIWYG) graphics, and the easy-to-use graphical user interface (GUI) of personal computers. (Not surprisingly, Apple was at the forefront of that advance, too.) You may remember a world of mimeograph machines, carbon paper, and mechanical paste-ups. It was a world in which the look of printed communications clearly separated the "pros" from the hoi polloi. That world is gone forever. High-quality printed communications are within everyone's reach (although not everyone chooses or is able to achieve the highest standards).

WebObjects (at its new, lower price) promises a similar revolution. Many individuals have tried (and succeeded to varying degrees) to put up e-commerce sites and dynamic pages. It is always a shock to someone with a small Web site to discover the difficulty of implementing e-commerce, shopping carts, or even a welcome page that greets a returning user by name. It *can* be done, and it *is* done. However, many of the solutions are jury-rigged; furthermore, they are often profoundly unscalable. That is, they work (barely) for the intended purpose, but it is hard to change or expand them. WebObjects is not only powerful but also scalable (as witness the many corporate sites that use it). For smaller users, WebObjects is the beginning of a reliable, flexible, and powerful development and production environment; it replaces other environments that aggressive and innovative small-scale users have pushed to their limits.

How will this change the computing environment? Most likely, the Web equivalents of mimeograph machines and mechanical paste-ups will seem quaint in a few years. Those equivalents are handcrafted HTML pages, scripts written in Perl or other scripting languages, and awkward bridges to and from legacy systems and databases. The rapid application development tools of WebObjects can yield significant productivity improvements to Web site designers and implementers.

In addition, like the desktop publishing revolution, the overall quality of the output (in that case, printed communications, but in this case, Web sites) will probably improve. As the new technology becomes more widely available and accessible to more people, it will be feasible and cost-effective to use it for even the smallest project. (If you don't believe this, look in a file or archive for a church or school newsletter from 20 years ago; you will probably be shocked at the low quality—by today's standards—of the design.)

Finally—and again, just as with desktop publishing—many intermediaries will disappear from the picture or find their roles redefined. This does not mean that everyone can become a Web designer overnight (or ever). What it does mean is that the possibility of experimentation is open to all; it also means that everyone has more control over the work that they do or want done. A complex Web site may still have a large staff devoted to creating and maintaining it; however, less and less of that work will be the drudgery that is the nasty little secret of Web site development today.

Another intermediary whose role may well be changed is the Web site host. The advent of broadband connections (including cable and DSL) and of highly reliable Web servers at low cost means that it is feasible for many individuals and small businesses to run their own sites. In the excitement over the growth of the Web, it is not often noted that most Web sites get very little traffic. Many sites may get only a few hits (if that) over the course of a week. Because of the overhead involved in creating and maintaining a Web site, many smaller sites are unable to be managed on their own; people use "free" pages on commercial services such as AOL instead. Coupled with the broadband connections, the deployment tools of WebObjects can change all of this.

Those are the changes that Apple set in motion. As a result of the lower pricing, a vast market of individuals and small businesses has access to the functionality, development, and deployment tools that heretofore were the sole dominion of large corporations. The consequences of this breakthrough are likely to be significant improvements in productivity in creating and maintaining Web sites, an increase in the overall quality of Web sites (at least those that use WebObjects), and an increase in efficiency as intermediaries and barriers to Web site development and support are reduced.

Notwithstanding the vast expansion of the WebObjects world, the traditional WebObjects users remain at the core of the Apple market. For existing and new corporate customers, WebObjects continues to provide the features they are accustomed to using. Productivity improvements and efficiency are all relative: in a one-person operation, they may mean the difference between being able to support a Web site and not doing so, but in a global enterprise, they may mean the difference between profitability and the reverse. (Note, too, that as with desktop publishing, ease-of-use and widespread access to new technology also empowers individuals and small workgroups within the organization.)

WebObjects: The Big Picture

What exactly is WebObjects and where did it come from? The answers to those questions help you understand how to use WebObjects.

WebObjects is an application server. It is software that runs on a Web server and generates HTML pages to be downloaded to users' browsers. In generating those HTML pages, it uses templates, and it draws on connections to databases and other applications.

One of the features that makes WebObjects distinctive is its rich suite of development tools and its adherence to object-oriented design. These provide an easy-to-use and powerful development environment. In addition to being an application server, WebObjects is also a development environment.

WebObjects originated at NeXT, which Steve Jobs started after he left Apple Computer in the late 1980s. The company manufactured computers; in the process, it developed its own operating system. The hardware part of NeXT was dropped, but the operating system (called NeXTStep) was ported to Intel and other hardware. NeXTStep gained a reputation of being an excellent development platform and of being very stable, and it gained a new name—OpenStep. In the late 1990s, Apple Computer purchased NeXT to obtain the operating system, which became the basis for its next-generation operating system, Mac OS X.

WebObjects arose at NeXT in the early 1990s as an outgrowth of their database kit that let developers easily integrate databases into NeXTStep applications. When Apple bought NeXT, WebObjects came along.

Apple's long-standing leadership in computer graphics and video played a role in the evolution of WebObjects as a tool for providing rich graphics. To its two original roles—application server and development environment—you can now add Web publishing, particularly for sophisticated media.

The next step for WebObjects is its widespread availability. No other product of this sophistication or complexity is priced at this level (although other application server vendors are in the process of rethinking their pricing).

WebObjects: The Details

WebObjects has a number of components and features. Each is described in depth later in this book. These components and features interact with one another, and you will find that you may need to jump back and forth, depending on your specific needs and background, so that you get all of the pieces together in a way that makes sense for you. For now, here is a brief guide to WebObjects components and features.

Enterprise Objects Framework

Enterprise Objects Framework is a framework—an object-oriented set of components—that encapsulates database data and the operations you need to perform on it. You write WebObjects code that interacts with Enterprise Objects Framework, which defines the specific database for use by WebObjects but without any of the product-specific concerns for the database manager that actually is to be used. Separately, you connect Enterprise Objects Framework to a specific database and database manager. Your WebObjects code is thus immune to most of the vagaries of distinctions among database managers.

Databases today are remarkable for their similarity and stability. They are, after all, among the most mature products of the computer age. All major databases today use SQL and they use the relational model.

Using Enterprise Objects Framework, you can describe the data that you need to work on in a WebObjects application. In a sense, Enterprise Objects Framework lets you define the nouns of your application: WebObjects—with its operations—defines the verbs.

Development Tools

Project Builder, Interface Builder, WebObjects Builder, and Enterprise Objects Modeler are the tools that you use to develop WebObjects applications. Each has a powerful and sophisticated graphical user interface that lets you drag and drop objects, draw connections, and otherwise implement your application with a minimum of typing. Each tool focuses on a different part of the WebObjects application:

▶ **HTML pages**   Use WebObjects Builder to create HTML pages and to link their elements to business objects from the database or within the application.

▶ **Java Clients**   Use Interface Builder to design your interface and to link its elements to your Java code.

▶ **Business objects**   Use EOModeler to create business objects and interact with your database.

▶ **WebObjects projects**   Manage the entire WebObjects project with Project Builder.

Deployment Tools

In addition to development tools, WebObjects comes with powerful deployment tools: Monitor, and Record and Playback Manager. These tools were developed to support WebObjects in its original environment: large-scale Web sites in large enterprises. They are among the most powerful deployment tools available to Web site and Web application developers.

Monitor provides a means to manage and create configurations for your WebObjects application. WebObjects can run in very complex environments with multiple copies of itself running on multiple servers. Tuning network-based applications is extraordinarily tricky, and Monitor helps you do that.

Record and Playback Manager does just what its name says: it lets you record individual Web sessions and play them back later for testing. Using Record and Playback Manager, you can create test suites to test not only the functionality of your WebObjects application, but also its stability and performance under stress (when you play back multiple sessions at the same time).

Production Environments

WebObjects itself runs on Mac OS X, Windows 2000, Solaris, and HP-UX. WebObjects 5 for Java is the first version written totally in Java. That means that it runs on any computer that supports Java; however, Apple certifies it with thorough testing only on some platforms.

NOTE

The WebObjects software that runs on all platforms under Java is the runtime software that interacts with a Web or HTTP server. The development tools run on fewer platforms. But the WebObjects applications that you develop can then run on any of the supported runtime platforms.

Development Environments

Most WebObjects applications interact with databases. WebObjects uses JDBC adapters to access these databases. In this book, OpenBase is used for all database examples.

Database Environments

A lot of WebObjects applications interact with databases. This interaction is through the use of adaptors for various data sources. The data sources supported directly by WebObjects are Oracle, Sybase, OpenBase, and Informix. Data sources can also be legacy and enterprise systems; WebObjects supports adaptors for PeopleSoft and SAP. In addition, WebObjects adapters are supported for open database connectivity (ODBC)—an open interface to relational databases ranging from mainframe products to personal computers.

OpenBase

WebObjects serves up rich data over the Web and usually that data comes from a database. Since 1991, OpenBasehas been a leading relational database on platforms such as Mac OS X (before that on NextStep), Windows, and Linux. It has been used with WebObjects and with Enterprise Objects Frameworks on many projects, including some of the examples that ship with WebObjects. Although its functionality is comparable in many ways to that of larger, enterprise-scales databases such as Oracle and Informix, its pricing makes it a feasible choice for small to medium sized enterprises, as well as for larger enterprises that need its reliability and ease of installation and support.

Although adhering to platform-neutral SQL standards, OpenBase takes advantage of the Aqua interface to Mac OS X as well as WebObjects and Enterprise Objects Frameworks. It is tied to those products and supports them more than any other database. It can be used with other applications servers and frameworks, too. Because of its integration with and support of WebObjects and Enterprise Objects Framework and in view of the fact that it is readily available (trial versions are available with WebObjects itself and for free download from http://www.openbase.com), OpenBase is used in the examples in this book.

In addition, the second part of this book focuses on the use of OpenBaseManager in creating and maintaining databases. You can use it for stand-alone databases as well as for databases accessed by other software applications than WebObjects. That part of the book will help you in each of these situations.

Before You Start: Two Cautions

Before getting started with WebObjects, you should note two cautions. Its ease of use does not always translate into reduced development and implementation time, and it can live quite happily on a private intranet or local area network (LAN) as well as on the Internet.

Some people look at the ease-of-development and think it means brief development time. In many cases, that's true. However, it can also mean significantly higher quality because more iterations of design, development, and testing can fit into a project's schedule. (In practice, both brief development time and high quality are often achieved.)

This book describes the development process primarily as a straight road from project inception to deployment and maintenance. In reality, however, there are many detours, experiments, and false starts. This is an absolutely normal part of development, and WebObjects makes it easy.

You can use WebObjects to deploy applications on individual computers and on various networks that are not connected to the Internet. You often use the Internet, but it's not necessary. Likewise, although you often use databases in WebObjects applications, they are not required.

The World of Application Servers

IN THIS CHAPTER:

Internet and Web Basics

Multi-Tier Application Design

This chapter explores the world of application servers—of which WebObjects is a significant part. The following are major aspects of this world:

- ▶ Object-oriented programming (the subject of Chapter 3)
- ▶ Relational databases (the subject of Chapter 4)
- ▶ The Internet and the World Wide Web in particular
- ▶ Multi-tier application design

Chapter 1 discussed WebObjects and its components. The names and terms covered in that chapter are specific to WebObjects. This chapter, on the other hand, addresses the general world of application servers. The terms and concepts discussed here are generic: they apply to WebObjects, to other application servers, and, in fact, to other software that is widely used today.

Internet and Web Basics

WebObjects is designed to run on the Web or to use Web standards to run on a local area network (LAN). Commercial use of the Internet is barely a decade old, and the World Wide Web itself is only slightly younger. Today, hundreds of millions of people around the world use both the Internet and the Web—often with little effort. (Ongoing updates of worldwide Internet use, along with details of the methodology in gathering the information, can be found at http://www.nua.ie/surveys/. According to information posted on this site, about 7 percent of the world's population have used the Internet in the last three months.)

Pioneers (that is, users from the early 1990s) know much more about the innards of the Internet than many sophisticated users today. Much of the complexity of the Web has been hidden inside wizards and assistants for the user; Internet functionality is now incorporated in word processors and a host of other programs. As a result, some of the basic terms, as well as some of the architecture, of the Internet and the Web are not widely known.

This section is not a complete guide to the Internet and the Web; rather, it touches on only those aspects and terms that you must know to work with WebObjects.

The Importance of Standards

The Internet and the Web are widely used because they rely on simple standards that define interfaces that people can easily master (such as e-mail and the World Wide Web). Anyone who has tried to connect computers and terminals by using technology other than the Internet can attest to the fact that simple standards are essential.

NOTE

An interesting sideline to the history of the Internet is the rise — and fall — of IBM's System Network Architecture (SNA). SNA was a powerful and sophisticated network design; many people believe that it was far superior to Transmission Control Protocol/Internet Protocol (TCP/IP), which became the Internet standard. TCP/IP, however, has one outstanding advantage over SNA: it is much simpler. The moral is that simplicity is paramount, particularly relative to technologies that are to be widely used by many people. Complexity — either sophistication or poor architecture — carries with it large costs in terms of training, development, and support. The Internet standards demonstrate this.

RFCs

Originally, Request for Comments (RFCs) were documents that presented rough suggestions for Internet standards; over time, however, RFCs have themselves become the standards. They pass through a variety of stages until they are final. A standard format exists for RFCs, which includes references to other standards—and, in particular, to standards that are made obsolete.

When in doubt about how an Internet standard works, consult the appropriate RFC. When you wonder if a proprietary product implements a feature that is over and above (or inconsistent with) an RFC, the RFC will help you to find out.

Standards Bodies

The major Internet and Web standards bodies all have Web sites (of course). The following are the standards bodies to which you might occasionally need to refer:

- ▶ **World Wide Web Consortium (W3C) (http://www.w3c.org)**   This body sets standards for the World Wide Web. It manages protocols, including HTTP, eXtensible Markup Language (XML), and other Web-specific standards.

▶ **Internet Corporation for Assigned Names and Numbers (ICANN) (http://www.icann.org)**   This body licenses registrars of domain names. From the ICANN site, you can find a registrar to license an unused domain name for you.

▶ **Internet Society (http://www.isoc.org/)**   This group is the umbrella for Internet standards. The following two groups are chartered by the Internet Society.

  ▶ **Internet Engineering Task Force (IETF) (http://www.ietf.org)**   This group consists of network designers, researchers, developers, and others interested in the evolution of the Internet. RFCs can be found on this Web site. (They are also located on many other sites throughout the Internet.)

  ▶ **Internet Advisory Board (http://www.iab.org)**   This group provides architectural oversight of the Internet (as opposed to the lower-level, more hands-on work of the IETF).

Transitions and Advances

A particular concern with Internet standards is that they be able to evolve. Note that most standards are backward-compatible with prior versions—that is, new versions of standards can be implemented without breaking older versions that are in use. Version control is essential for the smooth running of a network with a variety of devices operating at a variety of locations.

This concern was built into the Internet standards process from the start. You should also build it into your WebObjects applications from the start. Unless you are creating a deliberately short-lived WebObjects application (for example, to support a political campaign or the release of a movie), you should plan for how your WebObjects applications will grow and evolve.

Dealing with Nonstandard Features

Standards make life easier for everyone—but they are not the be-all and end-all. The standards used on the Web and the Internet all allow for controlled exceptions. Particularly when dealing with legacy systems, you may need to take advantage of these exceptions. However, try to minimize the nonstandards and use as much of the standards as possible.

TCP/IP

TCP/IP is the core communications protocol for the Internet. It specifies everything from *IP addresses* (Internet protocol addresses—the quartet of numbers that specifies an individual node on the Internet) to the format of messages.

TCP/IP deals only with communications; it does not specify the medium over which the communications runs. TCP/IP can run over twisted-pair wires, coaxial cable, wireless media (infrared, satellite, or wireless LAN), or other media (experiments with electrical power distribution lines for the use of telecommunications are underway in some places).

The communications medium for your WebObjects application may change—particularly when you take into account the rapidly-changing wireless technology. Developers and designers have gotten used to computers that only get faster and monitors that only get larger. The rather limited power and screen size on a personal digital assistant or wireless telephone represents an enormous step down in capabilities. Because TCP/IP is independent of the medium, all of the technologies that take advantage of TCP/IP—that is, all Internet protocols—are capable of running over wireless networks and winding up on portable devices.

HTTP

HTTP is used to request Web pages and to transmit them back to the requestor. Two particular aspects of HTTP will become important to you as you use WebObjects: the request/response cycle and sending data.

NOTE

Strictly speaking, HTTP lets you request a resource from a given location on the Internet—a Uniform Resource Identifier (URI), which is normally a Uniform Resource Locator (URL). (A URI is a more general form of URL.) The resource is normally a Web page, but it can be much more (or less).

Request/Response

An HTTP request is a sequence of requests and responses. Browsers take care of this behind the scenes, but you should be aware that your single request is converted into this sequence. The request can, for example, ask that the resource be returned if it has been modified since a certain date and time. (This is how your browser's cache gets the latest version.) The response can consist of the Web page requested; it can also consist of an error code such as the ones you see on many sites (404 for Not Found, for example).

Both an HTTP request and a response contain header fields: the parameters for the request are placed in these fields (`if-modified-since`, for example), along with status codes for the response (204—No Content, for example).

NOTE

RFC 2068 contains the allowed values for request header parameters and status codes for responses. This matters because browsers handle these status codes. If you want to return an error or some other notification to the user, using a status code means that this can be handled at the HTTP level. Creating your own status codes—such as one indicating "Your account is overdue"—requires coding at the HTML level.

Each request/response cycle is separate from the others. As a result, the Web is said to be *stateless*: it does not preserve the state of an individual user over time. Some software other than the Web protocols needs to keep track of what is in your e-commerce shopping cart, what your last search was in a database, and so forth.

TIP

Managing state is an important part of WebObjects.

Sending Data

Frequently, data must be sent along with the HTTP request. For example, when you enter data into a form on a Web page, that data needs to be transmitted when you click the Submit button.

There are two ways of sending data in HTTP requests: in searchparts and in forms.

Using Searchparts   In their headers, all HTTP messages specify a method. The most common one is GET: you use it to get a particular resource (usually a Web page). The HTTP request may be followed by a searchpart. After the URL, a question mark (?) introduces the searchpart. The searchpart consists of one or more pairs of named values. The syntax is specified in the HTTP standard, and it is quite simple. The name of each data pair is entered, it is followed by an equal (=) sign, and the value completes the pair. If more than one pair is entered, an ampersand (&) separates each pair. For example, here is a searchpart with two data pairs that follows a URL: `http://www.yourbusiness.com/ personnel&name=jose&division=sales`.

Keep the following in mind:

▶   A searchpart is part of the HTTP request, and it must consist of valid text characters. Invalid characters must be *escaped*—that is, preceded by a backslash (\) and the hexadecimal equivalent of the invalid character. A space, for example, is escaped as \80.

► The data transmitted in a searchpart can be visible in a browser's history and in other locations.

► It is impractical to transmit large volumes of data (as well as nontext data) in a searchpart.

Forms   For large volumes of data, nontext data, or data that you want to keep reasonably secure, you can use the HTTP `post` method. This transmits the data as part of the message part of the HTTP request (not in the URL). Forms use the `post` method.

NOTE
Forms frequently contain hidden fields, the contents of which are transmitted when the Submit button is clicked.

HTTP and Web Servers

HTTP requests are transmitted over the Internet; they are routed to the IP address of the computer specified in the URL. This routing is accomplished through the Internet's Domain Name System (DNS), which consists of domain name servers with routing tables throughout the Internet. Most Internet nodes have some form of DNS support to route their own traffic; if they do not, they rely on an upstream domain name server. (*Upstream* refers to a server that is far away from the end user and close to Internet backbone networks.)

Once the request arrives at the appropriate location, it is routed by local configuration files to the software that will process the request. That software is called an *HTTP server*; it is sometimes called a Web server, but because its business is processing HTTP requests, HTTP server is the more appropriate term. Examples of HTTP servers in common use are Apache, Microsoft Internet Information Server (IIS), and iPlanet (formerly Netscape's HTTP server).

The function of the HTTP server is to process the request and return the resource requested (or an appropriate error message). How the HTTP server fulfills the request is up to the server: the standards and protocols specify *what* it does, not *how* it does it.

And here lies the key to WebObjects. When a WebObjects page is requested, the HTTP server communicates with the WebObjects application; it passes along any incoming data to WebObjects. WebObjects does whatever processing is necessary, and it returns an HTML page to the HTTP server; the HTTP server, in turn, sends that HTML page back to the requesting user.

This pattern is the key to application servers. In fact, protocols govern the communication between an HTTP server and the software that processes HTTP requests in this way. The most common protocols (which are all supported by WebObjects) are as follows:

▶ **Common Gateway Interface (CGI)**   This interface usually relies on interpreted code. It is the oldest and simplest interface.

▶ **Internet Server Application Programming Interface (ISAPI)**   This is a set of dynamic-link libraries (DLLs) that can be called by the HTTP server. Being compiled rather than interpreted, its operations can be faster than CGI. It is used in the Windows environment.

▶ **Netscape Server Application Programming Interface (NSAPI)**   Similar to ISAPI, NSAPI is also compiled; it is used in the Windows environment as well as others.

▶ **Web Application Interface (WAI)**   This CORBA-based interface to Netscape Web servers is supported by WebObjects.

▶ **Apache**   The Apache module API is code that is compiled and linked into Apache. One of the Web's most used HTTP servers, Apache runs on UNIX, Windows NT/2000, and Mac OS X.

The application that delivers the requested resource to the HTTP server can do anything: it can interact with legacy systems, it can access databases, and it can even send its own HTTP requests to other HTTP servers and process the returned resource for retransmittal.

TIP

Make sure you understand the request-response process: everything else in this book depends on it. If you think you are missing something because it seems too simple, you are not. It is simple, like the Internet, and that's why the simple request-response process works and why this architecture has become so important today.

HTML

HTML is the basic language in which Web pages are written. It is a simple, text-based language designed to be processed easily by browsers. HTML combines content and formatting instructions into elements that are surrounded by tags. A paragraph consisting of the words "Welcome to our site!" looks like this:

```
<P>
Welcome to our site!
</P>
```

The opening and closing tags are identical in this case, except for the slash (/) that appears in all closing tags. Tags do not necessarily have to be paired: some tags can stand on their own. A nonbreaking space, for example, is often coded like this:

```
<NS>
```

Originally, Web page designers had to create HTML by hand, using word processors and basic text editors, but today, specially designed Web software does it for you. Graphically oriented Web-page-creation tools include Microsoft FrontPage and Adobe DreamWeaver. These products let you design a Web page just as you would create any other document; the underlying HTML is generated automatically for you.

For some reason, many Web page designers foreswear the use of such graphical tools. Perhaps they feel that because they had to suffer with the complexity and inefficiency of handcrafted HTML, others should, too. They do have one important point: sometimes the HTML generated in these programs contains stray tags that do not affect the appearance but can potentially cause problems.

Particularly as text is modified and rearranged, you may wind up with empty paragraphs such as the following:

```
<P></P>
```

There is nothing in the paragraph, and it does no harm to the appearance of the page. However, seven extra characters need to be transmitted, and the receiving browser needs to receive, process, and parse them. This is not a significant amount of processing, but for heavily used pages, it can add up.

TIP

Use graphically oriented HTML authoring tools, but review the resulting HTML code for the most time-critical pages that you create.

WebObjects works from HTML templates that you create. Special WebObjects elements are defined, and you can use them as you create your pages. When WebObjects responds to a request from the HTTP server, it does whatever processing is necessary to translate the WebObjects elements into HTML.

XML

Like HTML, XML is a Standard Generalized Markup Language (SGML). When used in conjunction with cascading style sheets (CSS, described next), it can be quite powerful. XML is similar to HTML but differs from it in two important ways:

▶ Its syntax rules are stricter than HTML. In its tags, for example, capitalization (case) matters.

▶ It is used to describe data; the formatting is handled in a style sheet.

XML can be used in quite complex ways; it also happens to provide a very efficient and portable way of transmitting data with descriptions of it. Just like a searchpart for an HTTP request can contain a data pair such as

```
Name=jose
```

XML can contain the following data:

```
<name>
jose
</name>
```

The definition of data elements such as this is described in Chapter 12. What matters here is that—as with a searchpart—plain text is used to structure and identify the data. (XML data can be something other than text, but its identification—its element name—is text.)

XML is widely used on Web pages; it also is becoming a lingua franca for parameters and other meta-information that needs to be transmitted from one user to another. XML is used extensively within WebObjects.

NOTE

In days of slow computers and communication and small disks and memory, free-format text-based architecture was wildly inefficient. It was much more efficient to specify character positions 17–26 as the name. That information was coded into programs and not transmitted with the data. Hence, there was less data to store and transmit. Of course, there was more programming to do, but the tradeoff was wise. Today, transmitting the location and name of data elements does not impose an undue burden on the resources making up the Web and its users.

Cascading Style Sheets

Cascading style sheets are often used as a companion to XML, but they can also be used with HTML. They remove formatting information from the basic Web page.

As a result, the Web page can specify a format such as Confidential, and it can be implemented (in the style sheet) as red, bold, and italic. Style sheets can override one another in a given user's environment. The Web page need only reference the basic style, and it will appear differently according to each individual's style sheet.

LDAP

The Lightweight Directory Access Protocol (LDAP) is just what its name suggests: a basic directory protocol. Data in LDAP consists of named pairs (name/value). WebObjects supports LDAP as a data source.

Multi-Tier Application Design

After half a century of the computer age, certain trends stand out even to the most casual observer. Computers get smaller, faster, and cheaper; more and more people use them; and they get easier to use. All of these facts are related: much of the increased power of computers goes into sophisticated interfaces that make them easier to use.

Yet another trend is less apparent, but it is at the forefront of every technology manager's consciousness. Writing computer code is very expensive. Each line of code needs to be designed, written, tested—and then maintained for the life of the system. A variety of methods have attempted to reduce these costs, but none is more effective than this: write as little code as possible. That strategy lies in large part behind the change of computer software design from monolithic, primordial ooze architectures to modern multi-tier architectures (using WebObjects, of course).

Primordial Ooze

At the dawn of the computer age, each program was custom written from scratch. There were no operating systems: there was nothing but a collection of vacuum tubes (usually) and crude input/output devices. Everything that the computer needed to do had to be coded into each program.

Before long, the coders (as programmers were called then) realized that they were rewriting the same code over and over. They found ways to share snippets of code. Not only did this cut down on coding time, but it also improved efficiency. After all, if code to compute a trigonometric function had been written—and debugged—it could be used without additional work.

Code libraries arose during the late 1950s; they contained common functions and routines. At the same time, the architecture of the computing environment was evolving; one of its design goals was to maximize the reuse of code. Thus, operating systems were developed. One critical role of an operating system was to manage the computer. Therefore, the code for printing, reading from tape, and so forth was moved out of individual programs into the operating system.

Separating the entire program into smaller units that could be reused helped to manage the task of programming.

This process relied on standard interfaces; without them, programming segments could not be reused. Without standards, you have a more complex situation than you had before; with standards, you can reuse code.

The Rise of Transaction Processing Operating Systems

By the 1960s, programs could be written that were quite complex. Operating systems, too, became more complex as the logic to support sophisticated processing was added to them. IBM's Customer Information Control System (CICS—informally pronounced "kicks") remains in use today in many organizations such as banks.

NOTE

After having marketed CICS for 30 years, IBM has discovered that it is an application server. The term did not exist when CICS was developed, but that is how it is marketed now.

At that time, computers were used only in large organizations. They were run by professional operators, and for the most part, they were programmed by in-house programming staffs. While some common packages existed for functions such as payroll, most software was custom-written.

The concept of a transaction was essential to CICS and similar operating systems. A *transaction* is a set of operations—usually involving values—that all occur as a group. The individual steps may be assembled over time (an operator may go through several screens' worth of data to complete your airplane seat reservation, for example), but at one moment, all of the information is processed and accepted— or rejected—in toto. If a transaction is processed and accepted, it is said to be *committed*. If it is rejected, any intermediate database updates need to be undone; they are said to be *rolled back*.

Most data processing in the 1960s (and much of it today) consisted of transactions. The freewheeling world of the personal computer is much less transaction oriented. When you type a document in a word processor, for example, saving a version has some aspects of a transaction, but normally you think of a continuing flow of operations.

The Web was designed for this freewheeling, "surfing," and linking kind of behavior. As e-commerce has moved onto the Web, it has become necessary to implement transaction processing, but the basic Web protocols do not support transactions.

WebObjects does support transaction management so that you do not have to worry about its implementation. You do, however, need to define transactions: what they are, when they start, when they stop, and what happens when they are committed or rolled back. This is typically not so much a programming task as a task for the business managers. Ideally, it is done as a joint endeavor.

Client/Server

With the development of ways to reuse code as well as the rise of sophisticated operating systems that could handle transactions, more sophisticated applications were created. One way this sophistication was manifested was in easier-to-use interfaces. Instead of preparing data on punched cards, operators could use screens with advanced features (eight colors, for example) to highlight and organize data. Naturally, these complicated applications required more powerful computers on which to run.

The development of desktop and personal computers helped to bring hardware costs under control. Instead of using a mainframe computer to handle the user interface, a program could run on the personal computer. That program could communicate with the mainframe, and it needed only to transmit and receive data; the screen backgrounds could be generated on the personal computer. This two-tier architecture was named client/server. It spread throughout the corporate computer world, and it remains in common use today. (The browser on a personal computer communicating with an HTTP server at another location is basically a client/server implementation.)

The client (personal computer) was responsible for the display and entry of data as well as for its transmission to the mainframe. At the mainframe end, the data was manipulated as necessary. The separation of client hardware and software from server hardware and software added complexity to system design; however, this separation made it easy to increase the number of clients (and the complexity of their interfaces) because you could simply add more terminals. (In the old, monolithic architecture, additional computing power was needed on the mainframe.) This architecture is shown in Figure 2-1.

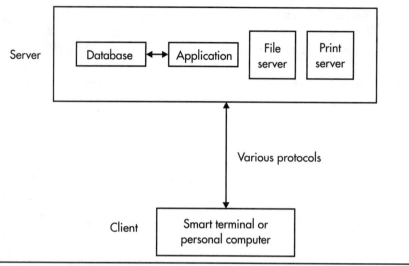

Figure 2-1   *Two-tier client/server architecture*

On the server, the application software often took advantage of existing functionality. Three types of servers were commonly found: file, database, and print servers.

▶   A file server read and wrote files in any format under the direction of the program on the personal computer or on the server.

▶   A database server (often a database management system—DBMS) stored and retrieved data at will. Its standard interface was usually SQL, and requests were sent from the application on the personal computer.

▶   A print server received instructions to print data as needed. The data was transmitted from the user interface application on the personal computer.

Client/server architecture looks quite clear on paper; however, in practice, implementation has not always been simple. Some people thought that the server software could be sharable among enterprise systems: a common corporate database, for example, might be used by payroll, inventory, and other applications. With this notion, customization for a specific business application could be done solely on the clients and their software.

In practice, though, this did not happen. Client/server systems almost always involve custom-written code on both the clients and the server. And the business logic winds up being distributed to both sides as well. However, on both the clients and the server, significant savings could be achieved by using file, database, and print servers as well as by using interface components that could be reused (more or less) from application to application on the clients. Furthermore, in addition to these benefits, the client/server system was less expensive than having a single computer capable of powering all the terminals in a large system.

Three-Tier Architecture

The next refinement of the architecture used three tiers: in addition to client and server tiers, an intermediate tier devoted solely to managing communications was added. This tier consisted of an HTTP (or Web) server. Figure 2-2 shows three-tier architecture.

This architecture was a tremendous improvement over traditional client/server architecture. For example, the HTTP server could work as a switch among a variety of applications—after all, its only role was to process HTTP requests one after the other. Client/server applications frequently used dedicated terminals.

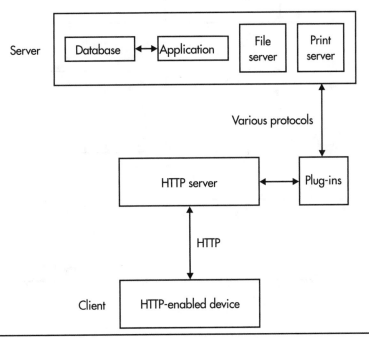

Figure 2-2   *Three-tier architecture*

Still, all was not well. Custom code in the form of plug-ins or other extensions needed to be added to the HTTP server to interact with databases and other traditional servers. Enter multi-tier architecture.

Multi-tier Architecture

The architecture of application servers emerged—multi-tier, as shown in Figure 2-3. In this architecture, the client level, personal computers, cell phones, or other HTTP devices communicate via TCP/IP with an HTTP server.

The communications between the client tier and the HTTP server is via HTTP. Another tier—the application server—was added to interact with databases and the

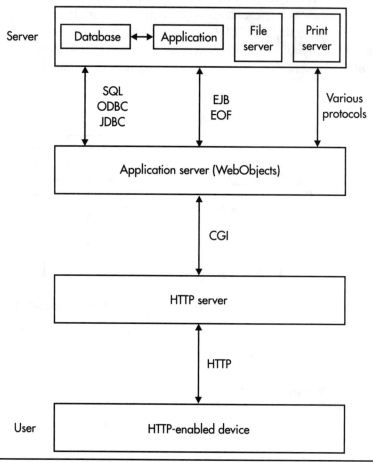

Figure 2-3 *Multi-tier architecture*

like. The application server communicates with the HTTP server via CGI or one of the standard interfaces.

NOTE

CGI, ISAPI, NSAPI, WAI, and Apache are all supported by WebObjects. CGI is used to refer to all of them unless a specific reference is needed. That eliminates the ambiguity of the generic word interface while avoiding the prolixity of a more complex phrase.

Adding a tier made the entire second tier (the HTTP server) totally generic because it consists of HTTP, CGI, and related protocols. This also made the software quite portable. All of those protocols are designed to work equally well around the world or in a single room.

The application server—WebObjects in this case—is also remarkably portable. On one side, it communicates with the HTTP server using CGI or a similar protocol; on the other side, it uses SQL, ODBC, or JDBC to communicate in a product-neutral, standards-based manner with databases.

The multi-tier architecture is powerful and efficient not only because the inter-tier communications are based on standard protocols, but also because the operations are factored into self-contained tiers and servers. The multi-tier architecture can be extended indefinitely. Additional tiers communicate with one another and with WebObjects as needed. Clients can be personal computers or devices such as cell phones; they can be network computers (thin clients). Their functionality can be confined to running a Web browser. Issues such as power, platform, and the like can be ignored. (Of course, specific applications can require more or less functionality on the client.)

This architecture can be—and often is—extended. The application server may communicate directly with legacy systems and terminals using protocols other than HTTP or CGI. Application server architectures, however, always assume at least HTTP and CGI interfaces.

The multi-tier architecture described here is powerful and valuable for a variety of reasons. It separates functionality as much as possible into standards-driven components. It also eliminates as many dependencies as possible that are not essential to the business operation. (For example, the choice of client terminal is limited only by the browser capabilities required.) As a result, application-specific code is not only minimized, but, because it is typically business-oriented, its specification and review at a detailed level can be done by the user.

Factoring the business logic out of the interface and operations of the back end is one of the greatest cost savings of multi-tier architecture.

Note, however, that the architectural diagrams shown in this chapter (particularly the three- and multi-tier diagrams) are conceptual representations. It is misleading (and generally wrong) to think that customized business logic can be confined to a single middle tier or even to several of them. Customized business logic might well need to be implemented on the client as well as in databases and other bottom-tier "standardized" tools. You may need JavaBeans, AppleScript, and various browser plug-ins on the client to carry out business logic operations. Likewise, you may need to implement customized field edits and other database features in a shared database just for a specific application. You can confine business logic largely to one or more intermediate tiers, but it pops up in the top and bottom tiers, too. Thus, although the databases and other bottom tiers are standardized in their architecture, these additions might be needed to customize them.

CHAPTER 3

Object-Oriented Programming

IN THIS CHAPTER:

Object-Oriented Programming Defined

Object-Oriented Programming Terms and Concepts

Advantages of Object-Oriented Programming

Components and Frameworks

L ike Chapter 2, this chapter presents concepts that underlie WebObjects but that are not specific to it. These concepts underlie all modern programming techniques and languages.

NOTE

If you are going to program WebObjects, you must be familiar with the concepts presented in this chapter. If you are going to use WebObjects to create a Web site and are not going to add custom-written code to it, you can safely skip this chapter; however, understanding these concepts will help you to use WebObjects and to appreciate how its tools work.

Object-oriented programming is yet another step toward the goal described in Chapter 2: do not write new code. If you do not write new code, you do not have to design, develop, test, or maintain it. Clearly, one way to avoid writing new code is to reuse existing code and to use standard routines as well as generic databases and the like.

However, sometimes the existing code will not suffice. In such cases, object-oriented programming can help by providing an architecture in which code can be reused with slight variations. The slight variations are carefully defined so that you only have to write, test, and maintain the changes to the code; the basic functionality (that has already been developed and tested) remains.

This structure—which allows you to deal with exceptions and modifications to code in an orderly manner—is very powerful. Most modern programming languages are object-oriented: C++, Objective-C, and Java are three popular examples.

Object-Oriented Programming Defined

Early programming languages were *procedural* (or *imperative*—a synonym in this sense). They consisted of instructions that were carried out one after the other. Conditional tests sometimes changed the sequence of instructions, and transfers from one part of the program made the sequence variable; nevertheless, the code was basically executed one step at a time.

Object-oriented programming, which began in the late 1960s with Simula and Smalltalk, takes another approach. This approach is based on *objects:* data structures encapsulated with routines that operate on them. Each object behaves in some ways like a small, self-contained program with its own data and operations.

Each object consists of data elements and methods (or functions). Most objects have both data and methods, but some objects have only data or methods (and some special objects have neither).

NOTE

Object-oriented programming languages have varying roots; as a result, their routines may be called either methods or functions. The terms are interchangeable.

Data elements can be any fundamental data types such as integers or arrays; they can also be other objects. Indeed, some objects are designed solely to manage other objects: list objects, for example, are common tools for object-oriented programmers.

Objects can be abstract or they can have parallels in the real world or in the programming world. For example, applications frequently have customer objects, invoice objects, and so forth.

Object-oriented programming is more complex than traditional procedural programming. It certainly requires more learning and experience to write successfully, and it also requires more up-front design and analysis. However, the benefits, such as code reuse and easy maintenance, pay off enormously.

Object-Oriented Programming Terms and Concepts

Object-oriented programming is not only more structured but more carefully defined than traditional programming. This section introduces the terms and concepts of object-oriented programming, which include the following:

- ▶ Encapsulation and accessor methods
- ▶ Interface access
- ▶ Inheritance
- ▶ Polymorphism
- ▶ Initialization
- ▶ Destruction
- ▶ Other methods
- ▶ Multiple inheritance
- ▶ Classes versus objects
- ▶ Instantiation, identification, and location

Encapsulation and Accessor Methods

An object's methods can perform any operation they want (subject to the constraints of the programming language, of course). One common operation is to access the data within the object.

The data elements within an object are normally not exposed to other objects and programs; they are said to be *encapsulated* within the object. As a result, other objects need to use *accessor methods* to access the data. Accessor methods come in two varieties known colloquially as setters and getters. *Setters* usually take one argument and set the encapsulated data element to that value; *getters* usually return a value that is the current value of the data element.

Not all of the data elements in an object will have a setter and a getter: some data elements are totally private and are used only by methods of the object. Others may be read-only or write-only and will therefore have only a getter or a setter.

NOTE

In most object-oriented programming languages, you can design objects whose data elements (or some of them) are visible to the outside world. Totally encapsulating data elements is a design principle that is usually enforced by programming standards within an organization. You certainly must write more code to use setters and getters, but experienced programmers can usually cite one or two war stories involving setters and getters that came to their rescue as code needed to be modified quickly.

Accessors can often come in groups, with several of them accessing the same data element. For example, an object might contain an individual's first and last name; you could devise two hypothetical accessors to return the name in conventional form and in reversed order (last name first—suitable for alphabetizing). In this scenario, `GetNameConventional` would in fact be an accessor that accesses two data elements (first and last name); `GetNameLastNameFirst` would access those same two data elements and return them in reverse order.

Accessors can also manipulate the data in an object. A loan payment object, for example, might have a method called `GetPayOffAmount (paymentDate)`, which would—for a given payment date—calculate the amount due based on the principle, interest owed, and other information within the object.

NOTE

Accessors get and set data elements at the behest of the programmer. When you need to modify data in response to user actions, you can create changers: accessors that modify the data and also mark the document as "dirty" or needing to be saved. Changers often call accessors. Mixing the two functions—data access and dirtying records—is poor style.

Interface Access

An object's methods and data elements make up its *interface*. You can manipulate the access to that interface by declaring methods (and, in some cases, data elements) to be of different security levels.

In all object-oriented languages, public interface elements are visible to anyone using the object. Private interface elements are usable only within that object's methods. Protected interface elements are visible to that object and to its descendants. In Java, final interface elements cannot be overridden.

A well-implemented object has a variety of access levels: if everything is declared as public, it is either a small utility object (and well-designed), or it is a poorly implemented object that does not hide its innards appropriately.

TIP

The reason for hiding an object's data and some of its methods is to control access to them. By doing so, you allow yourself freedom to modify the object later. If only certain accessors are made public, you have carte blanche to change how you process the object's data and otherwise manipulate it. If everything is public, programmers (and perhaps you in a moment of carelessness) may start to rely on how the processing is done. As a result, modifications to the inner working of the object can break other code. Hide everything you can!

Inheritance

So far, you have seen how objects are structured with data elements and methods; however, you have not yet seen how they can minimize the amount of code that you must write when minor exceptions are made to existing code. *Inheritance* is the feature that achieves that goal.

An object can be said to inherit from another. In that case, it has all the methods of the original; however, the descendant can override or reimplement some or all of the methods. This is how you can create an object that behaves just like another one, with the exception of a certain (carefully controlled) change. And this is how well-tested code (in the original object) can be reused with controlled changes. Inheritance is the key to the productivity benefits of object-oriented programming.

In addition to overriding or reimplementing methods of an ancestral object, descendants can implement entirely new methods. Descendants can themselves be overridden, forming a chain of inheritance from a fairly basic object to more and more complex or specific descendants.

NOTE

The design of objects for a given system is a matter of trial-and-error (as well as experience).

Polymorphism

Polymorphism goes hand in hand with inheritance. *Polymorphism* refers to the situation in which the method of an ancestor object is reimplemented in descendants. You call the method and the appropriate object responds in the appropriate way.

Thus, you can write code in which you call a customer object's `GetCustomerStatus` method. A descendant of the customer object—perhaps a preferred customer object—would respond differently from another one.

Sometimes, a method is declared but not implemented in an object. Its implementation is left to the descendants. Such a structure occurs in the case where each descendant needs to implement the method in its own way, but there is no default behavior that the ancestor could implement.

Such cases occur when the ancestral object is designed not to be implemented by itself. This is referred to as an *abstract base class:* one that is designed only to be overridden.

NOTE

See "Classes vs. Objects" later in this chapter for more on abstract base classes.

Designing object structures involves deciding which data elements and methods are common to all objects in a set and which are different. You can handle distinctions among related objects by creating new types of objects as well as by adding data elements to objects. For example, you may have a basic object that contains a name and address; a descendant of that object could be a customer object, and another descendant could be a vendor object.

Each object would call the ancestor's `GetNameAndAddress` method, but only the customer object would have a `GetCreditLimit` method. Furthermore, both might have polymorphic implementations of a `GetCurrentBalance` method; in the case of the customer object, it would return the balance the customer owes, and in the case of the vendor object, it would return the balance that you owe to the vendor. In this case, `GetCurrentBalance` would be declared but not implemented in the basic name and address object. It would be said to be *stubbed* in that situation.

TIP

If you are not used to object-oriented programming, you may be tempted to use a variable to identify distinctions such as that between a name-and-address record (in traditional parlance) that refers to a customer and one that refers to a vendor. You might have a variable called `typeofrecord` *with values such as* `customer` *and* `vendor`. *That solution is hardly ever as good as having two different types of objects. They may share a common ancestor (such as* `person` *or* `company`*), but having separate customer and vendor objects makes object-oriented programming simpler.*

Initialization

Initialization methods are used to set the data elements of a newly created object to predefined values. Some languages (such as C++ and Java) have *constructors:* methods with a specified name (the name of the object class) that are called automatically when objects are created. Constructors are used to set data element values to a known state—often zero or blank.

Initialization methods are often called later to set data element values to specific values for a given object. (Initialization methods are often no more than a sequence of calls to setter methods.)

NOTE

When constructors are used, they must function quickly and must not fail. Their purpose is to leave the object in a known state as expeditiously as possible. Initialization routines can afford to access databases, make calls across a network, and perform other tasks that can take time and might fail.

Destruction

Destructors are the flip-side of constructors. They are part of the garbage-collection process to reclaim no-longer-needed memory. Destructors can also set references in other objects to states in which they no longer point to the destroyed object. Destructors are written in C++ if they are needed, and they are called automatically in that language. In Objective-C, `dealloc` is automatically called to do garbage collection. In Java, this is all done automatically.

Other Methods

Other common methods and sets of methods handle *persistence*—reading and writing as well as other types of object storage. Some objects have methods to display themselves; many objects have debugging methods.

Many similar objects have sets of methods—protocols in Objective-C and interfaces in Java. Such sets of methods allow for objects that are not related in an inheritance hierarchy to share sets of methods (which they must implement for themselves).

Multiple Inheritance

Multiple inheritance is an object's ability to be descended simultaneously from two ancestors. Multiple inheritance is supported in C++ but not in Java or in Objective-C; as a result, it is not used in WebObjects applications (which do not support C++), but the concept is included here for the sake of completeness.

Protocols (Objective-C) and interfaces (Java) implement many features of multiple inheritance without the ambiguities and conflicts that sometimes occur in C++.

Classes vs. Objects

In object-oriented programming, *classes* are defined in programs. When those programs run, *objects* are created from those class definitions. (See the following section for more details.)

The distinction between the definition or concept of an object (its class definition) and the actual object that exists at run time is important to bear in mind; in practice, however, few people have trouble with it.

Instantiation, Identification, and Location

Where do run-time objects come from? Many wonderful and complex diagrams of object-oriented systems exist, but it is not always clear how all those arrows get implemented and how each object is connected to each other object. In the world of WebObjects and application servers, this concern is particularly relevant. Multiple copies of WebObjects may be running on a single computer, and multiple databases may exist. The details of development and deployment include keeping all of this straight.

From within a given program, you create an object from a class either by calling a method of a factory object whose responsibility it is to create *instantiations* or *instances*—which is what these newly-created objects are or by invoking an operator such as new. (This differs from language to language.) In either case, the constructor— if there is one and if the language supports constructors—is called automatically and the object that is returned to you is in a safe condition.

In a complex environment, the situation is more difficult. You may need to issue a call to an intermediary that will create an object in another application and pass a reference to it back to you. In such cases, you need to be able to identify an object in another process's environment. The process of identifying objects—particularly remote objects in distant locations and/or objects created by other applications—is an important issue in object-oriented programming.

NOTE

This topic is discussed further in "Components" later in this chapter.

Run-time objects, once instantiated, usually must be explicitly destroyed or released. This is different from simple variables such as integers or even arrays, in which their storage locations are released on exit from the block or procedure in which they are declared.

In a multi-user environment, releasing objects can be difficult. The person who created the object may be done with it before other people are finished. You can use reference counts and other mechanisms to handle this issue. Basically, you do not destroy an object when you are done: you merely indicate that you are done with it. The language and/or environment takes care of actually releasing memory when the last user is finished with a given object.

TIP

In Java, garbage collection and the destruction of objects at the appropriate time is done automatically. If you are reading or revising code written originally in Objective-C or C++, you can skip these steps in Java.

Advantages of Object-Oriented Programming

Object-oriented programming is widely used because it has proved its value in simplifying code and maximizing code reuse.

Simplifying Code

Methods in objects tend to be shorter—shorter than functions and procedures in traditional programs. A good method performs one task simply and straightforwardly.

Distinctions between similar but different processes and data are usually represented by different objects; in traditional programming, status or case variables frequently represent those distinctions. Thus, in traditional programming, you might have an account type variable that distinguishes between checking, savings, and investment bank accounts. Throughout the application, case statements or if statements would switch to separate sections of code to correctly implement the needed functionality.

In an object-oriented environment, you can create an abstract base class—account. You can create instances of checking account, savings account, and investment accounts as subclasses. Within each subclass account, there need be no if or case statements: the processing is alike for all instances of the subclass.

The absence of if and case statements is significant because it means that methods can run in a straightforward manner from the first line of code to the last. Conditional execution frequently generates errors. Furthermore, a change to an account type in this scenario would require changes to many procedures; in object-oriented programming, you can create a new account type that descends from the initial account type and in which only the modified behavior changes. Here is what such a hierarchy might look like:

▶ **BankAccount**   Abstract base class

▶ **CheckingAccount**   Class that is instantiated under business practices of the bank

▶ **CheckingAccount2**   Class that is instantiated after a certain date under revised business practices

`CheckingAccount2` in this scenario might implement only one method—perhaps an override of an interest calculation in `CheckingAccount`. `CheckingAccount2` might reflect bankwide policy changes (in which case, all `CheckingAccount` objects would be converted). It also might reflect accounts opened only after a certain date. Managing this complexity in a traditional environment is much more complicated.

Maximizing Code Reuse

Object-oriented programming provides a way to reuse code by making differences between different objects and implementations manageable, as the example given previously has shown. In practice, methods are easily separated into those that implement business logic and those that implement internally necessary functionality (such as display or persistence). Code for methods implementing business logic is usually so simple that users can review it—even line by line.

TIP

In designing object-oriented systems, learn to distinguish between the similar and the different. You may define abstract base classes (or abstract intermediate classes) to codify common data elements and methods that descendants will use. The simplification of the executable code in object-oriented design is accompanied by a complication of program structure: but in almost every case, the tradeoff is well worth it. Program structure can be reviewed once; code needs to be reviewed every time it is modified.

Components and Frameworks

When objects are reused, they can be reused singly or in collections. Two types of collections of objects are pertinent in object-oriented programming: components and frameworks.

NOTE

Although objects are run-time instantiations of classes, it sounds peculiar to many people to speak of collections of classes that can be reused. In fact, it is, indeed, the classes—the abstract definitions of not-yet-instantiated objects—that can be collected and reused.

Components

Components are objects or collections of objects that are intended for use in a distributed environment. They frequently correspond to real-world objects or to elements of business logic.

The meaning of component varies in usage, but the most widely used is the one presented in this chapter: objects or collections of objects that are intended for use in a distributed environment and that may or may not correspond to real-world objects or to elements of business logic. Microsoft's Component Object Model (COM) is an example of a somewhat confusing jumble of the words *component* and *object*. Using the word *object* to refer to objects within your own application and *component* to refer to objects within other applications or on other computers may help clarify what you are talking about; however, be aware that this distinction is not acknowledged in the world of object-oriented programming.

Three architectural models for components are currently used. They allow you to interact with components in a variety of environments. Each model provides a mechanism for giving your application a reference to a component in another environment; it also provides a mechanism for exposing your components to other applications in other environments.

WebObjects supports all three architectures; this means that your WebObjects applications can interact directly with objects and components from other environments.

NOTE

You do not have to understand all three architectures: you need only investigate those that are used by applications with which you have to interact.

CORBA

Almost all vendors support the Common Object Request Broker Architecture (CORBA) except Microsoft. It is managed by the Object Management Group (OMG) (http://www.omg.org), a major player in setting object standards in a platform-neutral and networked world.

CORBA was developed from IBM's System Object Model (SOM), which was first released two decades ago. Version control, security, and networking are among its strengths: not surprising when you consider its IBM mainframe heritage.

Although Microsoft does not support CORBA, an interface between Microsoft's object model, COM/DCOM, does exist.

COM/DCOM

The Common Object Model (COM) and the Distributed Common Object Model (DCOM)—sometimes combined as COM/DCOM—are Microsoft's first approaches to shared objects and components. COM was envisioned as a desktop model: it was designed to manage the interactions among applications sharing objects on a single personal computer. DCOM extended that functionality to networks.

This evolution meant that networking, security, and version control—strengths from CORBA's mainframe heritage—were retrofitted onto COM. These are precisely the three most difficult features to retrofit into an architecture. Complaints about COM/DCOM have abounded over the years; nevertheless, the architectures have been widely used, particularly in Windows applications.

SOAP

Microsoft announced a new architecture, .NET, in 2000. It is superior to COM/DCOM in that it does design in networking, version control, and security from the start. In addition, because it is based on eXtensible Markup Language (XML), it appears to have a more open and logical architecture than COM/DCOM. At its heart is the Simple Object Access Protocol (SOAP) that was proposed as a World Wide Web Consortium (W3C) standard by DevelopMentor, IBM, Lotus, Microsoft, and Userland Software. Also parts of .NET are SOAP Contract Language and SOAP Discovery Language—both tools to work with distributed objects.

Object Request Brokers

Diagrams involving the identification and use of remote components and objects often include an object request broker (ORB) that actually does the work. If you want to track this down to its roots, do not worry about looking for an ORB as a running process or application. ORBs do not exist as separate entities. They are compiled into application programs that need their functionality as libraries.

IIOP

OMG's Internet InterORB Protocol (IIOP) takes ORBs one step further, from libraries inside individual applications to fully networked entities that can communicate with one another and with one another's objects. WebObjects supports IIOP so that you can get to objects in other environments and across the network.

Frameworks

A *framework* is a collection of classes that implements a certain type of functionality. WebObjects, for example, is a framework.

Other commonly used frameworks are Microsoft Foundation Classes (MFC), MacApp (the original framework on the Macintosh and the most widely used framework in the late 1980s), PowerPoint (a cross-platform framework from CodeWarrior), and Cocoa (formerly NextStep and OpenStep, the development framework on Mac OS X).

General-purpose frameworks typically provide classes for objects, display, command handling, and so on. Specialized frameworks—such as WebObjects— address specialized concerns (such as the management of dynamic Web pages, file transfer, e-mail, and so on).

The WebObjects documentation provides a guide to the major classes of WebObjects; this book focuses on the most critical ones. You may feel that you need to override some classes to do precisely what you want to do, but first make sure you understand exactly what is happening. You typically call WebObjects methods, but you do not frequently override them in basic WebObjects applications. You do, however, create (and override) objects of your own.

A second framework comes with WebObjects called the Foundation framework. It provides general-purpose classes for manipulating text (including Unicode strings) and handling a variety of programming chores.

Enterprise Objects Framework

Enterprise Objects Framework (EOF) is part of WebObjects. It encapsulates business logic and data, and it interacts with WebObjects using objects.

Databases (along with most legacy systems) are not object-oriented. They consist of fields and records that need to be assembled into objects to interact with WebObjects. Enterprise Objects Framework does this.

Enterprise Objects Framework also provides an array of standard classes to manage editing, persistence, and contention. It is the subject of the third part of this book.

Enterprise JavaBeans

In some ways similar to EOF, Enterprise JavaBeans is "a component architecture for the development and deployment of component-based distributed business applications," according to the specification document. Based on JavaBeans and through them on the Java language, it provides a platform-neutral way of addressing many of the same issues that Enterprise Objects Framework addresses.

Based on the Java Development Kit (JDK), the java.rmi.Remote interface (for remote processing), the java.io.Serializable interface (for persistence), and the Enterprise JavaBeans interfaces (such as EJBMetaData, EJBHome, EJBObject, EnterpriseBean, and SessionBean) provide the basis on which application-specific components such as shopping cart, customer accounts, etc., can be developed.

Databases Today

IN THIS CHAPTER:

Overview

Terminology

Database Design

Aspects of Database Programming

T his chapter completes the introduction to WebObjects and its underlying technologies by focusing on databases. Long at the heart of enterprise computing, databases remain massive and critical components; they have also quickly claimed a powerful role in the development of the Web. (Some would say that databases have remained at the center of large-scale computer operations: it is the Web that is new.)

This chapter discusses database technology, the terminology you need to know, database design, and aspects of database programming. If you are approaching WebObjects as an experienced Web master, this information may be new to you; if you have basic knowledge of databases, you may also find a new perspective here. In either case, the terms and design issues described are used throughout the rest of the book.

Overview

From the start, computers have been called on to handle three tasks: computation, communication, and data management. Of these, computation is the least-performed task; computation-heavy applications include simulations (of weather, for example) and processing of massive amounts of data (in generating and manipulating images, for example). In most cases, though, computation and other features are used to support networking, communication, and data management.

Databases are among the oldest software products in the computer world: they certainly are decades older than word processors, spreadsheets, and other products familiar to PC users. The maturity of database products and database architecture means that you can count on a stability that can be quite a change for people who have spent the last decade dealing with the evolving Web.

The Database Market

If you are embarking on a WebObjects project and you have a database in place, you will probably use that database. On the other hand, if you are starting out with WebObjects but you do not have a database, you need to understand the following distinctions between the products.

The database market today is split into three major segments: desktop products, high-end products, and midrange products. Products in each of these categories can interact directly or indirectly with WebObjects; in addition, many of them have their own Web capabilities built in. The distinctions are somewhat arbitrary. (Microsoft, for example, considers SQL Server a high-end product.) However, the chief distinction among the products is their pricing structure.

Desktop Products

Desktop products such as Microsoft Access and FileMaker are designed to run on individual or networked personal computers. Desktop products are normally priced per computer; access over a network is often included in the purchase price. Prices are normally less than $1,000, and each product has an entry-level version that sells for less than $500. These products are sold like most PC software: you license the product, but in practice, having purchased/licensed it, it is yours to use as you see fit. Upgrades are issued routinely and can be purchased.

High-End Products

High-end corporate products such as Oracle, DB2, Informix, and Sybase are geared primarily to enterprise customers. High-end corporate products are licensed for use—often on specific computers—for a given period of time. Annual licenses are common, and they frequently are negotiated on an individual basis. In addition, limits to the number of processors and volume of transactions are common. These products are normally installed and maintained by IT staffs.

Midrange Products

Midrange products, including Microsoft's SQL Server, OpenBase, and FrontBase, target networked personal computers. Midrange products are typically purchased (like desktop products) and may come with transaction restrictions based on their price. Upgrades from one level of transaction to another can be done simply by paying an additional fee.

The Roles of Databases on the Web

A database contains a compendium of data. On the Web, that data is used in a variety of ways:

▶   It can power e-commerce sites.

▶   It can provide information as an end in and of itself.

▶   It can be used to publish content and support Web sites.

Powering E-Commerce

In some ways, powering e-commerce is one of the simplest uses of databases on the Web. Although implementing e-commerce on the Web is complex, the actual database support—invoices, inventory, and the like—is quite similar to that of traditional commerce. What differs with e-commerce is the need to support intermediate steps—a shopping cart, for example.

If you are going to be working in the e-commerce world, it is worth your time to look at existing commerce solutions to study their database designs. Invent only what is unique to your endeavor—and it will probably not be much. There really are not many variations on commerce. Furthermore, you may see some features that you can easily add to your operation.

Providing Information on Demand

Databases store and manipulate data: the Web (particularly using WebObjects) can provide an easy-to-use front end to these databases. This information can be made available to the public; it can also be used for internal information that must not be seen by others on the "outside" (such as personnel information). The database, its information, and its operations become the goal (or in some cases, the product).

Examples of in-demand use of databases include online banking and in-house and online human resource data systems. Whereas e-commerce relies on the same types of databases as offline commerce, providing information on demand is different from traditional forms of providing information.

When someone calls a corporate human resources office to inquire about the status of accrued vacation time, a clerk checks the data (often in a database) and provides the response—as well as the answers to other employee questions. When the employee accesses the information directly, however, those questions can go unanswered—or a mechanism needs to be in place to provide the answers. This supporting information (which people expect) often substantially enlarges the scope of an online publication project.

TIP

In planning an in-demand type of application, make sure you prepare for the need to supply vast quantities of additional data to support those who are less sophisticated data users.

Using a database to provide information also brings up questions of privacy, security, and accuracy. By providing people with direct access to a database, you remove the intermediation of skilled people with knowledge of the data, and therefore reduce some of the privacy concerns.

TIP

A system that allows direct access normally needs much more stringent error checking support than an internal system. In addition, this kind of system is subject to a far greater variety of mistakes and adventures from people who use it perhaps once a year rather than those who are paid to use it every day.

Publishing Content and Supporting Web Sites

The final role for databases on the Web is in publishing content and supporting Web sites. In this case, databases are as behind-the-scenes as they are in their support of e-commerce (and traditional commerce); however, database support is directly for Web sites.

Web sites, after all, are usually collections of large quantities of data, and databases are designed to manage large quantities of data. It makes sense to store traditional data, such as names, addresses, and inventory items, in databases for presentation on the Web, but it also makes sense to store purely Web site–based data in a database to present the information. For example, you can store the text of variable Web pages in this way, which can be much more efficient than updating Web pages every time some information changes.

Imagine, for example, a database that corresponds to an HTML form on a Web page with the following fields:

► Text to display

► Web page on which to display it

► Date/time at which to start displaying it

► Date/time at which to finish displaying it

Entering data onto a database form is much easier than routinely creating and/or updating an entire HTML page and then loading it onto a Web server via FTP. To upload a page manually to a Web site, someone needs FTP access to that site. Either all changes must be routed through a trusted uploader (thereby possibly delaying the process in the case of illness or vacation), or a variety of people need to be trusted with FTP access. In addition, the database strategy is a much more secure way of working: databases and WebObjects implement security very well.

Terminology

As befits a mature technology, databases have a settled terminology. The main elements of database jargon are defined in this section. They are used in the book to describe databases, and they also appear frequently in the discussion of WebObjects.

NOTE

Relational databases are described in the section that follows. Some of the terms here are defined from the relational point of view. Because most databases today are relational, the exclusion of other types should be excused.

What Is a Database?

The first term to define is *database*. It can refer to a specific database—as in a database of artwork for a gallery—or it can refer to the product that runs that database—Oracle, DB2, OpenBase, or the like. To be correct, the product is a database management system (DBMS).

Metadata and Schemas

A database contains data as well as *metadata* about that data (data about the data). The metadata is typically called a *schema*. A schema defines the layout of the database for a specific project—a database of animal medical records for a veterinarian, for example. It identifies the data elements, their characteristics (integer, text, and so forth), and the relationships among them.

Other Nondata Data

A database may contain reports, data-entry screens, or other features that are developed as part of a database project. DBMSs can support a variety of tools. Furthermore, databases often contain edits and constraints on data. (See "Integrity" later in this chapter.)

TIP

If you are asked to "put a database on the Web" using WebObjects, make certain that you identify every report that the user expects to see. Posting the data on the Web may be the least of your problems. More than one project has gone wildly over budget because users and developers have not understood what the other meant by "the database."

Database Administrators

In large IT environments, a *database administrator* (DBA)—or a team of them—is responsible for managing databases, implementing security, and performing other routine database maintenance. You may be a DBA who is using WebObjects to move into the world of the Web; on the other hand, you may be a Web master who is dealing with databases and DBAs for the first time.

Data Design

The terms in this section identify the data in a database. They are the most basic—and most precise—terms.

Database data is structured; it normally consists of the same type of data for a variety of individuals or cases: for example, first and last name together with grades for each student in a class, or planting date and crop yield for each field on a farm. Two parallel sets of terminology exist.

A physical database is divided into two basic parts—rows and columns—that contain two types of storage units—fields and records. If you think of a database as a table (or spreadsheet), each *row* of the database contains one observation (one student, one field, and so on), and each *column* contains one type of data (first name, crop, and so forth). You can also describe each observation as a *record* and each type of data as a *field*. This terminology is left over from the days of formatted reading and writing of media (before databases); however, it is still commonly used.

Tables

Databases normally contain many *tables*—each of which has its own rows and columns. The database combines all the tables. For example, a single corporate database's only common thread to its tables may be that they are all part of the organization. Or a database for human resources might contain a table for names and addresses, another for employment history, and still another for pension information.

NOTE

In some desktop database products—notably FileMaker—database is used to refer to an individual table. Many users also refer to a database when they mean table. Be aware of this: it is yet another way in which project requirements are misunderstood and can go out of control.

Indexes

Indexes are usually maintained by the DBMS. The most common type is an *inverted* index, in which the data in a table is flipped on its side. That way, instead of reading a given row with all its data, the DBMS can read a column (the inverted index) that contains all the data values for that column. With this single read, the DBMS can determine which rows have a certain data value and then read only those rows. The alternative is for the DBMS to scan each row to determine if it contains a given value.

DBMSs carry out many of their operations solely by using indexes. When you specify a complicated criterion for the retrieval of data, the relevant indexes are read and combined in whatever way you have specified (and/or) to produce a list of the rows that need to be returned.

Indexes take up disk space (the data, after all, is stored twice), and when they're included, database updates take longer (because each index must be updated as well as each data record). However, indexes help speed up data retrieval. DBMSs vary in their use of indexes, and you can control how they are maintained. (One common strategy is to turn off indexing during batch updates and then to regenerate the indexes when online processing is to continue. Many a computer spends the wee hours of the morning indexing its databases.)

TIP

In developing a WebObjects project, you may be manipulating data in a way that differs from how previous applications have worked. You may get improvements in your WebObjects application's performance by adding (or removing) indexes from the tables in your database. Even if you do not control the database, you can often request that indexes be revised, and if these revisions do not adversely impact other users, you may be able to reap the benefits.

Processing

In addition to the descriptions of data in the previous section, database terminology includes concepts for processing that data. Three critical processing issues are integrity, contention and concurrency, and security.

Integrity

Integrity in the database world means exactly what it does in real life: trustworthiness. You can add integrity to a database in a variety of ways, including using appropriate field definitions, field edits, relational integrity, and user-supplied edits.

Field Definitions   You can guarantee that an account balance is numeric, for example, by defining it as a numeric field (rather than text). You can likewise force the database to insure the integrity of a date field by defining it as a date—rather than as text or as a set of numbers (month, day, and year). Such *field definitions* help you improve the integrity of your database.

NOTE

A significant part of the Y2K computer problem was caused by date information being stored in nondate fields, where it was manipulated by home-grown date routines, not all of which dealt with the year 2000 properly. In all fairness, this situation was caused in some cases by the fact that until relatively recently, many DBMSs did not explicitly support date fields.

Using an appropriate data type may seem an obvious point; however, it is amazing how often data types are set inappropriately. An extremely common scenario is as follows:

1. Create a numeric field to store age data.

2. If the data is unavailable, you change the field type to text so that it can store "no response (n/a)." Right away, you have lost the error-checking that a numeric field would provide (a DBMS will simply not store nonnumeric data in a numeric field).

3. Alternatively, you use a special value to indicate no response (perhaps –1). This, too, is an unsatisfactory solution. Fields should contain the data that their names imply. Special values—that is, values that "never happen"—are the root of many program bugs.

If you are designing a database, you can avoid creating such problems. If you are working on a WebObjects application that interacts with an existing database, you may encounter such situations and have to work around them. Watch for text fields that really should be numeric (or other types), and watch out for special values: these problems abound in databases, and they can cause you endless debugging grief.

In the old days of computing, memory, disk, and communications were very expensive; every bit and byte was expensive in terms of storage and transmission. As a result, data fields often served multiple purposes—as in the case of special values. The proper way to design a database (or to redesign it if you are using a legacy system and have the opportunity to do so) is to separate the data into different fields. For example, use one field for age, another for data status (this field can contain *n/a* or codes indicating how it was obtained), and even more fields to indicate other characteristics of the data. Do not jumble everything together, and particularly do not put metadata into the data fields themselves.

Field Edits   You can set up field edits in many DBMSs. *Field edits* (or validations) need to be programmed or specified in some way; they form a barrier to the storage of invalid data. Common field edits require a field that's not to be blank (or to be blank), to have a value within a certain range, to have a minimum number of characters (in the case of text fields), and so on.

In some DBMSs, you can also specify whether the field edits or validations can be overridden. It is best not to allow overrides; therefore, you can be certain that all the data characteristics specified in field edits will be adhered to.

NOTE

Field edits can be changed over time; you cannot always be sure that the validations and field edits in place today apply to the data that has previously been stored in the database.

Referential Integrity   *Referential integrity* refers to integrity based on data in other tables or records; field edits normally refer to data within an individual record or field. Referential integrity is discussed further in the section "The Relational Model" later in this chapter.

User-Supplied Edits   Finally, *user-supplied edits* can support the integrity of a database. User-supplied edits may occur anywhere in the systems that update the database: frequently they will be located in your WebObjects application.

User-supplied edits support the quality of the data more than its integrity. They usually address judgmental issues. For example, field definitions and field edits can guarantee that a monthly sales figure is numeric. Or user-supplied edits might examine whether this month's sales figure differs by more than a certain percentage from the previous months; if so, user intervention would be requested.

Contention and Concurrency

From the start, databases have not only been designed to store and manipulate large quantities of data; they have also been designed to handle multiple users. These issues are generally discussed in terms of *contention*—two or more users trying to get the same data—and *concurrency*—the ability of two or more users to work at more or less the same time on the same data. The terms have slight nuances of difference, but each refers to the same general issue. Concurrency is used here for the general concept; contention is used only for a specific problem that may arise in the process of ensuring concurrency.

To support concurrency, databases support the concept of locking resources. Typically, the resource that is locked is a row or record; field-level locking is also implemented in many DBMSs, but it can become problematic for programmers and designers in many cases.

You would lock a record to prevent other people from accessing or changing it while you are making changes to it. The key design issue here is to determine the scope of the lock—both in time and in the amount of data that is locked.

Consider the case of someone who is thinking of making an airplane reservation. If three flights are going to the right place at the right time, the passenger might make a choice based on price, meal service, or other factors. Is it appropriate to place some kind of hold on all three flights while the passenger cogitates? Clearly, doing so is not in the airline's interests: other potential passengers could be locked out.

This type of situation plays out over and over in the database world. The goal is always to lock the smallest possible unit for the briefest period of time. Depending on the application, this may mean that failures occur when you come to act: the seat reservation you want, for example, may have been taken by someone else. That problem, however, is usually preferable to turning others away and winding up with unsold seats.

In addition to minimizing the resources locked and the time for which they are locked, you normally have a choice of the type of lock that you can implement. Exclusive locks prevent anyone else from doing anything in the database. Less restrictive locks allow others to view but not update data you are about to manipulate; even less restrictive locks allow you to notify others that you might be about to issue a lock.

WebObjects and Enterprise Objects Framework both deal with concurrency and locking.

Security

When multiple users are accessing a database and access is available over a network, issues of security often arise. DBMSs have implemented various security mechanisms over the years, but all center around the concept of *data ownership*: one person owns each set of data (usually a table) in the database.

That owner sets (or has a DBA set) the security access that others can have to the data: security access can be set by field or by column indicating who—or which groups of people—can read the data and who can update it.

In the world of WebObjects, it is critically important to recognize that you will often be bypassing the database's normal security mechanisms. In traditional systems, individual users run application programs under their own names and access the database in that way. In the world of application servers—including WebObjects—WebObjects itself (or occasionally the HTTP server) accesses the databases under the privileged user ID under which it is running. As a result, users who access WebObjects have access to databases under a different user ID than their own—and it is a user ID that normally has more privileges than individual users have.

NOTE

Security is discussed at length in Chapter 27.

Mirroring

Modern databases—particularly high-end products—support mirroring of databases. *Mirroring* is one of the techniques by which a database is physically replicated on a variety of computers—often in a variety of locations—so that many users can access the data at the same time.

When data is not updated online, the process or mirroring is relatively easy. However, when online updates are allowed, it is far from simple to make certain that all updates (and their associated locks) are correctly implemented. When administering your DBMS, be aware that these mirroring & locking capabilities exist, and for the most part, deal with mirrored databases as you would with an individual database; that is, treat this mechanism as internal to the database.

TIP

If you are working on a WebObjects project that may need mirroring capabilities or that may need to scale up to include them, make certain that mirroring capabilities are in place. Going from a single-machine database to one that is mirrored is a much bigger step than increasing the number of mirrors. Some low-end DBMSs do not support mirroring features, and you may find yourself moving from one DBMS to another under great time pressure.

Database Design

Armed with a understanding of the basic terminology of databases, you can now turn to the basics of database design. Following are the principles that govern most database projects today. Understanding these principles can help you appreciate why the databases you deal with may have been set up in one way or another; knowing these principles can also help you to set up your own databases.

The two key concepts of database design are the relational model and normalization.

The Relational Model

In the 1960s and 1970s, as computers were adopted throughout businesses, much software was written and many databases were developed. It became clear that with each additional line of code and each additional database, complexity grew almost exponentially. In the world of computer programming, structured programming and (later on) object-oriented programming helped to bring order and control to this world of spaghetti code and idiosyncratic architectures.

On the database side, the *relational model*—a model based on mathematical set theory—was devised and rapidly adopted for the same reason: to bring order and control to a world of loose ends and confusing and inconsistent data structures. The relational model has one overriding principle: *everything is a table*. Furthermore, this model includes three important features: objects, integrity, and operators.

Everything Is a Table

All data is stored in tables, every database operation acts on tables, and every operation on a table produces another table. A table can be the raw data that contains your data; it can be the result of an operation that brings two or more tables together in a larger (but transitory) table, or it can be the result of an operation that generates a new and smaller table—perhaps even a single row and column (one cell).

Objects

The *objects* in the relational model consist of tables, rows within those tables (records, or *tuples*, in relational terms), and columns within those tables (fields, or *attributes*, in relational terms). As noted previously in the discussion of indexes, columns can be used to retrieve data; they are referred to as keys. A *primary key* is a column that is designated to identify uniquely each row in a table; the values of a primary key are unique. That means that if the field CustomerID is to be a primary key, no two CustomerID fields can have the same value.

NOTE

In large and distributed systems, the requirement of unique values for primary keys can lead to problems, because a field that should be unique may not remain unique after you combine two data sources. Many techniques are used to force uniqueness of data values. One common technique is to add identifying information to the value. Similar to a telephone area code, this additional information creates a larger data element but maintains the key's uniqueness.

Integrity

Integrity and the rules to create and maintain it are part of the relational model. *Integrity* refers to the correctnesss of the data within a database. Integrity can be defined and described in general terms: you can specify that someone's age must be greater than 0, but you cannot specify (in the database integrity descriptions) exactly what the value for an individual person's age is.

In fact, the relational model is in some ways a descriptive programming model rather than a procedural one. In other words, you describe the data, the relationships among the data elements, and the characteristics of the integrity, and then you force the DBMS to implement all of this automatically.

NOTE

Some people are impatient with the rules and structures of the implementation of integrity in the relational model. They want to get right to work and start setting up a database system. They don't realize that these rules and structures are the work, and mistakes in setting up the model and its integrity can jeopardize a system for years to come. This problem may be why DBAs often find themselves at odds with developers.

Operators

Operators in the relational model work on tables and produce tables. These are basically mathematical set operators that implement intersections and unions. Almost from the start, SQL has been used to implement these operations. SQL is described in "Aspects of Database Programming," later in this chapter.

Normalization

The next element of database design that you should be aware of is normalization. *Normalization* is a set of rules that help you design databases and their tables for efficient use. Understanding normalization can help you understand not only how to develop your own databases, but why and how the databases that you are dealing with have been organized the way they have.

The point of normalization is to structure data in a way that minimizes its duplication. It may use more disk space and processor power, but it helps to keep databases running smoothly. Use Enterprise Objects Framework to mask the complexity of normalization. Using the framework can help a variety of people deal with normalized data in their own idiosyncratic ways without corrupting the underlying databases.

NOTE

Normalization provides efficient database processing in part because today's DBMSs expect their tables to be normalized. Normalized data sometimes takes more processing to access than unnormalized data, but the DBMS designers have optimized the steps used in dealing with normalized data so that this performance penalty is minimized. Tests have repeatedly shown that the performance degradation of normalized data is almost invisible. Nevertheless, some people still contend that normalized data is inefficient.

Five types of normalization exist. Each deals with a different type of organizing data to avoid duplication. These types are progressively more complex (types four and five are not covered in this book because they are beyond its scope).

First Normal Form

First normal form is the most basic type of normalization, in which you eliminate repeating groups of data. In a sophisticated personal information system, you may have a variety of telephone numbers, for example. For each one, you might include four data elements:

▶ Telephone number

▶ Type of telephone (wired, cellular, fax)

▶ Location (home, office, weekend)

▶ Comments (use only for emergencies, voice mail available)

These four data elements make up a set of repeating fields; as such, the elements should be pulled out onto their own. Instead of a personal record with space for (perhaps) five sets of telephone numbers (each with its own four data elements), you should set up a personal record that is related to any number of records in a related table.

The added complexity (of creating two tables) provides many advantages:

▶ The personal record need not waste space for unused phone numbers (space for five if only two are used).

▶ The personal record doesn't break if the arbitrary limit of five is exceeded.

▶ You can easily search the subsidiary table for weekend phone numbers, fax numbers, and so forth. In the unnormalized model with all of those fields jumbled together inside the personal record, you would need to test a variety of fields to find these results.

To implement this normalized data structure, you need to make certain that a primary (unique) key exists in the personal table, and that the key is used to identify data in the related table. Note that the primary key in the personal table—a person's ID—is not a primary key in the subsidiary table. No primary key may exist in the subsidiary table, although it is generally a good idea to invent one for future use.

TIP

The slightly increased complexity of data adhering to first normal form can be hidden with the use of Enterprise Objects Framework. The objects that you create and use can be constructed from multiple records; you may never know exactly which underlying data structures you are dealing with. This applies to all forms of normalization.

Second Normal Form

Second normal form encourages you to eliminate redundant data. Consequently, data should be stored in only one place in your database. For example, if you have a customer database with name, address, and telephone number, as well as a vendor database with name, address, and telephone number, you should consider having a common database with name, address, and telephone number, and then having specialized customer and vendor databases with links to the common database.

In this example, you can see that normalized data is more complex: instead of two databases, you have three. However, there is an advantage to having all names and addresses in a single location. For example, many companies deal with the same entity as both customer and vendor, and in many universities, graduate students are also teachers. If a person's or vendor's telephone number changes, only one update is required.

Third Normal Form

Another form of redundancy arises when you have data stored in a record that does not depend on a key. Keeping data that is not dependent on the key out of a particular table is the objective of *third normal form*.

Consider the personal data record again; you can assume that all the data in that record depends on the key; that is, it is part of an individual's data. However, a set of data may be redundant. Given a postal code, for example, you may be able to derive the person's town, village, state, or province (or several of them). You need only the postal code in this case; the other items that are derivable are unnecessary—in fact, not only are they unnecessary, but they can be incorrect. Many online order-entry systems ask customers for their postal code (which is stored) and then use the other geographic information to validate the postal code (but this information is not stored).

Aspects of Database Programming

Your actual work with databases generally revolves around SQL, the ODBC and JDBC database connectivity APIs, and the concepts of transactions. They are discussed in this section.

SQL

SQL is used to manipulate relational databases. It is often hidden from you by Enterprise Objects Framework; however, you should be aware of the basic method by which database programming in SQL is carried out.

In traditional procedural programming, you process data by reading one record at a time from a file or database. You check certain fields—balance, perhaps—and based on that record and on input data, you take certain steps. You then read the next record, repeat the process, and continue until all records are processed.

With SQL, the structure is reversed. Instead of a loop in which tests are made for conditions, the tests are incorporated into the SQL retrieval query that you write. You retrieve all of the records that have certain characteristics (credit balances, balances owing, or the like), and then you loop through the resultant records, *performing the same operation on each*. Checking for condition is primary and the loop is secondary.

This means that the code is simplified: you no longer test for this or that, and you know that all the records retrieved need the same action. (To get a set of records that all need the same action, you may need to retrieve several sets of records, each set corresponding to a different condition.) Eliminating complicated if statements and conditional processing simplifies the code, testing, and maintenance.

This processing is reflected in WebObjects applications. If you are used to traditional procedural programming, you will need to adjust to the WebObjects way of working.

ODBC and JDBC

The relational model is now standard for databases, and SQL is the standard language of manipulation. These concepts are further encapsulated in Open Database Connectivity (ODBC) and Java Database Connectivity (JDBC). They provide abstractions of databases so that applications can be written against generic databases rather than against individual products.

In WebObjects, *adaptors* let you connect to specific databases: Oracle, DB2, and so forth. Adaptors provided with WebObjects also let you connect to any ODBC or JDBC database. As a result, you can use WebObjects with almost any database.

Transactions

Although not strictly a database concept, *transactions* are often implemented using database technologies. A transaction is defined as a set of operations that may take place over time but that are to be considered as a single unit. A purchase, for example, may require an update to an invoice and to inventory records. If the transaction fails, though, all of its operations need to be undone, or *rolled back*.

Transaction processing is a common online activity, and WebObjects supports transactions. Many DBMSs implement a transaction architecture in which you can specify the beginning and end of a transaction; all database calls within it are processed as a group, even if they occur over a period of time. Transactions often, though not always, involve an exchange of value.

Building a Database
with OpenBase

OBJECTIVES

▶ Use OpenBaseManager

▶ Create database schemas

▶ Manage database users and environments

Creating and Using
a Database

IN THIS CHAPTER:

The SiteDemo Database

Working with OpenBaseManager Schema Editor

Building Relationships

Modifying Data with OpenBase

Creating and Running Queries in OpenBase

The first part of this book dealt with the overall concepts behind WebObjects and OpenBase: application servers, object-oriented programming, and databases today. This part of the book hones in on OpenBase and how you use it to build, maintain, and manage databases.

If you are using another database manager, you will find that the tools and techniques that you have at your disposal are very similar: after all, relational databases are a very stable and mature technology. Furthermore, the terminology is consistent across all products. As a result, you can use this chapter as a roadmap to working with products other than OpenBase.

The book uses a basic application design for most of its examples. Built on the SiteDemo database that is described in this chapter, it implements a reusable database-driven Web site. In addition, its functionality can be applied to a variety of other architectures and applications: these are pointed out in this chapter.

After a description of the SiteDemo database and the application to be built, this chapter shows you how to work with OpenBaseManager's Schema Editor tools; it then focuses on the critical aspect of building relationships. In the final section, you will see how to use OpenBaseManager to enter and modify data in the database as well as how to use it to perform queries against the data.

These processes—entering and modifying data as well as performing queries against the database can be done using OpenBase, using EOModeler and Enterprise Objects Framework, and using WebObjects itself. This part of the book looks at OpenBase, the next part looks at Enterprise Objects Framework, and the third looks at WebObjects. Using each of these tools can help you not only to develop a robust application but also to understand how it is working (and how it is going wrong as you develop it).

Users normally work only with WebObjects itself; WebObjects builds on the Enterprise Objects Framework model that you create, and that, in turn, rests on your database—OpenBase for this example. If you have any doubts about whether or not a particular section of code in WebObjects is working or not, try the same thing in EOModeler or in OpenBaseManager: the logic may be the same in each case, but, if the results differ, you know you have implemented it incorrectly. If the results are the same in each case, either your fundamental logic is flawed, or the database itself has a problem.

The SiteDemo Database

The SiteDemo database and demo is designed as a step-by-step tutorial as well as a model that you can use for a variety of other projects. This section describes what you can do with it—as is or with your own modifications—as well as how it is designed. While this section in no way is a complete guide to database design, it includes a number of tips for fields that you may want to include in your own tables.

Some people treat database fields as precious commodities: they economize by shortening text fields and by combining variables into single fields. This adds complexity to applications and ultimately winds up costing more money in maintenance than it may save in relatively-cheap disk space. OpenBase optimizes its data storage so that text fields use only the amount of disk space they require: defining a field as char(100) uses up to 100 characters for each record's field, with the actual number of characters determining the storage used.

The ease with which you can add columns to databases and to your data model means that you do not have to piggy-back fields. If you have a perfectly good field in which to store status and you later need to store a new data element, you are much better off adding a column to the database and to the model than deciding that status values in the range 20-30 don't mean status but actually mean something else.

What You Can Do with SiteDemo

SiteDemo implements a database-driven Web site. Such a site has a minimum of handwritten HTML pages: most of its content comes from a database either automatically or in response to user requests.

The data on the pages are *items*. Each item has a title (which is normally displayed in boldface type) and some content (usually no more than a paragraph or two). Items may have graphics associated with them, and they may have URL links. A variety of management information is stored in them; for example, one variation on SiteDemo identifies each item by the page on which it is to be seen.

Some items can be *discussed:* that is, people can post comments and responses to them. Each individual response is stored in the Discussion table.

In order to implement security and various other site features, a third table— *user*—keeps track of names, addresses, and security levels for visitors to the site. In the implementation described in this book, anyone can see items and search the items table; you need to register (that is, create a record in the User table) in order to discuss items. You need a specific security code to be able to modify discussions or items and to delete them.

This little application handles all of the functionality that you need for almost any Web site: retrieval, additions, updates and modifications, and user identification. You can combine these basic features into e-commerce sites, discussion groups, online catalogs, or whatever you want. There are only so many basic building blocks to database-driven Web sites.

SiteDemo Design

The three basic tables are described in this section. (Note that the screen shots in this book show the database during its implementation: not all fields are present in each screen shot.) The basic fields are described and named here.

Item Table

An item consists of five important data elements:

▶   **Title**   This is normally displayed in boldface type on the Web page. If you are implementing a Web site based on this design, you may want to indicate that this field is required. To do so, you mark it not null in Schema Editor (you will see how to do this later in this chapter). Another way of accomplishing the same goal is to make EOModeler and your Enterprise Objects Framework require that the title field is not blank. Still another way of accomplishing this is programmatically in your WebObjects code. This is a very common situation: you need to identify the requirements, and then you can choose which level of the project to implement them in. In the case of databases that are shared among a WebObjects application and other applications, you can thus enforce rules universally or only in one context.

▶   **Information**   This is the text of the item; it ranges in length from a word or two to a paragraph or two. It, too, may need to be a required field. If you want to require either a title or information to be present, you must implement that type of edit in your WebObjects application. It would be done as part of data validation, which is discussed in Chapter 12. The name of the validation method would be validateInformation.

▶   **URL**   Optionally, a link can be associated with the item. This is an example of a field that must not be marked as not null since it is optional and null values are legal.

▶   **URLname**   If a URL is present, it can be named with text such as "Further information," "Report," or the like. This helps customize the display. You may want to implement a WebObjects application edit that checks that URLname is not entered if URL is blank (null). Likewise, you may wish to place the text of the URL in the URLname field if nothing has been entered by the user. If you implement these rules, they need to be carried out in record-level (object-level) validations of the entity in Enterprise Objects Framework that is based on the

Item table. You would implement them in a method called validateForSave (or validateForInsert, and so forth); these methods are described in Chapter 12.

▶ **imageURL** An image can be associated with the item. If so, it is not stored in the database, but instead is identified by its URL from whence it is fetched when the item needs to be displayed.

A variety of housekeeping data elements are added to each item. It is not unusual for this type of information to overshadow the number of basic data elements.

▶ **Timestamp** OpenBase maintains timestamp information for each record; this keeps track of its latest revision.

▶ **Version** It is sometimes useful to keep track of the version of your software that creates database entries. If you are forced to change the meaning of a database field (never a good idea, but sometimes inevitable), the version number will let you know which meaning applies to the data that is stored. This is a poor programming technique, but, alas, it is something that happens in the real world—particularly when you do not control the database.

▶ **Category** Items can be arranged in any way that you choose. For a discussion forum, categories would be different discussion areas. For an online e-commerce catalog, categories would be different types of merchandise.

▶ **Status** You need to keep track of each item's status. This allows the database to hold in-progress or out-of-date items. It is normally good database design to have a value such as this: it means that you do not have to delete and re-add items to your database as you work on them.

▶ **Type** Some implementations of a database-driven Web site identify items by type: one set of values for type could be news, want-ads, reference, and so forth. (Note that you can combine categories and types so that you can use types within categories. At a school, for example, categories could serve for different departments; within each department, types of items could represent news, class descriptions, homework assignments, and the like.)

▶ **Visibility** Finally, a visibility field lets you control where an item is displayed. It provides an easy way for sorting items on a page: you can assign numbers starting from 1 and going up so that items are ordered.

▶ **User** This is the field identifying the user who has posted an item.

Note that a frequent modification to this type of design is to maintain information about the original entry as well as the last modification: this applies to the user and to the modification date fields.

Discussion Table

The Discussion table contains discussions about individual items. It is similar to the Item table—and, in fact, could use the same structure, or even be the same table. The structure described here is a simple implementation.

For each discussion, the following data fields are kept:

▶ Title

▶ Information

▶ ItemID   A reference to a record in the Item table.

Some status information is needed, just as for an item record. However, by having the reference to the item record in ItemID, you do not need to repeat the information that is available from that record—category and type, for example. The other status information is needed because it refers to the discussion record, not the item record:

Timestamp

Version

Status

Visibility

User

User Table

The User table contains basic name and address information. Three design choices are of note for this type of data storage.

The name is stored in three fields: first name, last name, and name. While you can use your WebObjects code to attempt to split up the name into first and last names, there are enough exceptions and special rules to make it worthwhile to store the (sortable) lastname field separately from the user-defined name field.

Standard four-line addresses are now used by both private delivery services and many post offices. In addition to the name (first line) and city/country information (last line), the two middle lines provide for both a post office box and for a street address. Thus, a single address can be used by both types of services. Be aware that this type of address requires the two address lines to be on separate lines. Some programs combine the two (with a comma, most often) that converts a compliant four-line address into a non-compliant one.

Note the privacy code. Increasingly it is important (and often required by law) to keep track of the conditions under which you have collected data and how it can be reused.

Working with OpenBaseManager Schema Editor

You use OpenBaseManager to create and modify a database schema. This section walks you through the process. To begin with, you need to create and start a database (instructions for this are in the OpenBase documentation as well as in Chapter 7). Select the database from the list and then click Start if necessary (it is the top button at the right of the window). After a few moments, the other icons should be enabled. If they are not, the database may not have been started properly.

Launch Schema Editor by choosing Schema from the Database menu or clicking the button shown in Figure 5-1.

The design window will open. It has two display modes: Figure 5-2 shows the tabular display, and Figure 5-3 shows the graphical display. You switch between them using the buttons at the left of the toolbar in these figures. As you can see, the tabular display focuses on an individual table; the graphical display shows a number of tables along with the relationships (if any) among them.

In tabular display, each entry in the table defines a single column. You click the Add Columns button to create a new column. You can then enter or change the name, and you use the type pop-up menu as shown in Figure 5-4 to select the type of the variable in that column.

The following data types are available; they are standard SQL data types available on most relational databases:

- ▶ char   Use for character strings. You declare the maximum length in Schema Editor; OpenBase uses only as much storage space as is required for the current contents of the string.

- ▶ boolean

- ▶ integer

- ▶ long

- ▶ longlong   Use for record ID numbers to avoid possible overflow. OpenBase assigns unique numbers, which can grow large.

- ▶ float

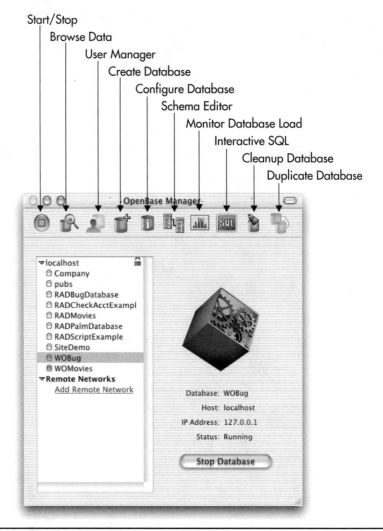

Figure 5-1   *Launching Schema design*

► **money**   The formatting of this field is set in preferences for the host on which the database is running. Set it in Preferences in OpenBaseManager.

► **date**   Formatting depends on host preferences.

► **time**   Formatting depends on host preferences.

► **datetime**   Formatting depends on host preferences.

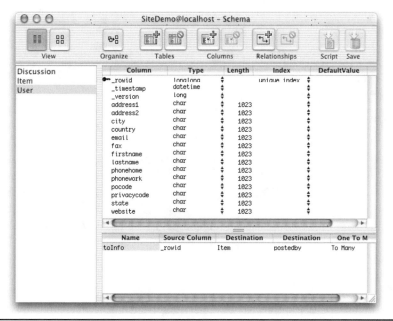

Figure 5-2   *Schema design: tabular display*

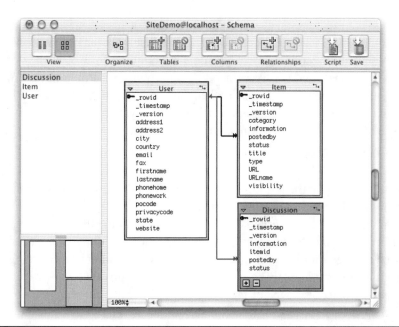

Figure 5-3   *Schema design: graphical display*

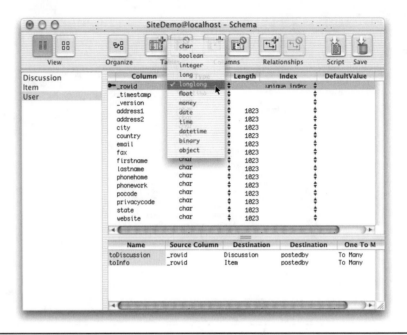

Figure 5-4   *Selecting a column type*

▶   binary   Binary Large Objects (BLOBs) are just that—any collection of bits
that you want to store. They can be data in your own format, or they can be
images, movies, and the like. Encoding your own data structure into BLOBs
hides the data elements and makes them unsearchable in the database. BLOBs are
commonly used in data conversions from older systems where application code
is used to access data structures, not data records.

▶   object   OpenBase uses this type in its management of BLOBs.

You also can click in the left margin to make a field the primary key for that table.
The primary key is identified with a key icon: in Figure 5-4, _rowid is a primary key.
Note that a primary key has certain characteristics—including the fact that it must be
unique. Normally, you use the OpenBase _rowID field as a primary key. (Internal
OpenBase variables start with the underscore; that is a common programming
technique to let others know that a variable is essentially private.)

You also can select the type of index—if any—for that column as shown in
Figure 5-5.

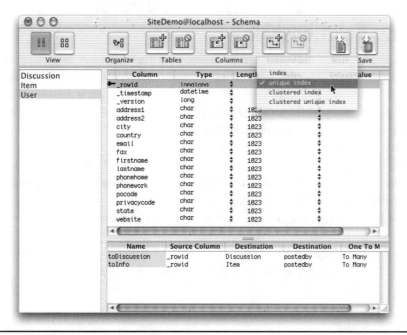

Figure 5-5   *Selecting an index type*

Indexing a column makes retrieval faster; it also may make updating slower, since the index needs to be updated in addition to the underlying data.

A clustered index forces the records in the table to be stored in the sequence of the index. If you have ID numbers that increase by one for each new record, this will cause records 1, 2, 3, and 4 to be stored in that order. Clustering an index is a way to improve processing for databases that are accessed sequentially. A customer table, for example, is likely to be accessed randomly as various customers' data is handled. An invoice table, though, may typically be accessed in chronological order—in which case clustering an index on a date field may be a good idea. Since clustering affects that actual storage of the records in the table, only one clustered index can be used in the table.

Unique indexes allow only one occurrence of each value. If you try to insert a second Customer 154 record, you will get an error if the customer ID is a unique index. If you are relying on the uniqueness of a value in the database, a unique index can help to preserve data integrity.

Building Relationships

The heart of a relational database is its relations. OpenBaseManager helps you build and maintain these easily. If you are working in tabular view, click the Add Relationship button. The relationship definition window will open as shown in Figure 5-6.

You can select any of the tables from the pop-up button at the top of the window. In each table, one and only one primary key is defined. Thus, when you have selected a table, that key is shown in this window.

You then select the table to which the first one will be joined. If it is a one-to-one relationship, you identify the table and then the field with the second set of pop-up buttons. Note that the field at the bottom can be selected, or you can type in a new field name. If you do so, when you click the Create button, that column will be added to the second table.

You can also create a relationship in the graphical schema view by control-dragging a line from the primary key to the foreign key as shown in Figure 5-7.

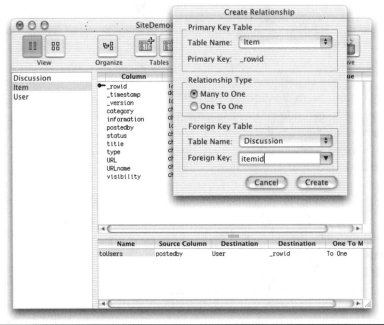

Figure 5-6   *Creating a relationship*

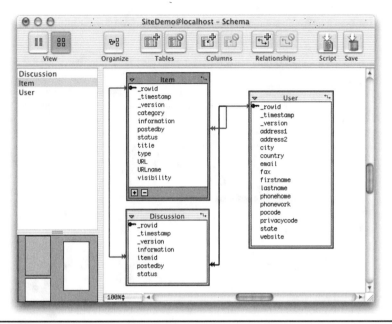

Figure 5-7   *Creating a relationship in graphical view*

Once you click the Create button, the window shown in Figure 5-8 opens. It diagrams the relationship and provides a sentence describing it.

The two other tabs in the window let you examine the two sides of the relationship as shown in Figures 5-9 and 5-10. You can specify the behavior to use when adding or deleting records to one side of the relationship or the other. (This is demonstrated in the following chapter.)

The tabular view lets you provide default values for each column; it also lets you specify that the column is non-null as shown in Figure 5-11.

Furthermore, if a relationship has been specified, it is shown at the bottom of the display as shown in Figure 5-12.

The other side of the relationship is shown in the other table's view as you can see in Figure 5-13.

One further feature of Schema Editor is that you can combine the tabular and graphic views. Clicking on the triangle at the top left of each table in the graphical view shows it in tabular view within the graphical view as you can see in Figure 5-14.

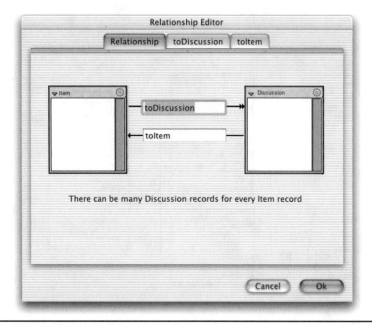

Figure 5-8 *Relationship description*

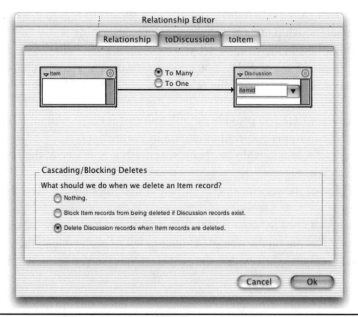

Figure 5-9 *Specifying the toDiscussion end of the relationship*

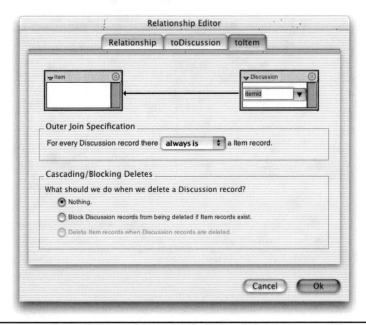

Figure 5-10   *Specifying the toItem end of the relationship*

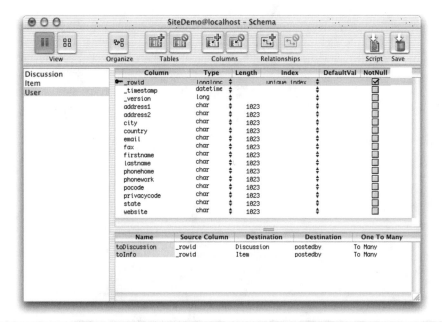

Figure 5-11   *Column information in tabular view*

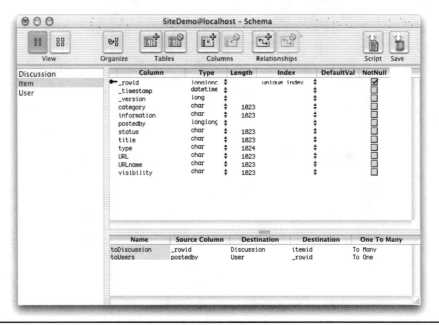

Figure 5-12   *Relationships are shown in the tabular view*

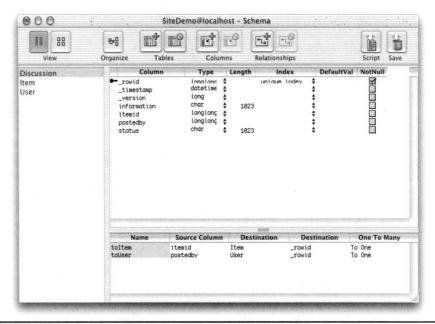

Figure 5-13   *Relationships are shown in both related tables*

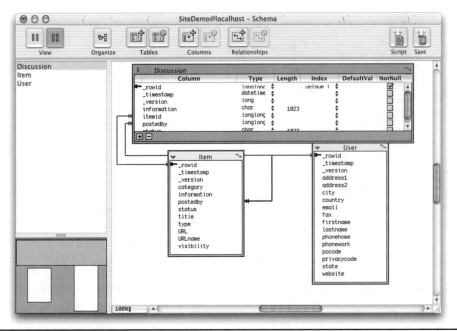

Figure 5-14   *Graphical views can combine tabular and graphical views of individual tables*

Modifying Data with OpenBase

To begin, make certain that your database is started in OpenBaseManager. (There is more about starting databases in Chapter 7.) Open the Data Browser by clicking the Browse Data button.

The Data Browser opens, as shown in Figure 5-15. In the center of the window is an area that displays data or queries from your database. The two tabs let you switch between those displays. At the left, the tables in your database are shown at the top, and queries that you have constructed with Data Browser (if any) are shown at the bottom. Everything is resizable: the main display can be enlarged both as you resize the window and also as you move the divider between the left-hand display of tables and queries and the main display. You can also resize the table and query lists by dragging the divider between them.

To begin with, the three tables of your database are shown as you can see in Figure 5-15.

Click on the name of a table to show its data: the number of records to be displayed is specified in the Display box in the upper right of the window. You can change this to display more or fewer records. You can further customize the display by dragging column names back and forth to change their order.

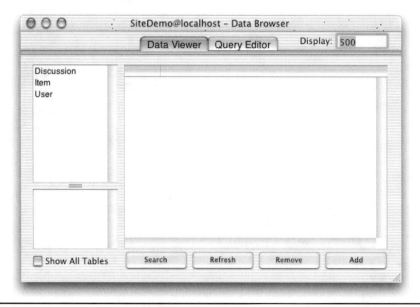

Figure 5-15 *Data Viewer has two tabbed displays*

To add a new record to the database, select a table at the left by clicking on it, then click the Add button in the lower right of the window. A new record will be created. Automatic-entry fields such as _rowid will be filled in, and you can fill in other fields as you wish. In Figure 5-16, record 4 has been created (the 4 is generated by OpenBase as a unique ID), and the Itemid column has had a value of 44 manually entered into it.

This illustrates how relationships in OpenBase are used: they are stored in the database for use by EOModeler, but they are not enforced at the database level (this enforcement is referred to as *referential integrity*). In Figure 5-16, an Itemid value of 44 has been entered, but there is no such Itemrowid to match the Itemid value. EOModeler will help you catch such errors.

In addition, note that Data Browser does necessary type conversions so that if you enter a value such as "abc" in a numeric field, it will be converted to a numeric value. This may be what you want, but it may be a user input error. You can use your WebObjects code to distinguish between the two (that is, to either automatically convert from one type to another or to ask the user what is meant).

Figure 5-16 *Enter data directly into Data Viewer*

Creating and Running Queries in OpenBase

You can check the data in your database directly from OpenBaseManager using Query Editor. This is helpful not only in developing your application but also in debugging it once it is running. Start from the Data Viewer window, and then click the Query Editor tab.

Default Database Queries

At the right, a pop-up button lets you select basic queries for a number of tables—including those in your database. (Your database tables appear at the bottom of the list as you can see in Figure 5-17.)

The default queries select all columns from each table. They are generated using standard SQL, which is described further in the following chapter. Once you have selected a query template, its SQL is displayed in the editor window. You can modify the SQL if you want; you also should name the query and save it as shown in Figure 5-18.

Figure 5-17   *Use Query Editor to create template queries*

Once you have saved a query, it appears in the lower left of the Data Viewer tab. If you click on it, the query will be run as shown in Figure 5-19.

You can scroll horizontally to see all the data in the record. You also can resize each column by dragging the vertical separators between column names to enlarge or reduce column sizes. If you will be using a query regularly, you may want to modify the query itself to omit columns that you normally do not care about.

Note that by default, all columns are retrieved for the first records in your table—the number being specified in the Display box at the upper right of the Data Viewer window. By running a query, you can select records on a logical basis, viewing records from the middle or end of the table, or from various places in between.

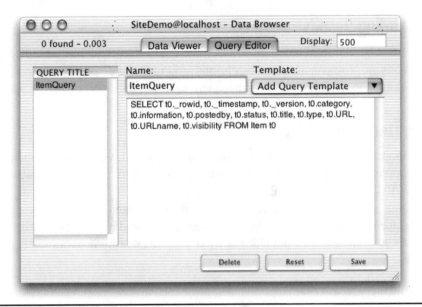

Figure 5-18   *Name and save template queries*

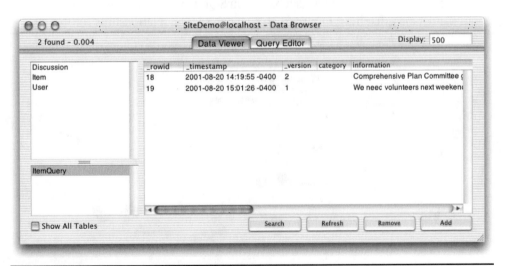

Figure 5-19   *Run template queries from Data Viewer*

Manipulating Results

If you click on the title of any data column, the query results will be sorted based on that column. You can also move columns around in the display; your reordering of the columns is remembered for subsequent searches until you change it again.

Customized Queries

In addition to running canned queries that you have saved, you can dynamically create simple queries by clicking on a column title to open the dialog shown in Figure5-20. Use it to dynamically create your queries.

Remember that OpenBaseManager is a database-oriented tool that is designed for developers to use during development, debugging, and maintenance. The user-friendly graphical user interface is what you are creating in WebObjects.

System Table Queries

The Show All Tables checkbox at the bottom left of the Data Browser tab lets you run queries against the system tables in OpenBase. As you will see in the next chapter, everything about an SQL database is an SQL table—including the information about the database itself. In Figure 5-21, you can see the relationships for the

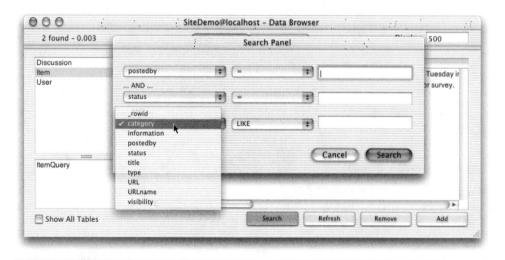

Figure 5-20   *Create customized queries by clicking a column title*

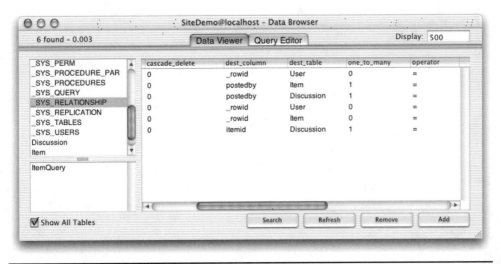

Figure 5-21   *Database metadata is stored in SQL tables*

databases that were described in the previous chapter. They are all stored in a table. You should not modify this data, but you may want to look at it to help in debugging strange database errors.

The Data Viewer in OpenBaseManager is an excellent low-level debugging and development tool. As you can see, it provides you with direct access to the database without the error-checking that you implement explicitly in WebObjects and implicitly in your rules in EOModeler.

The heart of OpenBase and most modern databases is SQL. You have seen SQL queries in action in this chapter; the next chapter provides more information on SQL and what you can do with it.

Using SQL

IN THIS CHAPTER:

This chapter provides an introduction to SQL, the basis of the relational database model. Depending on how you use OpenBase and WebObjects, you may need to know much more than is described here—or you may only need to know the very basics that are described in the overview and the section on retrieving data.

Although you may spend your time in WebObjects, Enterprise Objects Framework, and OpenBaseManager, remember that ultimately every database access that you write explicitly or implicitly is going to be executed using the SQL syntax described in this chapter.

High-volume database applications need their database tables tuned carefully, and it is critical that they be designed for the fastest throughput of the entire system (which sometimes does not mean the fastest throughput for certain operations). For many database applications—including many WebObjects projects—performance is not the primary consideration. Rather, the ability to store, retrieve, update, and manage data in a responsive manner and with a minimum of high-powered programming support is what matters. The combination of SQL, OpenBase (or another relational database), Enterprise Objects Framework, and WebObjects help you maximize your productivity and get the work done quickly.

NOTE

SQL and databases (like WebObjects itself) are used in many very advanced applications such as the Apple Store, and in a variety of critical Web sites supporting very large corporations. The fact that these tools work for such demanding applications should not be taken as an indication that they are not also appropriate for smaller-scale projects. They are, and the weeks of study that you need to learn enough about the tools to build a large-scale application are proportionately reduced for smaller-scale projects such as the basic ones that use WebObjects to publish rich media on the Web or on intranets that use Web technologies.

SQL Overview

As you saw in Chapter 4, the heart of SQL is its tables: sets of data stored in rows and columns. All data in SQL resides in tables: they may be simple tables such as those that have been shown so far in this book. They may also be complex tables created dynamically during the course of data retrieval; such tables exist only at run time as a result of a query. In addition, they can be the simplest possible tables that also are created at run time: a single data value is a table with one row and one column.

Thus, whether a table that you describe is a database schema or a table created on the fly, everything is a table.

You operate on tables using operators that are similar to basic set operators. The primary operator is the *select* statement, which you use to retrieve data. It is described in the section after this.

In order to get data into tables, you *insert* it; in order to modify data that already exists, you *update* it. This is an important distinction. In the first case, until you actually insert the data, you do not have to worry about what else is in the database; at the moment you insert it, the database will have to check that unique keys in the new record do not conflict with other keys, but that is all the checking that is needed other than standard data editing.

In the second case—updating data—there is a period of time during which you know that you will be updating a record. You retrieve the existing data, modify it, and then perform the update. In an environment in which many people can be using the database at the same time (an environment that is usually the case with WebObjects applications), you need to make certain that the data has not been changed by someone else during the period that you are modifying it. Enterprise Objects Framework takes care of this; you can also use OpenBase to lock records during this period.

Two forms of data locking are used: optimistic and pessimistic locking. In the case of optimistic locking, a before image of the data is kept when the user retrieves it. When an update is requested by the user, the before image is checked against the current image; if they are the same, the change goes through. If another user has made a change in the meantime, the before and after images will not match, and the update will fail.

Enterprise Objects Framework lets you implement optimistic locking below the level of the record. You can specify for each attribute (column or field) whether or not you want it to be checked—you do this with a little lock icon next to the name in EOModeler. If it is not checked, changes to it will not cause an optimistic locking failure.

Pessimistic locking prevents failure by not allowing a second user to attempt to update data while the first user is in the process of updating it. While this prevents collisions between users updating the same record, it can severely slow down performance, since the locked records are out of bounds to users during the update—and that update might include a lunch break!

In general, optimistic locking works for databases in which the updates are scattered. Pessimistic locking is best for updating small amounts of shared data used by many users (such as an ID number) and when the update cycle can be controlled (such as when it does not wait on user input).

You need to consider issues of updating data from the very start of your database design. In addition to modeling your data using the rules of normalization described in Chapter 4, you should make certain that the data elements likely to be updated together will be able to be isolated during updating, and that multiple updates at more or less the same time do not cause conflicts. This is one reason to sometimes denormalize data slightly: you may divide a single logical row of data into two parts so that each can be updated separately if the real-world environment is such that those two parts are frequently updated at more or less the same time by different people.

Retrieving Data with SELECT Statements

The SELECT statement is the workhorse of SQL. In it, you specify the columns that you want to retrieve and the table or tables from which to retrieve the data. Its most SQL statement basic retrieves all columns for a specified table:

```
SELECT * FROM MyTable
```

This is the basic SQL statement that EOModeler uses in preparing its model. You never see it, but you do see its results in EOModeler: all of the columns for each of your tables are shown there, and you can work in EOModeler and in WebObjects to manipulate your data further. For many people, this is the most common way of using their database data in EOModeler and thence in WebObjects.

However, you may want to use more complex select statements in debugging, system development, and prototyping. You can use them directly in OpenBaseManager, or you can incorporate them into your application. In addition, select statements represent the ultimate description of a what a database does. Together with the database schema, they frequently provide the most accurate—and sometimes the only—documentation of a database. For that reason, if you are converting a legacy application to WebObjects, you may need to read the existing select statements in order to find out what happens in the database.

There are three major additions to the select statement:

1. The ability to combine and manipulate columns during retrieval
2. The ability to retrieve data from several tables at once—to do a *join*
3. The ability to select only that data that fulfills a logical condition

In addition, there is an order by clause that you can use to sort the retrieved data, but sorting is covered in EOModeler and WebObjects in most cases.

Combining and Manipulating Columns

You can use basic SQL operators to combine columns in a select statement. An example of this is a select statement to retrieve both the address1 and address2 fields from the Users table. In the following select statement, each of them is retrieved separately:

```
SELECT address1, address2 FROM Users
```

However, you can combine them into a single derived column as they are retrieved:

```
SELECT address1 + " " + address2 FROM Users
```

By combining columns in a select statement, you can reduce the postprocessing you need to do programmatically; you can also reduce the number of columns that need to be moved into EOModeler. In general, the lower the level at which you combine data, the more efficient the operation is; also, the more absolute it is. In other words, if the columns are combined before they go into Enterprise Objects Framework and thence into WebObjects, there is no way that the individual underlying columns can be manipulated in those environments. Combine columns at the most basic level that you can, recognizing that the decision ripples through the other users of the database.

SQL functions (described later in this chapter) allow you to perform additional manipulations on one or more columns as they are retrieved in a select statement. These functions let you manipulate strings and modify values.

Remember that each select statement is, in fact, the definition of a new table that is created during the performance of that select statement.

Combining Tables Using Joins

The power of relational databases comes in large part from the ability to execute joins during queries; that is, to retrieve data from more than one table at the same time. The result is, as always, a new table, and in that table the origins of the data are lost: the two tables are joined together.

Joins require the use of primary keys; you can specify them in your database scheme using OpenBaseManager and its relationships. The simplest joins combine single records with identical values: a customer billing record with a customer address record, for example. In the case of one-to-many relationships, there is a row of the results table for each of the many records; the data from the one side of the relationship is repeated in each of the appropriate rows.

For example, in the SiteDemo example, each row of the Items table can have zero, one, or many Discussion records associated with it:

Item 1 has no Discussion records

Item 2 has 1 Discussion record (Discussion 1)

Item 3 has 2 Discussion records (Discussion 2 and 3)

If you construct a joined select statement, you can come up with a new table as its result:

Item 2 —Discussion 1

Item 3 —Discussion 2

Item 3 —Discussion 3

This is an *inner join:* a join in which each resulting record is complete: thus, Item 1 does not appear, since it has no Discussion records. By specifying relationships in OpenBaseManager and/or EOModeler, you can let Enterprise Objects Framework construct these records for you. You also can construct them yourself using SQL. And, as noted previously, you may need to read existing code in order to find out how legacy systems are constructing joined records.

Joins are the way in which you denormalize data in order to use it in your operations. The records in the results table would be prime candidates for normalization if they were the actual records in a table that is stored; when retrieved in a join, all the data that you need is where you need it, even if it is duplicated in a way in which you would not store it in the database.

In order to construct a join, you can simply specify the columns that you want:

```
SELECT address1, address2, title FROM User, Item
```

The address1 and address2 columns are retrieved from Users, and the title column is retrieved from Items. However, to perform the join described here, you need to retrieve title and information columns from both Items and Discussions tables. As a result, you need to be able to specify which column comes from which table, since they have the same names in both tables. You do that by identifying each table and column with an identifier. Assign any identifier you want to each table, placing it right after the table name; place the appropriate identifier before each column name, separating the identifier from the column name with a dot as shown here:

```
SELECT t0._rowid, t0.title, t0.information, t1._rowid, t1.title,
t1.information, t1.Items_id FROM Item t0, Discussion t1
```

If you execute this query, you will discover that it is not yet complete: it generates too many records. The actual join must be limited to those records in which the primary key in the Items database equals the Items_ID column in the Discussions table:

```
SELECT t0._rowid, t0.title, t0.information, t1._rowid, t1.title,
t1.information, t1.Items_id FROM Items t0, Discussions t1
WHERE t0._rowID = t1.Items_id
```

This statement returns the appropriate records.

Specifying Retrieval Conditions with Where Clauses

The *where* clause in a select statement limits the results of the query to those that fulfill the criterion. Simple where clauses let you pinpoint individual records in the database, as is the case in:

```
SELECT name FROM Customers WHERE Customer_ID = "425"
```

This statement retrieves the single cell containing the name of customer 425 (it may also return nothing if such a record does not exist).

The where clause in the previous section is more typical: it compares the values of one column to the values of another (possibly in another table). All of the records that fulfill that criterion—no matter what the values happen to be—are returned.

Where Clause Operators

The operators that you can use in where clauses are the standard comparison operators (=, !=, <, <=, >, and >=). In addition, five other operators are provided:

▶ **SOUNDSLIKE**   You can compare two values using the SOUNDSLIKE keyword. It compares the sound of the two values.

▶ **IN**   The IN operator lets you check if the value for a given column is either in a comma-separated list of values or in a subquery (described in the following section). A variant is the NOT IN operator, which does the reverse.

▶ **EXISTS**   This operator checks to see if a correlated subquery returns any values. If it does, then the where clause is true and the record is returned. Note that EXISTS checks only that the result of the subquery is not null: if you need to check whether a specific value exists, you use IN.

▶ **LIKE**   This is a wildcard operator that compares a column in the candidate record to a pattern you provide in the where clause. Patterns can include * or % to indicate wildcard strings; "_" indicates wildcard characters and lists of characters within brackets (for example: [abc] or [_]) and checks a single character against the possible values in the bracket.

▶ **BETWEEN**   This operator lets you specify upper and lower bounds of a range of values to be checked against.

Database Programming Versus Procedural Programming

If you are not used to database programming, you may be tempted to retrieve records individually. Once you are used to database programming, you will be comfortable retrieving all records that fulfill a criterion and then looping through them in your code. In WebObjects, *display groups* let you display the results of a query where a variable number of records need to be displayed.

Subqueries

A select statement creates a table when it executes; you can use that table as a source of criteria for a where clause. There are two basic forms. In the first, known as a *noncorrelated subquery,* you simply use the subquery to find the value or values that you want to use in the test. Its general format is:

```
SELECT t0.column1, t0.column2 FROM MyTable t0 WHERE t0.column3 IN
(SELECT t1.column4 FROM OtherTable t1)
```

The subquery is executed, and it produces a table consisting of one column—the values of column4. (Of course, the subselect can be far more complex than this.) The outer query then selects all rows from MyTable in which the value of column3 is found in the subquery; that is, those values of column3 that also appear as values of column4 in OtherTable.

This query uses aliases to identify the tables from which the columns are drawn. If there is no ambiguity, they are unnecessary. If column1, column2, and column3 occur only in MyTable and column4 occurs only in OtherTable, you do not need the aliases. However, to avoid breaking queries as columns are added to tables, it is a good idea to use them. They are omitted from subsequent queries in this section only for reasons of readability.

Here is a query that returns the names and addresses from a Customers table of those customers whose customerIDs are associated with unpaid invoices:

```
SELECT customerName from Customers WHERE customerID IN
(SELECT customerID FROM Invoices WHERE balanceDue>0)
```

A *correlated subquery* requires an additional database access for each record that is considered for retrieval. This is because the where clause in the subquery uses a value from the main query. Here is an example:

```
SELECT column1 from MyTable t0 WHERE column2 IN
(SELECT column3 FROM OtherTable t1 WHERE t0.column1 = t1.column5)
```

Because correlated subqueries require an additional database access for each potential row that is to be returned rather than a single additional database access for the query itself, they can be very inefficient. In many cases, they can be converted to noncorrelated subqueries.

Other subqueries use the EXISTS and NOT EXISTS operators following WHERE. One very common use of this is to check if a given ID exists in a database table. In set theory terminology, subqueries allow you to implement *intersections,* which are a companion to joins.

Adding Data to the Database

You can add data to the database interactively with OpenBaseManager. You can also use the SQL insert statement to do so. The format is very simple:

```
INSERT into MyTable (column1, column2, column5) VALUES (val1, val2, val5)
```

You do not insert rows into any given physical location in the table: they wind up wherever the database manager wants to put them, and you retrieve them using the keys you have defined in the database schema. The insert statement lets you insert a single row with some or all of its columns: in the example shown here, only some columns are provided.

In practice, you very rarely use the insert statement. Once the database has been constructed, you use WebObjects to enter data; you use OpenBaseManager and its Data Browser to enter small amounts of test data.

Updating Data

Because database records have no fixed location, when you want to update one you first need to find it using the same query language that you use in a select statement. The *update* statement combines the retrieval and the modification in one:

```
UPDATE MyTable SET column5 = newValue WHERE balanceDue > 0
```

The query, which can be complex, is placed in the where clause. Because the query returns a table, it may return more than one row. Thus, an update statement can (deliberately or not) be used for batch updates, deletes, or inserts to the database.

Deleting Data

Deleting data is similar to updating it: you locate the records you want to delete, and then you delete them. The delete statement does both at once:

```
DELETE FROM MyTable WHERE balanceDue = 0
```

Again, note that the query in the where clause may return more than one record, and the delete statement will delete all of them.

SQL Functions

There are two broad categories of SQL functions:

▶ Data conversion and manipulation functions
▶ Summary functions

The first group provides conversion among different numeric and string types. In addition, it provides string manipulation functions such as length, replace, substring, upper, lower, and the like.

These are standard programming functions; they are also described in the OpenBase documentation or the documentation for the database manager that you may be using.

The other group of SQL functions summarizes the data that is returned. There are five summary functions:

- ▶ **COUNT**   This returns the number of records fulfilling the selection criterion. Note that count can be a very efficient operator, since it may be able to be completed by referring only to the indexes of the database.

- ▶ **SUM**   This is the simple summary of a given column.

- ▶ **AVG**   This is the average for a column.

- ▶ **MIN**   This is the minimum value.

- ▶ **MAX**   This is the maximum value.

You specify these functions in a query as shown in the following example, which returns the total unpaid balances in an invoices table:

```
SELECT SUM(balanceDue) FROM Invoices
```

The summary functions operate on all records retrieved, providing a single row in reeturn with the summary data. You can also *group* the records retrieved; if you do so, there will be one summary record for each group. For example, the following query would return several records; each will contain the total balance due for a category of customers:

```
SELECT SUM(balanceDue) FROM Invoices GROUP BY customerCategory
```

Summary functions and group by clauses are very important in ad hoc queries of databases. When designing a database, an Enterprise Objects Framework model, and a WebObjects application, you often need to allow access for ad hoc queries. You may even need to prepackage such queries for users and administrators.

Creating and Altering Tables

SQL is used to create tables within a database. The *create table* command does this. You usually use OpenBaseManager to create tables using its graphical user interface; however, you can save the commands in SQL scripts to rerun them later. You may want to modify the SQL code in the scripts to generate tables that are almost, but not quite, like the tables you created with OpenBaseManager.

You can also alter tables through SQL: just about everything you need to do to the structure of tables and the data contained in them can be done through SQL. You can rename tables and columns, add or delete columns, and change the type of the data in columns. In these cases, you need to rebuild your Enterprise Objects Framework model.

There are two further aspects to SQL that you need to be aware of: views and indexes. They affect both the performance of the database and the ease with which you can develop database applications.

Creating Views

Much in the same way that a subquery produces a temporary table that you can use in the main query, a view creates a virtual table that you can use in queries. Unlike subqueries, views are permanent parts of the database. Once you create a view, you use it just like a database table.

The view is created using a standard select statement. Thus, it can contain some or all columns from a table, it can contain derived columns that use SQL functions to change their type or manipulate their data, and they can contain joins that link two or more actual tables (or views) together.

You create a view by naming its columns and the view itself and then providing the select statement that populates the columns:

```
CREATE VIEW MyView (UserFirstName, UserLastName) AS
   SELECT (firstName, lastName) FROM Users
```

Views are a good way to expose parts of your database to users for ad hoc analysis. You can provide access to the views without having to provide access to the underlying tables.

Using Indexes

Finally, indexes provide a way to tune database performance in a significant way. An index is an inverted data structure for a column within a database. This means that, for the column involved, all of the data is stored together, separately from the main data storage, which is organized by rows. Each indexed data element may be stored twice: once in the row to which it belongs, and once in the index of its column. Updates are slightly slower: at least two updates may be required for each record that is added or modified: one to the main record and one to the index.

The issue of optimizing database accesses and index updating is a highly important one for performance. OpenBase addresses the issue by minimizing the performance impact through the use of slightly more disk and memory on the database server.

Since you can have an index on any or all of the columns in a database, a heavily indexed database can exhibit significantly slower update performance than a nonindexed one.

However, on retrieval, the matter is reversed. In finding all of the records that have a certain value (or range of values) in a given column, only one disk access is required: the index needs to be read. Unindexed, the table needs to be read record by record to find and check each of the needed column values.

Indexes can be *clustered* in OpenBase (and many other databases). A clustered index is one in which like values are physically clustered on disk; this further reduces disk accesses on retrieval.

Like all database managers, OpenBase uses the indexes that you create as best it can. Sometimes, a query can be entirely fulfilled using only an index: the database table itself never needs to be read. You can neither force OpenBase to use an index nor prevent it from doing so (although dropping the index obviously prevents its use).

In setting up your database, you should make certain that all keys (primary and foreign) are indexed. They are used constantly for data access, and they need the speed of indexing.

Special distributions of data in the database may adversely affect indexes. For example, a field with only two possible values (such as yes and no), should not be indexed. Early versions of DB2 reacted very badly to numeric fields with frequent occurrences of a single value such as 99999.

Indexing is a major area of differentiation among databases. OpenBase, for example, lets you index BLOBs.

7

Running and Maintaining the Database

IN THIS CHAPTER:

Where Are the Databases?

Using OpenBaseManager

Configuring the Database

OpenBase Preferences

Backing Up Databases

Restoring from Backups

Importing from Spreadsheets

Replicating Databases

The previous chapters in this part of the book have showed you how to create your database and its schema, how to manage data and queries, and how to use SQL. Those are one-time or relatively rare events. This chapter looks at running the database: the day-to-day operations that you need to perform.

If you are used to the world of desktop personal computers, realize that the world of application servers and databases (that is, WebObjects and OpenBase or other databases) is different. In the desktop world, you use an application to open a data file, and then close both of them when you are done. In the always-on world of application servers and databases, they run all the time that your computer is on, and they serve users from across the Internet or a local area network.

In this chapter, you work only within a database: you select it in the OpenBaseManager window and then proceed with the commands described here. This chapter rounds out the OpenBase chapters by focusing on the maintenance features that OpenBase provides. Running databases and a Web site normally requires 24 × 7 availability: everything should be running at all times. You accomplish that with redundant hardware and software as well as with regular maintenance procedures that prepare you for the inevitable glitches and make recovery from them as easy as possible.

Where Are the Databases?

You use OpenBaseManager to create and modify databases, but one familiar aspect of file maintenance is missing from the previous chapters. You can name databases, but you never specify their locations on disk. The OpenBase databases are stored in different directories on different operating systems:

▶   Windows 2000: \Apple\OpenBase

▶   Linux: /home/OpenBase

▶   Solaris: /opt/OpenBase

▶   Mac OS X: /Library/OpenBase

Within the OpenBase folder, you will find a subfolder called Databases, and that is where the databases live. You can browse that folder; you will find that each database is itself a folder. The files and folders within the database folders are private to OpenBase: do not move or rename them.

Most database managers function in much the same way: a given location on your computer is used to locate all databases, and the internal data storage structures are private to the data manager. You work totally through SQL and interactive editing tools such as OpenBaseManager to manage the databases.

Using OpenBaseManager

When you install OpenBase (or any other data manager), you specify where and how it runs. Normally, the database manager is started along with all the other housekeeping operations when the computer starts up. It continues running in the background until it and the computer are shut down.

Individual databases can be started or stopped while the database manager is running. Depending on the installation, this is done by a database administrator (DBA), operations staff, or—in many small installations—the Webmaster, WebObjects designer, DBA, and network manager…you.

You can manually start or stop a database by using OpenBaseManager as shown in Figure 7-1.

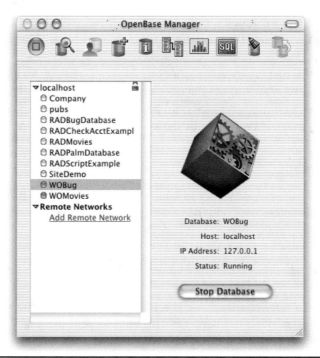

Figure 7-1   *OpenBaseManager*

There are three primary areas of the main window:

1. At the top, a toolbar provides access to frequently used commands through their buttons. If it is not visible, you can show the toolbar using the toolbar button at the right of the window's title bar; you can also use the Toolbar commands from the Tools menu to toggle its appearance.

2. At the left, a list of databases on your computer as well as on remote networks is shown. The indicator to the left of each database name is clear if the database has not yet been started. It is yellow while it is starting up, and it is green while it is running. When a database has been stopped, the indicator is red.

3. At the right, you will see status information about the selected entity— database, network, or local computer. In addition, a button will let you configure a host or start or stop a database, depending on what is selected.

Starting and Stopping Databases

As with so many aspects of the user interfaces and software described in this book, OpenBaseManager just works. Launch the application, select the database you care about, and you will see its status information. If it is not running, the button to start the database will be shown in the right-hand pane along with its status information. As you would expect, once the database is running, the button changes to a Stop Database button.

You can use this display to troubleshoot problems. If people have trouble accessing a database, check to see that it is running; if not, start it. If a database consistently is not running when it should be (and after you know that it has started), you may need to investigate further to see what is causing it to stop.

Using the Toolbar

The buttons in the toolbar may vary in your version of OpenBase from those shown here. However, although they may be in a different order, their icons will be the same. From left to right in Figure 7-1, here is what the buttons do.

▶ **Start/Stop**   If you have selected a database, the first button starts or stops it. The image on the button changes to reflect the action that the button will have.

▶ **Browse Data**   When a database is selected, you can browse its data (and even update it) as described in Chapter 6. This button opens the data browser window.

► **User Manager**   This button lets you manage security for users and groups. Its functions are described in Chapter 27. The users and groups apply only to the selected database, so if you have not selected a database, the button is dimmed.

► **Create Database**   This button creates a new database. It is always available.

► **Configure Database**   This button lets you adjust database settings for the selected database. It is described in the following section of this chapter.

► **Schema Editor**   Use this button to open the Schema Editor window for the selected database; its use was described in Chapter 6.

► **Monitor Database Load**   This opens a small window that shows the performance of the currently selected database. Once a second, OpenBase queries the database to find out what is happening. This is a highly optimized query, and so it does not degrade performance.

► **Interactive SQL**   Use this button to open a graphical or text-based SQL editor for your selected database.

► **Cleanup Database**   Cleanup checks integrity, rearranges disk storage if necessary, and generally prepares the database for further efficient use.

► **Duplicate Database**   This button does just what you would expect. It is available only if you have selected a database in the list that is not running (you cannot duplicate a running database).

Configuring the Database

You can configure the database when you create it, and you can modify its configuration later on. Select a database from the list in OpenBase Manager, and then choose Configure from the Database menu. The window shown in Figure 7-2 will open.

If the database is running, the only option that you can change is the option to automatically start the database when the computer reboots and OpenBase itself is started. The other configuration options must be changed when the database is stopped.

The most frequently used configuration option lets you move the database from one host to another. Typically, you start with the database on your local host computer as you design and develop your system. As it moves into production, you may move it to another computer on your local area network. Configuring the database requires a host password, that is, the password for OpenBase itself on your host.

Figure 7-2   *Configure the database*

OpenBase Preferences

OpenBase preferences allow you to set preferences for the OpenBase software that is running on a computer: you use OpenBaseManager to control these preferences. These apply to all tables within all databases on that computer; to set preferences for individual tables or databases, you use the commands described in the previous chapters.

Basic Preferences

When you select OpenBase Preferences from the OpenBase menu, the window shown in Figure 7-3 opens.

At the top, you select the host computer whose preferences you want to set. The following basic preferences let you specify a sort order as well as the formats of dates, times, and money. Finally, you can set maintenance options for your OpenBase server and specify the directory in which it places its logs.

NetworkPreferences

The Network tab of the Preferences window displays the pane shown in Figure 7-4.

In many cases, you can simply allow the local host information to be set automatically; however, you can also specify a name and IP address for the computer. You may need to do this if it has two or more IP addresses.

Figure 7-3   *OpenBase preferences*

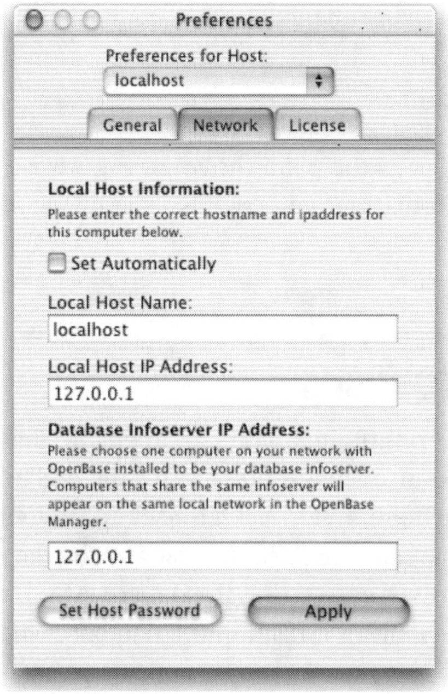

Figure 7-4   *Set Local Net preferences*

One computer on your network is designated as an infoserver; you do so with this window. All of the databases served by OpenBase on all of the computers that share the same infoserver appear on the same network in OpenBaseManager.

Host Password

You can add an infoserver on a remote network using this window. If you do, you then can administer that infoserver and its databases through OpenBaseManager on your own computer (the remote network's name appears in the pop-up button at the top of the Preferences window shown previously in Figure 7-4). You specify the IP address of the remote infoserver, and you can provide any name that you want for it. This is helpful because the name you may use internally on a network (such as "database server") may not be unique or even meaningful when viewed from the outside.

If you do not specify the IP address of an infoserver, OpenBase will locate the infoserver associated with the databases on the IP address that you have specified. However, it is much better to provide the infoserver's address directly.

At the bottom of the Network Preferences window, there is a button you can use to set or change the host password. Obviously, this is the most secure piece of information in the entire database system: once you have it, you can create or destroy users and groups for individual databases. Good database practice is to routinely change this password: a one-month or even one-week update is not unusual in important production environments.

License Preferences

Finally, the License tab opens the pane shown in Figure 7-5. Here you can see (and modify) your license information; you can also see which features are enabled for your license.

Backing Up Databases

While you want to do everything that you can to ensure that your databases are available at all times, you also should prepare for the endless variety of problems that can occur that will require you to have a backup of your database.

OpenBase database backups are ASCII copies of the database tables. The process of creating a backup involves converting the data to ASCII and then dumping it to a file; restoration involves pouring it back into a database (or creating a new database into which to put it).

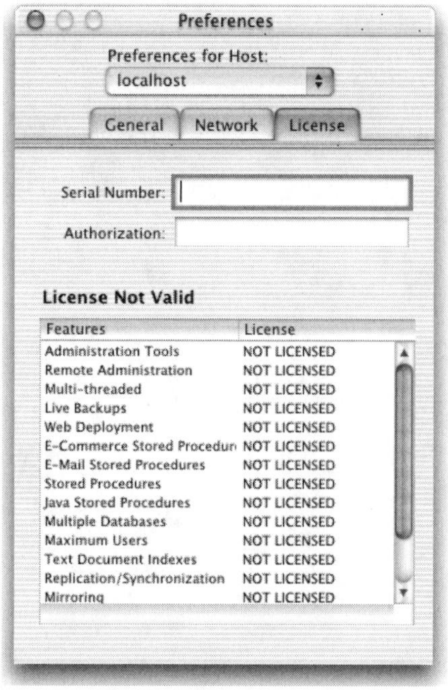

Figure 7-5   *Remote Net preferences*

You can back up any running database by selecting it in OpenBaseManager and choosing Backup to ASCII from the Tools menu. You will be prompted to enter a filename for the backed up data.

You can perform a manual backup at any time. However, the backup process in OpenBase is normally automated. You start by selecting a database that is not started in OpenBaseManager and then choosing Setup Backup Server from the Tools menu. This will open the window shown in Figure 7-6.

To add another database, click Add and open the window shown in Figure 7-7. You can specify a database and its host as well as the user name and password (if any).

All of the databases that you want to back up automatically must be selected in this way. Once you have selected them, you can then use Set Backup Schedule in the Tools menu to specify the backups you want, as shown in Figure 7-8.

You can create any types of backups that you want, and they will be run automatically on either a daily or weekly basis. Each backup that you specify can be active or inactive; thus, you can add databases to your backup server but only activate their backups periodically.

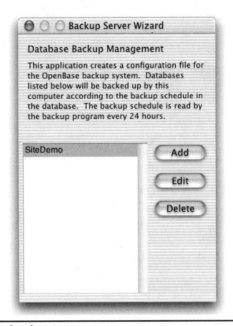

Figure 7-6   *Setting up a backup server*

Figure 7-7   *Select a database to back up*

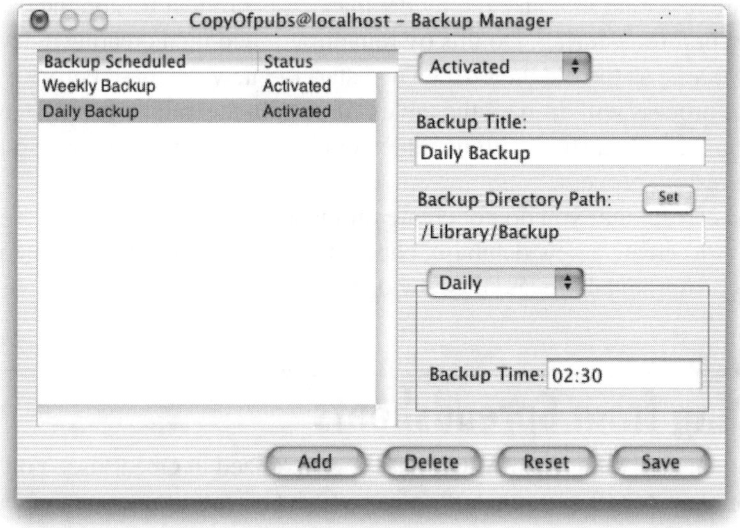

Figure 7-8   *Specify backups for each database*

Restoring from Backups

You can restore from a backup that has been created manually or one that has been created automatically. In either case, the process is the same: choose Restore from Backup from the Tools menu. The window shown in Figure 7-9 will open. As you can see, you have a choice to create a new database (which you will be asked to name) or to restore into a database that you selected before starting the restore command.

Figure 7-9   *Choosing the restore destination*

If you are restoring into an existing database, it is prudent to stop the database and duplicate it before restoring. Do this by renaming it and then creating a new database with a new name as the old database. Then start the new database before restoring. The restore process will drop all the tables (if any) in the database, so your new database can be only a shell with no tables in it. The structure will be imported during the restore process.

Also, be careful that you do not create duplicate data during the restoration. The safer case is to create a new database, check its contents, and then rename the old (possibly corrupt) database and the new one.

Importing from Spreadsheets

The process of importing from ASCII data is generalized in OpenBase. You can import from any ASCII file—including spreadsheets. This allows you to create an OpenBase database into which you import any data that can be found in a spreadsheet. You can generate spreadsheet files not only from programs such as Excel but also by using Save As options in word processing and desktop database applications.

Furthermore, you can copy and paste data from OpenBase into spreadsheets. Browse the data that interests you in the Data Browser, select it, open a spreadsheet, and paste it in.

Replicating Databases

The final maintenance procedure discussed in this chapter is database replication. This is the process by which multiple copies of a database are synchronized with one another. In the case of duplication or importing and exporting, the production database is primary, and the copy (or exported data) is secondary.

In the case of replication, all copies of the database are online at the same time when the replication occurs, and updates may be made to any of them. Replication propagates those changes through all of the databases so that they are mostly identical on all computers at all times. Replication need not happen in real time like this. You can take a copy of your database with you on your laptop and make changes to it. When you return, you can synchronize it with the master database by replicating the two: at that time, the changes in either database will be made to the other until they are the same.

In order to set up databases for replication, you need to prepare the database keys. Select the database in OpenBase Manager, and then choose Configure to open the window shown in Figure 7-10.

Choose Generate Replicated Keys. You will then need to specify the primary and secondary databases in a dialog that is presented next. Use the database numbers that were assigned.

The reason for this process is that, in a nonreplicated database, unique IDs need to be unique within that one database. In a replicated database, the ID numbers used need to be unique across all of the replicated databases; when they are synchronized, if there are two records with ID 4, they will be merged. Thus, Generate Replicated Keys will give you unique values that can be synchronized.

The second step in replication is to select the database to be a replicate and choose Replication Manager from the Tools menu. This will open the window shown in Figure 7-11.

Use the pop-up button in the upper right of the window to select the primary database; then, use the buttons in the lower right to specify the actions to be taken when apparently duplicated (but not identical) data is encountered.

Figure 7-10 *Configuring keys for replication*

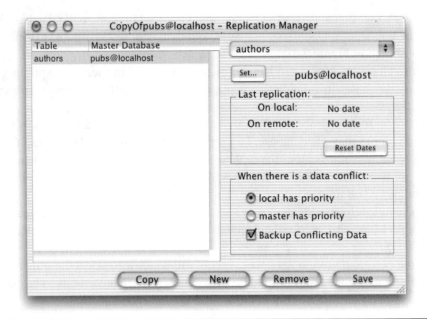

Figure 7-11   *Using Replication Manager*

Note that OpenBase uses the clocks on each computer in its synchronization. This is a good opportunity to use a NTS (Network Time Server) clock: that will make each machine's time as close to those of the others as possible. If your computers have their clocks set manually or via another mechanism, check periodically that their times are correct. OpenBase can manage mildly out-of-synch clocks, but severe discrepancies can cause unexpected results. (Discrepancies on the order of a year or more are the ones you need to worry about.)

Interacting with Databases Using Enterprise Objects

OBJECTIVES

▶ Learn about Enterprise Objects Framework

▶ Understand Enterprise Objects Framework design issues

▶ Manage persistent objects

▶ Use EOModeler

▶ Integrating the model with the database

Introduction to Enterprise Objects Framework

IN THIS CHAPTER:

Databases, Objects, and Enterprise Objects Framework

Factoring Applications and Data

Factoring Logic and Data

Design Strategies: Which End to Start From

How Enterprise Objects Framework Works with WebObjects

I n Part II of this book, you saw how to create and manage relational databases—particularly those using OpenBase. Relational databases are the core of most WebObjects applications. Not only do they store and retrieve data but their relational structure formalizes the data in a manner that is consistent from one vendor's implementation to another. In view of the fact that modern data management is so consistent, it is not difficult to build on top of it. Enterprise Objects Framework does so. It adds two important features to relational databases:

▶   It lets you manage relational integrity for the relationships in your database.

▶   It provides an object-oriented interface to the database. What actually are rows (records) are objects to the programmer. It is these objects that WebObjects applications use.

In this chapter, you will learn about the basic issues of integrating databases with object-oriented programs in general and with WebObjects in particular:

▶   **Databases, objects, and Enterprise Objects Framework**   This section deals with the basic issues of integrating databases with object-oriented programs in general and with WebObjects in particular.

▶   **Factoring applications and data**   Given the design issues described in the first section of this chapter, this section helps you separate your data from your programs.

▶   **Factoring logic and data**   Data that is stored in databases can include a variety of nondata resources; this section helps you identify what is data and what is not.

▶   **Design strategies: which end to start from**   Putting it together requires that you have the big picture, that you know how to start, and that you have a reasonable plan for carrying out your work. This section shows you how to do that.

▶   **How Enterprise Objects Framework works with WebObjects**   Finally, this section of the chapter shows you how Enterprise Objects Framework works with WebObjects. This chapter lays the groundwork for the rest of the chapters in Part III of this book.

Databases, Objects, and Enterprise Objects Framework

Personal computers and telecommunications have been the biggest advances in computer hardware in the last half century. On the software side, object-oriented programming and databases have had the greatest impact. (Arguably, structured programming could be added to this list; however, it is reasonable to consider the concepts of structured programming as precursors of object-oriented programming.) Object-oriented programming and database technology have dramatically increased programmer productivity; they have not only allowed faster development of projects, but they also have permitted larger and more complex projects to be managed than could have happened with their predecessor technologies. Unfortunately, object-oriented programming and database technology have developed fairly independently of one another; not only that, but until the late 1990s, they did not even work together particularly well.

The basic difficulty lies in the fact that both databases and objects store data in one way or another. An object encapsulates data and functionality—that encapsulation means that the object can manipulate its data. A database also stores and manipulates data—but in an environment that focuses on the data itself, not on functionality. The challenge has been to integrate these two overlapping technologies.

One approach to resolving this problem was to create object-oriented databases. In this concept, objects themselves would be stored (somehow) in databases and reconstituted as necessary. Whatever the merits of this approach, it did not catch on. One reason is that databases exist today and they store enormous volumes of information. Application programs have been written to handle the data in those databases. It is not feasible to wave a magic wand and convert all of that data to objects and all of those programs to object-oriented code.

The solution to the problem of integrating databases with objects is to create special types of objects that interact with databases on the one side and with the world of objects on the other. WebObjects has such a technology—Enterprise Objects Framework. The objects from Enterprise Objects Framework interact with databases by using adaptors that are specific to the database product involved. You program your WebObjects application by using objects from Enterprise Objects Framework, and you interact with them in a purely object-oriented way.

What is critical about this architecture is that the databases involved need not be designed specifically to interact with Enterprise Objects Framework. Both Enterprise Objects Framework and WebObjects can work with whatever the database is. This means that you can implement Enterprise Objects Framework and WebObjects applications (including Java clients) to access legacy databases without disturbing them—and without requiring rewrites of legacy software that may access the databases.

Factoring Applications and Data

Conceptually, it is easy to think of your data (which resides in a database) and of your applications (which are implemented in programming languages such as Java and deployed with tools such as WebObjects). The process of separating these two aspects of a project is known as *factoring*. (Factoring applies—in its mathematical sense—to any process of separating parts of a project. It is used to describe separating the user interface from the functionality of an application, for example.)

Although the concept of separating applications and data is apparently simple, in practice, it is not always so. Particularly when you are dealing with databases that you share with other applications or when you are interacting with legacy systems, you may find that the databases you must deal with have not been properly factored: you may need to read, write, and maintain information that is relevant to another application. To a large extent, you may be able to limit this intrusion of other applications to the inside of Enterprise Objects Framework objects, but you may not be successful.

By the same token, limit your application to itself: do not place application data into a database. Even if it is not shared with other applications today, it may be shared tomorrow—and your design choices can make that easier or harder.

Be on the lookout for the type of application data that creeps into databases. Anything that reflects the application (or its interface) rather than the underlying data is suspect. This does not mean that you cannot store application-specific information in a shared database; just make certain that it is isolated (in its own table, for example). Keep it out of the primary data tables. Follow this simple rule of thumb: if people understand the data and the business operations, they should be able to understand the database tables; they don't need to know about any programs that happen to access that data.

In particular, log data (who updated a record and when) is a prime candidate for the incursion of application information into a database. The who and when are legitimate, but adding an IP address, a WebObjects session ID, or a terminal identifier can bring inappropriate application information into the database. Ideally, the database should be designed so that it can be updated from a batch process on a mainframe, a remote user, or over the Internet. The logging information should not assume any one mechanism.

Another area in which application information seeps into databases is in caches and in-progress data stores. It can be very helpful to allow users to enter a complex set of data over a period of time. (A loan application, for example, may require users to stop in the middle to locate a prior year's tax return.) The intermediate data values may represent the stages by which someone enters data using a particular application or interface. The page-by-page Web interface may have eight steps; an interface that processes an uploaded file from a personal computer or handheld device may have one or two steps. As soon as the in-progress data store mirrors a particular interface, you will eventually have trouble when you accommodate another interface.

But by far the biggest culprit in muddying databases with application data is letting the interface intrude into the database. References to page numbers or screen identifiers do not belong in databases: they will change over time.

NOTE

Some databases still use formats that were designed for 80-column punch cards. In these legacy databases, the databases and all of the programs that access them have never been able to be converted to a more modern data layout.

Factoring Logic and Data

A more subtle form of factoring involves keeping inappropriate logic out of the data in the database. Most databases today allow you to program a variety of field edits so that inappropriate data is not stored. Those edits have a tendency to insert application logic into a database.

One approach to edits is to separate them into two categories: validity and quality edits. *Validity edits* are those that cannot under any circumstances be overridden or ignored. They can appropriately be implemented in a database because under no circumstances can they be avoided. A date, for example, may take many formats—normally, a database or its supporting software can do basic conversions. However, the date "Snowflake Butter" is invalid under any known calendar.

Only such validity edits should be implemented in the database, and before doing so, you should check and recheck that the assumptions expressed in the edits are always true.

TIP

Avoid using special values in data fields. A typical culprit is –1, which is often used to indicate missing data rather than a numeric value.

Quality edits are those that under some circumstances can be overridden or ignored. They should not be implemented in databases because they do not apply in all cases: their implementation belongs in applications. Examples of quality edits are range checks, period-to-period comparisons, and any other reasonable measures. Any operator overrides—credit limits, for example—are automatically quality edits.

TIP

If data that fails a validity edit can be stored pending resolution of the question, it is a quality edit, not a validity edit. One way to avoid confusion in database design is to store data as entered as well as data that has been edited. That enables you to park the input data in the entered fields while you go about editing and correcting it in the true database fields.

Design Strategies: Which End to Start From

If you are implementing a system that uses an existing database, you have no choice: you start from the database and work around it. If you are starting from scratch, you can start from either the database or the application: typically, you go back and forth, refining your design.

Once a database has been designed and deployed, it is much easier to change the applications that access it than the database itself. For that reason, the database design should be scrutinized as carefully as possible; be as hard-nosed as you can be about allowing data or logic into the database. Once there, the data and logic will have to be dealt with by every application and user that comes along.

Deliberately stretch your thinking. Will this design work when the access is via a wireless handheld with a very small screen? Does the database design require security restrictions that you cannot implement in the real world? The purpose of such mental exercises is to find any cases in which you have let your application, its interface, or its specific logic creep into the database.

NOTE

Chapter 4 presented a number of database design issues, including normalization. A properly normalized database makes your life much easier. If you have the chance to design (and normalize) the database you are working with, do so; if you have any input whatsoever, do not pass up the opportunity.

How Enterprise Objects Framework Works with WebObjects

Enterprise Objects Framework is an object-oriented framework that you use to create enterprise objects. *Enterprise objects* contain the business logic of your application or process; they contain no information about the database or the user interface (unless they must do so in very special circumstances to work around database design problems raised by legacy systems). You program your WebObjects application by using the enterprise objects; Enterprise Objects Framework provides tools you can use to integrate your objects with specific databases.

Using Enterprise Objects

From the WebObjects side, enterprise objects manage *persistence* (storage and retrieval) with a minimum of your intervention. For basic applications, you can assume that your objects are simply always there. For more sophisticated applications, you can take a more aggressive role in managing persistence and in handling contention and concurrency.

An Enterprise Objects Framework object can contain a single database element (that is, one field or column for one record), an entire row, parts of a row, or a dynamically created set of data that comes from several tables or that is derived from various data elements. The object should normally correspond to a real-world business entity, object, or concept such as a customer, an inventory item, a schedule, or a news item. (Note that the real-world parallel need not be a physical object.)

Because Enterprise Objects Framework lets you map database items to your enterprise objects, you need not be constrained by the design that a database has (which may not be optimal for your purposes). You need to accommodate only one constraint: a single database row cannot be part of two enterprise objects that are used in the same context. (For simplicity, consider that to mean a single WebObjects application for now.) An enterprise object may comprise information from two or more rows in two or more database tables, but each row must uniquely belong to a single enterprise object. (This is referred to as *uniquing*.)

Once you have mapped the database data to your enterprise objects, Enterprise Objects Framework takes care of keeping the objects organized. This includes storing and retrieving them as necessary. The Framework lets you work with enterprise objects that may not actually have data in them: its *faulting* process populates the objects with data when necessary.

NOTE

You can use an inventory object in preparing a Web page to display an e-commerce catalog; for that purpose, you may need the item's name, its image, and its price. You may not need to know the name and address of the vendor from which the e-commerce business can purchase additional stock, so the Framework may not get around to filling those fields in the objects. If those fields are necessary, they will be filled automatically by the Framework.

This mapping of database tables and fields to your enterprise objects is called a *model*. Together with your user interface (implemented in WebObjects), the enterprise objects themselves, the Framework's classes, and a database and its adaptors, you have a customizable and maintainable application.

The Enterprise Objects Framework Structure

When you use Enterprise Objects Framework, your application has five parts:

▶ **Enterprise objects**   The objects you create that incorporate data and logic as exemplars of real-world entities

▶ **Model**   The mapping of database tables and fields to enterprise objects

▶ **User interface**   The WebObjects classes that create Web pages and manage the request-response loop

▶ **Enterprise Objects Framework classes**   The classes that manage operations on the database and on Enterprise Objects Framework objects.

▶ **Database and database adaptors**   The adaptors (custom-written or provided by WebObjects) that let you access the databases that you use to support your application

These five parts work together most effectively when you clearly delineate their roles. Just as it is important to factor applications and data, you need to factor each of these parts and their functionality. For example, you can choose to implement certain data edits in any of several parts of your application. The invalid date previously cited in this chapter (Snowflake Butter) can be caught in the database itself, in the user interface, or in the enterprise object. Other edits that require checking against data in the database (that is, data in other enterprise objects) can also be performed in several places. Choose the editing environment that is most efficient and robust: sometimes an edit will be performed in more than one place.

DESIGN TIP

Edits that are not data-dependent can be implemented in the interface and can provide very fast response to a user. For example, you can check that a date or e-mail address is in the right format in this manner. The fact that you may need to repeat the edit in the database environment should not discourage you from doing it in both places. Just make sure that the two edits are consistent. They may not be identical, but there should be a logic to them. For example, the interface may check that a date is correctly formed. The enterprise object may check that the date is within a certain range (such as during a person's membership period). The database may perform both edits—or neither. Database edits should be unconditional (that is, they can never be avoided or overridden); therefore, they often cannot be done at the database level even though intuitively that may seem like the appropriate place to perform edits.

The WebObjects framework provides the basic functionality that you need to support the request-response loop and to dynamically create Web pages. Likewise, Enterprise Objects Framework provides the basic functionality for interacting with databases and for performing common tasks such as the following:

▶ Editing data can be implemented in the Framework; in addition, database infrastructure administration including referential integrity and key management are supported in the Framework.

▶ Storage and transaction management are also implemented in the Framework.

▶ The Framework supports adaptors so that you do not have to worry about the idiosyncrasies of individual database technologies when designing your applications and objects.

Enterprise Objects Framework Design Issues

W eb sites—particularly database-driven Web sites—quickly become very complex. This part of the book uses SiteDemo in order to show you how to build such a site and how to map the concepts of the previous chapter to the Web pages you see and build. Note that this example is stripped down to its basics of functionality both in code and in the pages that are shown. It is not meant to be an example of good interface design, but the code itself is meant to be a foundation on which you can build your own code.

NOTE

The ThinkMovies WebObjects example that is distributed with WebObjects is the basis for this example; it is more complex and complete, but both this and ThinkMovies have the same basic structure. Furthermore, wherever possible names of methods and variables follow the ThinkMovies naming patterns to make it easy for you to compare the two.

In this chapter, you will find a walk-through of the basic site pages as well as the WebObjects code that supports them. The detailed code to support persistence is described in Chapter 10. The full WebObjects project is available for download at http://www.philmontmill.com in the WebObjects section. As is so often the case with WebObjects, you can look at functionality from at least two sides: the Web interface side and the database side. This part of the book focuses on the Enterprise Objects Framework routines and the database, but the Web interface code is also provided. In the next part of the book, there are more details on the interface code, and some of the database code is repeated without the explanatory text. In short, you will see it twice, each time from a different perspective.

The WebObjects Application

Start with a WebObjects application in Project Builder. The Main component shell will be built automatically for you. You need to customize it by causing your start page to be loaded. Here is the code for Main:

```
import com.webobjects.foundation.*;
import com.webobjects.appserver.*;
import com.webobjects.eocontrol.*;
import com.webobjects.eoaccess.*;

public class Main extends WOComponent {

  protected EOEnterpriseObject item;
  protected WODisplayGroup itemsDisplayGroup;
```

```
public Main(WOContext context) {
  super(context);
  }

}
```

You need not add anything to the code that is created automatically for you in WebObjects for a basic application. However, for an application such as SiteDemo, you will need to add code. Fortunately, it is generally boilerplate code that is customized only for the names of your Enterprise Objects Framework model and its entities. In this case, you need to declare a display group and an item (both lines in boldface). They are used to display the dynamic results on this page (the most recent entries in the database).

Start Page

Figure 9-1 shows the start page for this example. It contains the data pulled from the database and shown in the display group ("Meeting on Tuesday…").

Figure 9-1   *Start page for SiteDemo*

Two basic functions are illustrated in this example: adding records to a database and searching for them. The links on this page are both links to WebObjects direct actions: AddItem and Search. Each of those direct actions creates a page that is a standard WebObjects component (the pages are AddItem and Search). Those are the pages that will be returned to the user.

To implement this page, work with the Main component that is created by default in your WebObjects project. Double-click Main.wo to open WebObjects Builder. Enter the title for the page and create two WOHyperlink objects—Add Content and Search. Specify the action class for each link as DirectAction, and identify the directActionName as "Search" or "AddInfo". Note that all of these properties are quoted strings: for example, the directActionName is "Search", not Search.

TIP

In an actual application, you need to decide at what point (if any) to implement gatekeepers for security purposes. Can anyone click Add Content, or are only registered users allowed to do so? Perhaps anyone can click Add Content, but only registered users can click the Submit button on the page it leads to. See Chapter 27 for more on security. Because these links use direct actions, they can be bookmarked. If they did not, users would have to come through the start page to get to them.

Entry Page

From the start page, users can go to the Add Content page shown in Figure 9-2.

In addition to their titles and other information, entry pages always contain one or more HTML forms. The form you see here is a simple one: it contains a title (NewContentForm), several data entry fields, a Reset button, and a Submit button (the Submit button is named Add Item).

Start by creating a new component (from New in the File menu). Name it AddItem. You need to write some Java code in Project Builder, and you need to create the page in WebObjects Builder. You can do these in either order.

Creating the Page in WebObjects Builder

Add a form to the page. It should contain eight strings and text fields (Category, Title, Information, and so forth) for the titles of the data and the data itself. (If you want, you can align these in a table.) You need to set up key bindings as follows (note that what follows is the contents of the AddItem.wod file—refer to Chapter 14

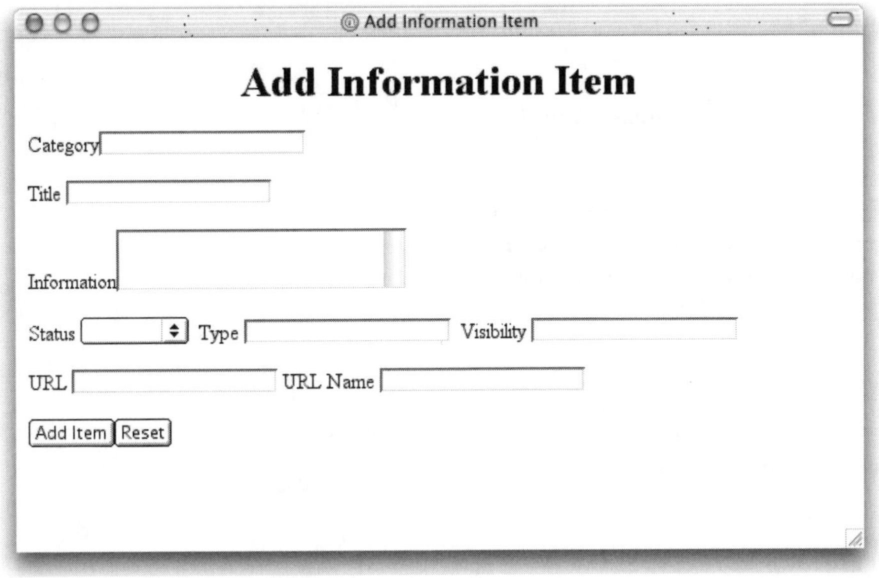

Figure 9-2   *Entry page*

for details of using WebObjects Builder). You can use the default names such as Form1, or you can change them in the Inspector window in WebObjects Builder.

The form itself as well as the Submit button are bound to the direct action ConfirmAdd and the actionClass DirectAction. Note, again, that these are quoted strings, as you can see in the following code.

Each of the data entry elements is bound to a name (a quoted string) and a value (a Java instance variable, described in the next section). The pop-up button is also bound to a method in the Java class: `statuslist`. The method and the variables are entered as values, not quoted strings.

```
Form1: WOForm {
 directActionName = "ConfirmAdd";
 actionClass = "DirectAction";
}

PopUpButton2: WOPopUpButton {
 name = "status";
 list = statusList;
 value = status;
 selectedValue = status;
```

```
  item = status;
}

ResetButton1: WOResetButton {
}

SubmitButton1: WOSubmitButton {
 actionClass = "DirectAction";
 directActionName = "ConfirmAdd";
 value = "Add Item";
}

TextField1: WOTextField {
 value = category;
 name = "category";
}

TextField3: WOTextField {
 value = type;
 name = "type";
}

TextField4: WOTextField {
 value = visibility;
 name = "visibility";
}

TextField5: WOTextField {
 value = URL;
 name = "URL";
}

TextField6: WOTextField {
 value = URLname;
 name = "URLName";
}

TextField7: WOTextField {
 value = title;
 name = "title";
}
```

```
informationTextArea: WOText {
 cols = 40;
 rows = 3;
 value = information;
 name = "information";
}
```

Writing the Code in Project Builder

You need two sections of code. The first is located in the AddItem.java file in the
AddContentPage component that was created for you automatically when you added
the component. The second is the direct action itself.

Code for AddContentPage Component

You need to add the boldfaced code to the file. The first section is the instance
variables to which the data entry fields are bound; the second section is the method
that returns the list of items for the pop-up button.

```
//
// AddItem.java: Class file for WO Component 'AddItem'
// Project SiteDemo
//
// Created by jfeiler on Mon Aug 13 2001
//

import com.webobjects.foundation.*;
import com.webobjects.appserver.*;
import com.webobjects.eocontrol.*;
import com.webobjects.eoaccess.*;

public class AddItem extends WOComponent {

  protected String category;
  protected String information;
  protected String status;
  protected String title;
  protected String type;
  protected String visibility;
  protected String URL;
  protected String URLname;
```

```
    public AddItem(WOContext context) {
      super(context);
    }

    public NSArray statusList () {
      return Application.statusList;
    }
}
```

This component displays the entry page shown in Figure 9-2; unloading the data and processing it is the responsibility of the direct action, ConfirmAdd—the direct action name specified in the .wod file.

Code for the Direct Action Component

Remember that all direct actions have "Action" appended to their name; thus, you must write a ConfirmAddAction to match the binding to ConfirmAdd you specified in the WebObjects Builder file. This method should be placed in DirectAction.java, which you may have to create if it does not already exist. (To create it, create a new Java class, DirectAction, which extends WODirectAction.)

The entire method is shown here; it is annotated inline.

This method will unload the data from the form and add it to the database. You will need a reference to the application itself; next call the request method to get the HTTP request that contains the form data from the user. Use this code as is.

```
public WOActionResults ConfirmAddAction () {
  Application anApp = Application.myApplication ();
  WORequest aRequest = request ();
```

Next, create an object into which to place the data from the user's form. In this case, you create an object called newItem, which is the object that will be stored in the database table Item. Note that this object is an instance of the Item class that you generated from EOModeler using the Java button.

```
  Item newItem = new Item();
```

Next, unload the request fields into the instance variables using the accessors created in the EOModeler Java code:

```
  newItem.setCategory ((String)aRequest.formValueForKey (categoryKey));
  newItem.setInformation ((String)aRequest.formValueForKey (informationKey));
  newItem.setStatus ((String)aRequest.formValueForKey (statusKey));
  newItem.setTitle ((String)aRequest.formValueForKey (titleKey));
```

```
newItem.setType ((String)aRequest.formValueForKey (typeKey));
newItem.setVisibility ((String)aRequest.formValueForKey (visibilityKey));
newItem.setURL ((String)aRequest.formValueForKey (URLKey));
newItem.setURLName ((String)aRequest.formValueForKey (URLNameKey));
```

All of these accessor methods are created automatically for you by EOModeler when it creates your Java class from the model. You merely need to keep track of the names you have used for the fields in WebObjects Builder. The keys are defines of the following sort:

```
private String informationKey = "information";
```

In each case, this string must match the string bound to the name property of the appropriate field in WebObjects Builder.

The editing context for your application is what handles persistence: it is discussed in Chapter 10. For now, it is sufficient to know that the following code—with one change—will insert your new object (filled with data from the user's HTTP request) into the editing context and thence into the database. The one change you make in this code is replacing newItem with whatever your object name is.

```
EOEditingContext anEC = anApp.lockEC();
anEC.insertObject (newItem);
anEC.saveChanges();
anApp.unlockEC();
```

While that will do the trick, you also can provide a more robust process if you check for errors. The following code adds error checking to the previous code. Again, simply replace the name of the object you are adding. You can add this error checking code even if you have not yet implemented your own custom validation. When you do, that code will be called; in the meantime, the default code will be called. In other words, there is no harm in adding this code as a routine matter.

```
EOEditingContext anEC = anApp.lockEC();
try {
    anEC.insertObject(newItem);
    anEC.saveChanges();
} catch (NSValidation.ValidationException ex) {
    exception = ex;
    anEC.undo();
} finally {
    anApp.unlockEC();
}
```

Finally, remember that you need to return a page to the user. You can create a confirmation page saying that the data has been added. As is commonly the case, a confirmation page is used for several actions: ConfirmAddEdit confirms both of those.

```
WOComponent aPage = pageWithName("ConfirmAddEdit");
return aPage;
```

Search Page

The search page is shown in Figure 9-3.

Creating the Page in WebObjects Builder

Here are the bindings from the .wod file that implement the search form.

All searches are combinations of operators (explicit or implied) and data values for which to search. This form is no exception. To search by the title of content entries, you select from a pop-up button to specify the type of relation, and you type in a value.

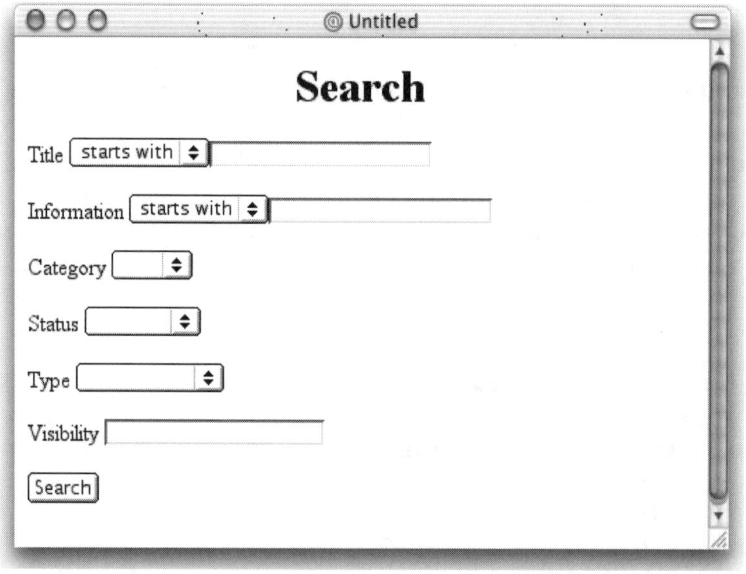

Figure 9-3   *Search page*

Every WOPopUpButton has a list of values; you bind `textOperatorList` (which you will write in Java) to that `list` key.

Rather than returning separate values for the search operators and values, this architecture returns everything in a dictionary—`queryDict`. It is created in Java when you instantiate this page, and it is returned in the HTTP request and processed by the direct action invoked by the form. Thus, you will see a number of bindings to `queryDict` key/value entries.

Here are the bindings for the pop-up button:

```
PopUpButton1: WOPopUpButton {
  name = "titleOpKey";
  list = textOperatorList;
  value = queryDict.titleOperator;
  item = queryDict.titleOperator;
  selectedValue = queryDict.titleOperator;
}
```

Next, you create a WOTextField into which users can type the value to search for. Note that its value will be placed in `queryDict.title`.

```
TitleTextField: WOTextField {
  name = "title";
  size = 30;
  value = queryDict.title;
}
```

All of the search form's operators and values are handled in the same way. Finally, you bind the form's direct action to Results, which you will implement as ResultsAction in DirectAction.java.

```
SearchForm: WOForm {
  directActionName = "Results";
}
```

```
SearchForm: WOForm {
  directActionName = "Results";
}
```

Writing the Code in Project Builder

Here is the code you write to support the search page. Once again, there are two pieces: the code to display the search page and the code for the direct action.

Code for SearchPage Component

You need to create the queryDict that will be used to pass data back and forth. The boldfaced code in this class is the declaration and then the creation of that dictionary. The only other code you add is the code to access the lists to populate the pop-up button.

```java
import com.webobjects.foundation.*;
import com.webobjects.appserver.*;
import com.webobjects.eocontrol.*;
import com.webobjects.eoaccess.*;

public class Search extends WOComponent {

    protected NSMutableDictionary queryDict;

    public Search(WOContext context) {
        super(context);
        queryDict = new NSMutableDictionary();
    }

    public NSArray textOperatorList() {
        return Application.textOperators;
    }

    public NSArray typeList () {
        return Application.typeList;
    }

    public NSArray statusList () {
        return Application.statusList;
    }

    public NSArray categoryList () {
        return Application.categoryList;
    }
}
```

Here is the code in Application.java that supports `textOperatorList`. Note that this type of code is commonly placed in Application.java rather than in individual components so that all pop-up buttons with similar types of values in an application have exactly the same values.

```
public static final NSArray textOperators = new NSArray
  ( new Object[] { "starts with","ends with","contains", "is" });
```

Code for the Direct Action

The direct action bound to the form is Results; you implement it in ResultsAction in DirectAction.java as follows. As usual, much of the code can be used as is. You start by setting up variables and getting the HTTP request. Nothing needs customizing here except the name of the page that will display a batch of data:

```
public WOComponent ResultsAction() {
  WOComponent  aPage = pageWithName( "DisplayBatchPage" );
  WORequest aRequest = request();
  NSMutableDictionary aDict = queryDictionaryFromRequest( aRequest );
```

This method will be used to process the Previous and Next links on the summary display page. For that purpose, batch numbers are needed (results 1 to 10 might be batch 1, 11 to 20 batch 2, and so forth).

```
  Number aBatch = numericFormValueFromRequest( aRequest, "batchIndex" );
```

The first time through, batch will not have been set, and it will be `null`. The following line sets it to 1.

```
  int aBatchIndex = (aBatch == null) ? 1 : aBatch.intValue();
```

The boilerplate code that follows does the actual retrieval. Nothing needs customization here.

```
  Application anApp = Application.myApplication();
  WODisplayGroup aDG = displayGroupFromRequest( aDict );
  try {
    EOEditingContext anEC = anApp.lockEC();
    aDG.qualifyDataSource();
```

From the display group, you obtain a list of objects to display.

```
  NSArray aList = aDG.displayedObjects();
```

You create the page to return and set the number of items per batch. Then, the display group just takes care of everything. The only thing you have to do other than to set the variables is to handle the special case in which the batch index is 0. The only customization that you need to do here is to change the name of the page that displays a batch of results (or you can use DisplayBatchPage as long as you name the page with that name).

```
aPage = pageWithName( "DisplayBatchPage" );
   aDG.setNumberOfObjectsPerBatch( 10 );

   int maxBatch = aDG.batchCount();

   if (aBatchIndex < 1) {
     aBatchIndex = maxBatch;
     }

   aDG.setCurrentBatchIndex( aBatchIndex );
   aPage.takeValueForKey( aDG, "displayGroup" );

   } finally {
   anApp.unlockEC();
 }
 aPage.takeValueForKey (aDict, "queryDict");
 return aPage;
}
```

As you can see, very little new code needs to be written to implement a search.

Summary Display Page

The summary display page is shown in Figure 9-4.

Creating the Page in WebObjects Builder

There are three important sections to this page:

1. Result summary information (number found, numbers shown)
2. Titles and links to add discussions or edit the item
3. Previous/next batches

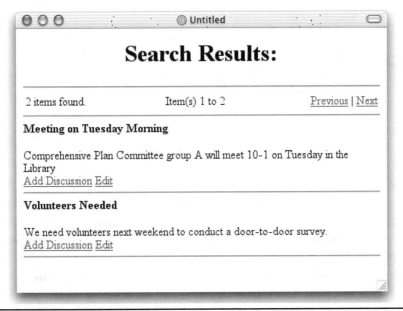

Figure 9-4   *Summary display page*

The heart of this page is a WebObjects displayGroup: an object containing database query results to be displayed. The ResultsAction method described previously set this for you. You will note these two lines in the center of that code:

```
aDG.setCurrentBatchIndex( aBatchIndex );
aPage.takeValueForKey( aDG, "displayGroup" );
```

The display group (`aDG`) is set with the batch index (1 to start), and the page that is being built—which is this page—has its `displayGroup` key set to `aDG`. You can therefore use the displayGroup object here.

Result Summary Information

You can bind WOString objects to displayGroup methods. These are standard WebObjects methods, and they require no implementation on your part. These are the bindings that produce the numbers 3, 1, and 3, as in "3 items found" and "Item(s) 1 to 3":

```
FromString: WOString {
  value = displayGroup.indexOfFirstDisplayedObject;
}
ToString: WOString {
  value = displayGroup.indexOfLastDisplayedObject;
}
TotalItemsFound: WOString {
  value = displayGroup.allObjects.count;
}
```

Titles and Links

A WORepetition object (available from the WebObjects Builder toolbar) handles the iteration that is common to these pages. You need to create two bindings for it: `list` returns the list of items to be displayed, and `item` is an NSKeyValueCoding object that provides your data. Note that this structure does not involve the use of a specific object: you can use generic Enterprise Objects Framework objects and rely on their key/value pairs to store your data. The list binding will always look like this; the item binding must match the declaration you will make in the Java code.

```
ListRepetition: WORepetition {
  item = item;
  list = displayGroup.displayedObjects;
}
```

Within the WORepetition object, you place a WOHyperlink object, and within that, a WOString object for the data fields. You bind the `value` of the string to the appropriate key of your object. As you can see, you can bind elements of the entity returned (item) as well as elements that are related to it (information in the discussions relationship to the item).

```
String1: WOString {
  value = item.title;
}

informationItem: WOString {
  value = item.information;
};

String6: WOString {
  value = item.discussions.information;
}
```

The links to add discussions or to edit the item are created as normal WOHyperlinks. The name of the actionClass is "DirectAction", and the name of the actionClassName is "AddDiscussion" or "EditItem". You need to add a custom binding such as ?itemid and bind a unique key such as item.rowid to it. That binding will then be passed on through the link, and you can use it to retrieve the needed data. Here, for example, is the code for the link to add a discussion to an item:

```
Hyperlink2: WOHyperlink {
  actionClass = "DirectAction";
  directActionName = "AddDiscussion";
  ?itemid = item.rowid;
}
```

Previous/Next Batches

Two other links are provided on this page: they let you go to the previous or next batch. Each one needs bindings as shown here. You provide a direct action—in this case, `Results` is used again (it was used for the first search, and it contains code to handle `batchIndex` variables if provided). You will need to implement `batchIndexPlusOne` and `batchIndexMinusOne` in your Java code. Remember to pass `queryDict` back so that it can be used in the direct action.

```
NextBatch: WOHyperlink {
  ?batchIndex = batchIndexPlusOne;
  directActionName = "Results";
  queryDictionary = queryDict;
}

PreviousBatch: WOHyperlink {
  ?batchIndex = batchIndexMinusOne;
  directActionName = "Results";
  queryDictionary = queryDict;
}
```

Writing the Code in Project Builder

As usual, there are two sets of code to implement in Project Builder. You need the support code for the DisplayBatchPage component, and you need to implement a direct action for each of the links—adding a discussion or editing an item. Creating those links is similar to creating any other direct actions, so this section concentrates on the code you have to write to display the batches.

Starting from the code generated when you create the DisplayBatchPage component, customize it to add three variables and the two batch processing methods required for the WebObjects Builder page.

```
import com.webobjects.foundation.*;
import com.webobjects.appserver.*;
import com.webobjects.eocontrol.*;
import com.webobjects.eoaccess.*;

public class DisplayBatchPage extends WOComponent {
```

The following are the three variables that you need to declare. The first (displayGroup) is set in the ResultsAction direct action; its contents are used by the WebObjects Builder page in displaying data. You do nothing here except declare it.

```
protected WODisplayGroup displayGroup;
```

The next variable, queryDict, is a dictionary in which query key/value pairs are stored. Again, you declare it here so that it can be used elsewhere.

```
protected NSMutableDictionary queryDict;
```

Finally, you declare a custom object, item, which is your custom object. It is created by EOModeler when you create Java classes from your model,

```
protected Item item;

public DisplayBatchPage( WOContext context ) {
 super( context );
 }
```

These are the two methods that increment and decrement the current batch index for next/previous processing. Copy them exactly:

```
public int batchIndexPlusOne() {
    return displayGroup.currentBatchIndex() + 1;
  }

  public int batchIndexMinusOne() {
    return displayGroup.currentBatchIndex() - 1;
  }
```

Persistent Objects

IN THIS CHAPTER:

Issues of Persistence

Faulting

Fetching Data with an Editing Context

Fetching Data with a Display Group

Database applications by their very nature deal with persistent data, that is, data that is available for the application to use whenever it wants to, whether that is after a few seconds of doing something else or after months or years of doing something else. Persistence is one of those things that just works most of the time, but you should know what is going on for those cases in which problems arise or you need to optimize an application. This chapter introduces you to persistence in general; it then goes on to describe the WebObjects faulting mechanism that is used to retrieve data on an as-needed basis.

WebObjects uses editing contexts to manage data, and that concept is explained in this chapter. (You saw display groups in action in the previous chapter.) Finally, you will see how to fetch data from a database using either a display group or an editing context.

Issues of Persistence

In dealing with persistent data, there are two issues you need to address:

1. You need to be able to map and remap the database data to your program's memory structures. Basically, this is an issue that plays out over time: you must be able to repeat the retrieval and mapping at will. Enterprise Objects Framework does this for you.

2. You need to work around changes to the data that have occurred outside your application's purview. This is a matter of data sharing because changes your application does not know about are, by definition, made by others. Changes made by various users who are working with your application may well fall into this category. Most database applications store data in a database and then ignore it until it is needed again. The architecture that keeps users out of one another's way relies on the database for coordination.

Because data can change without your application's involvement, your in-memory data must always be considered to be no more than probably correct. (Quite probably correct, but still not necessarily correct.) If you are experienced in writing systems for shared environments, none of this is new to you. However, if you are coming to WebObjects and Enterprise Objects Framework from the world of desktop computing or as a Webmaster who is starting to move into applications, you should appreciate the importance of persistence and the issues it raises. As a general rule, you cannot add in multiuser capabilities and data locking after the fact: you must build them in from the very beginning of your application design.

Fortunately, building persistence management into your application is very easy with WebObjects and Enterprise Objects Framework. This chapter shows you how to store and retrieve data, and it spends very little time on the architectures needed to manage persistence. In fact, for most purposes, there is only one thing that you need to know about persistence: all methods that can access the database may fail. WebObjects uses exceptions in Java to get out of these failures, and appropriate error messages are returned to the user in most cases.

You can customize the default WebObjects error messages to provide information to your users in terms they can understand. See Chapter 21 for information on customizing error messages.

NOTE

A related issue to persistence is that of security. See Chapter 27 for more on that topic.

Faulting

WebObjects uses a mechanism named *faulting* to optimize its performance. Faulting delays database accesses to the last possible moment, providing just-in-time data delivery to WebObjects applications. There are two benefits to this strategy:

▶ By getting the most recent data from the database, WebObjects reduces the possibility that the in-memory copy of the database data differs from the data in the database.

▶ Objects that incorporate database data can be instantiated quickly and used earlier if their database data is not retrieved until needed.

This architecture requires careful coordination between WebObjects and the Enterprise Objects Framework objects with which it deals. Fortunately, WebObjects is a mature product, and this architecture has been proven over many years: It works.

Faulting relies on objects communicating their data needs at the appropriate times. The default accessors of object properties in WebObjects all properly call methods named `willRead` and `willChange`. Your implementation of accessors for your own data automatically goes through these accessors (unless you deliberately change them); thus, you don't have to worry about notifying WebObjects that data needs to be loaded (the objects need to be faulted, in technical terms).

Two special faulting mechanisms can be used to improve your application's performance: batch faulting and prefetching.

Batch Faulting

Batch faulting applies to an Enterprise Objects Framework entity that is usually a database table. You can set it in EOModeler by selecting the Advanced Entity tab in the Inspector tool. Clicking the checkbox will turn batch faulting on for that entity. When a fault is issued against that entity (that is, when a row is requested from the database), a batch of records is returned; typically, they are related records from another table. (You can specify what the batch is to be by selecting an entity in EOModeler and clicking the Advanced Entity button in the Inspector window for that entity. See Chapter 11 for more on EOModeler.)

You can set up batch faulting programmatically; you do so with the batchFetchRelationship method of EODatabaseContext.

```
public void batchFetchRelationship(
  EORelationship relationship,
  NSArray objects,
  com.webobjects.eocontrol.EOEditingContext anEditingContext)
```

You pass in an array of objects as well as a relationship that they have (User to Item, for example). The elements of that relationship are retrieved for all of the objects in the array—that is, all User records for the Item objects are retrieved at once.

This can optimize performance if done properly, and it can cripple your application if not. For batch faulting of this nature to work, you need to know that:

- ▶ All of the data will be needed (do not retrieve all of the related records for 100 objects of which only 20 will be browsed by a user)
- ▶ You have sufficient memory to store the results
- ▶ You have a moment at which a possibly time-consuming database call can be carried out

There is more on batch faulting in the documentation of EODatabaseContext. The range of choices you have is large, ranging from the EOModeler-determined batching (if you choose that option) to your own programmatically controlled batching.

Prefetching

Prefetching retrieves related objects such as all Discussion objects for an Item object. You can set prefetching in the fetch specifications you create in EOModeler (they are described later in this chapter in the sections on fetching data). You specify which relationship you want to prefetch, and WebObjects does the rest.

The same considerations apply to prefetching as do to batch faulting: you need to know that you'll use all the data, you need the memory to store it, and you may be invoking a length database call. But, like batch faulting, prefetching can improve your application's performance.

Note that prefetching fetches the related data for a given object; batch faulting may do the same thing, but more often it is used to retrieve a number of objects' related data.

Fetching Data with an Editing Context

This section shows you how to use an editing context to fetch data. If you want to write SQL fetch statements, this is for you. If you want to have WebObjects and Enterprise Objects Framework automatically fill a display group for you, the next section should fit the bill.

Each WebObjects application that uses Enterprise Objects Framework needs an editing context (some use more than one). The editing context manages communication between the Enterprise Objects Framework objects and WebObjects.

You declare an instance variable in your override of WOApplication (usually called Application) as follows:

```
private EOEditingContext editingContext;
```

You create one in the constructor for using the following code:

```
editingContext = new EOEditingContext();
```

The editing context is passed around as a parameter in various database-related calls. You will see it used throughout this book.

In order to fetch data using an editing context, you first get the editing context, then create a query, and then execute it to fetch the data.

Getting the Editing Context

You can create an editing context as you need it, but for an application with shared data, the shared editing context from the application object is usually used. It is locked while each part of your application uses it, and an accessor is usually combined with a lock state call in the Application override of WOApplication as you can see here:

```
public EOEditingContext lockEC() {
  editingContext.lock();
  return editingContext;
}
```

The companion method is presented here for the sake of completeness:

```
public void unlockEC() {
  editingContext.unlock();
}
```

When you need an editing context, you can obtain the application's context and have it locked with these calls:

```
Application anApp = Application.myApplication();
EOEditingContext anEC = anApp.lockEC();
```

Make certain to unlock the editing context as quickly as possible with this code:

```
anEC.unlockEC();
```

Building the Query

There are two steps here: creating the qualifier (the WHERE clause in SQL) and creating a fetch specification. Building the qualifier often involves `qualifierWithQualifierFormat`.

This method is based on the `printf()` function in C. It contains a format string and an array of items to be output into the formatted qualifier. As with `printf()`, the format string itself may be complete, and there may be no items to output. Here is an example of that case:

```
EOQualifier qualifier =
  EOQualifier.qualifierWithQualifierFormat("City = 'Valatie'", null);
```

However, you may want to build the qualifier dynamically. The following code places two strings into the array to be printed; one of them is a constant, and the other is presumed to be a local variable—it could also be an accessor. This would allow you to bind an interface element to it so that users could type in data to be used in the search.

```
NSMutableArray args = new MutableVector();
args.addObject("City");
args.addObject(currentCity);
EOQualifier qualifier =
  EOQualifier.qualifierWithQualifierFormat("%@ = %@", args);
```

After you have created your qualifier, you create an EOFetchSpecification. There are several constructors for EOFetchSpecification; here is one of the most common. It takes three arguments: the entity name (from your Enterprise Objects Framework model), a qualifier, and an array of sort orderings. In the code that follows, there are no sort orderings.

```
aFetchSpecification = new EOFetchSpecification("User", qualifier, null);
```

Fetching the Data

You call `objectsWithFetchSpecification` to fetch the data. It is a method of your editing context, so you can simply write the following:

```
NSMutableArray theResults = new NSMutableVector ();
theResults = anEC. objectsWithFetchSpecification (aFetchSpecification);
```

The results (if any) will be placed in the array: they are enterprise objects and you can start using them right away. You do not have to map any data into variables.

Fetching Data with a Display Group

Although the previous method is not particularly difficult, display groups make fetching data even easier. This section walks you through the process of doing that. (You can also create a display group project using the New Project command from the File menu; that is even easier.) There are three things to do:

1. Declare the display group in your application.
2. Put it into a WORepetition on your Web page using WebObjects Builder.
3. Create a Fetch Spec in your Enterprise Objects Framework using EOModeler.

(WebObjects Builder and EOModeler are discussed later in the book, but these steps briefly show some of their uses.)

Declare the Display Group

In your Application object, declare a display group as follows:

```
protected WODisplayGroup itemsDisplayGroup;
```

Place a Display Group in a WORepetition

You use WebObjects Builder to create a display group inside a repetition. What you do is to add a repetition to your page and, as shown in Figure 10-1, bind its item property to your Enterprise Objects Framework entity component, and you will see something like what is shown in Figure 10-1. (In this case, the item property is bound to a variable called "item" which is of the class Item. You could just as well bind the item property to a variable called "myClient," which might be of the class Client.)

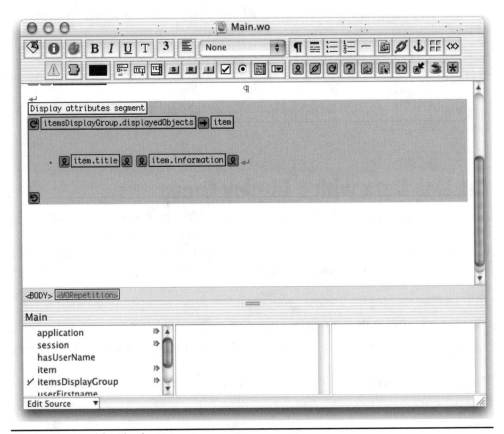

Figure 10-1 *Add a display group to your page*

You bind the WORepetition object's `list` to your display group's `displayedObjects` array. (Chapter 14 is devoted to using WebObjects Builder.) Then, double-click the display group in the browser at the lower left to open the Display Group Options window shown in Figure 10-2.

For simple cases, you can just click OK. Until you open the Display Group Options window, the display group is marked as not completed; the check mark next to its name in Figure 10-1 shows that the options have been set.

In this case, one change has been made: a Fetch Spec named FetchFront has been selected. It controls the data that will be shown. You create Fetch Specs using EOModeler, and you will see how to do that shortly.

The previous code is used on the Main component in SiteDemo: it automatically retrieves current information to be shown on the starting page. A more complex display group is shown next in Figure 10-3. This is the repetition loop containing a display group that shows the results of search queries in SiteDemo. You can see that for each repetition, the `item.title` and `item.information` strings are displayed. Then, a conditional statement is executed, checking to see if there is a URL in the record. If there is, it is displayed. Similarly, a test to see if there are discussions is made, and, if so, they are shown, too. Finally, links let you add or edit the item. Note that the WORepetition is repeated for each item.

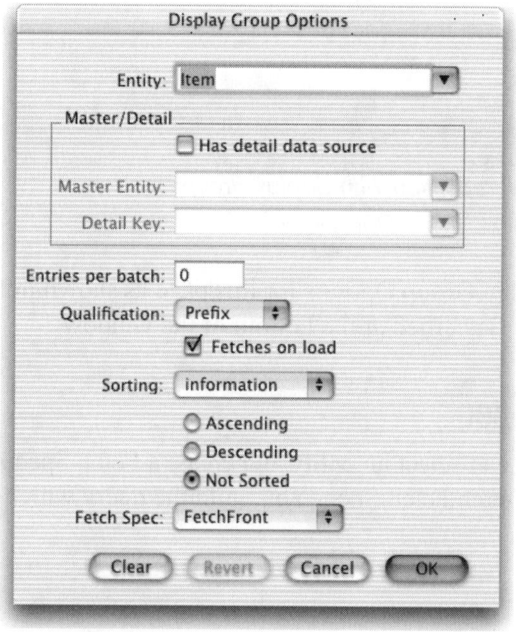

Figure 10-2   *Set Display Group Options*

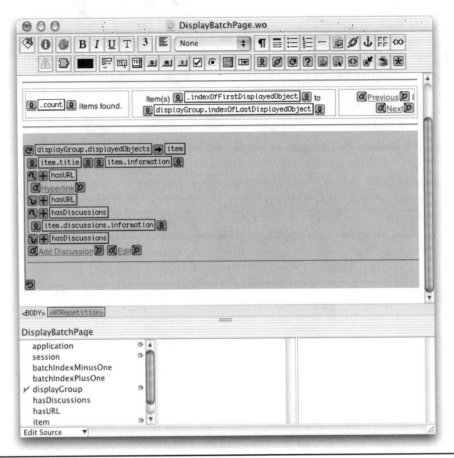

Figure 10-3 *Complex repetition with display group*

You set the Display Group Options for this page as shown in Figure 10-4. Note that no Fetch Spec is specified at the bottom of the window.

Create a Fetch Spec

In EOModeler, you can select an entity and create a Fetch Spec for it. Figure 10-5 shows the basics of such Fetch Spec. You build the query which the Fetch Spec will

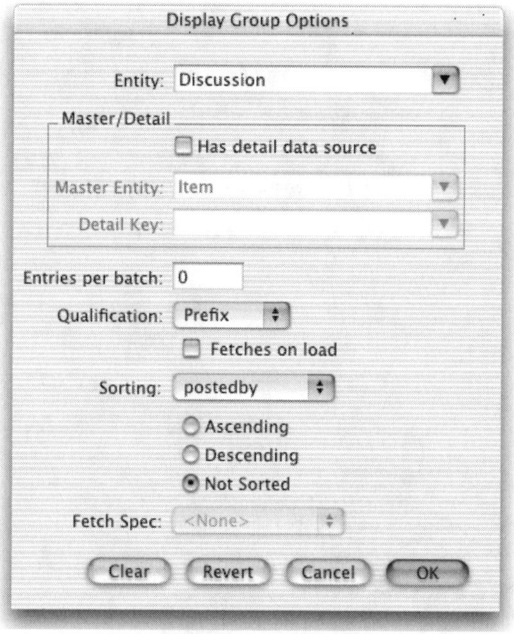

Figure 10-4   *Display Group Options without Fetch Spec*

contain by selecting variables (such as `status` and `visibility`) from the data browser; it will show you all of the attributes for the entity you selected and for which you are building a Fetch Spec. Note that related fields will be shown. You're on your own when it comes to typing the actual relations involved. At the bottom of the window, you can see the SQL that is being generated.

If you prefer, click the SQL tab and type in your own SQL as shown in Figure 10-6.

Sometimes, you know what you want to retrieve: this Fetch Spec retrieves the public items with visibility of 0 on the starting page. Other times, you need to build the query dynamically. Figure 10-7 shows how you construct a Fetch Spec that retrieves data according to a variable that is set at run time. It retrieves a record from the Item database where rowid is equal to a variable named theItem.

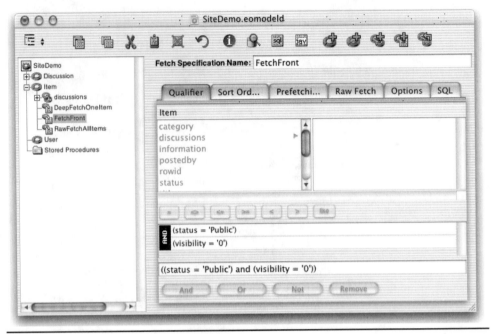

Figure 10-5   *Create a Fetch Spec*

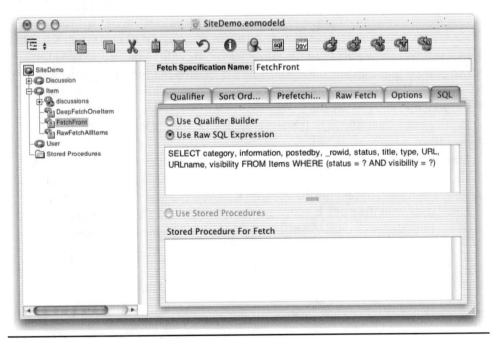

Figure 10-6   *Create your own SQL*

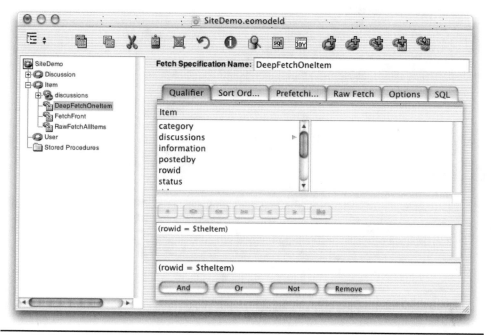

Figure 10-7   *Dynamic SQL in a Fetch Spec*

Back in WebObjects Builder, create a variable called theItem (using the controls at the top of the vertical scroll bar). Precede its name with a question mark. You can then bind this variable to an interface element; the value of that interface element will be used in retrieving the data for the Fetch Spec. Figure 10-8 shows you how this will look.

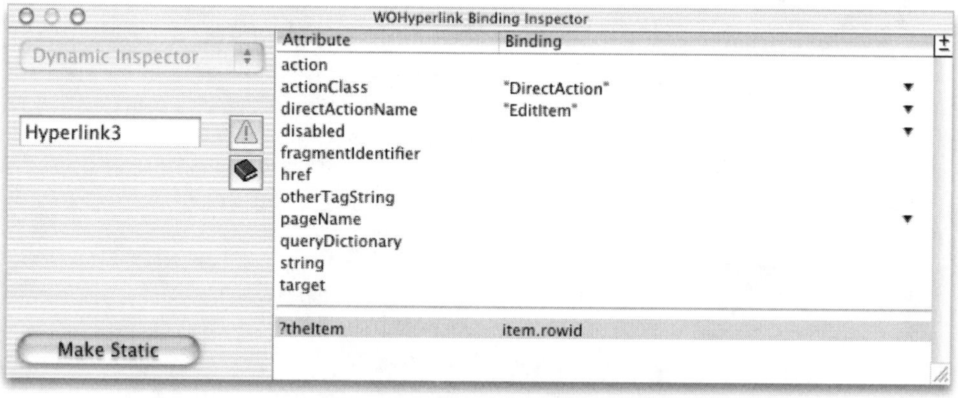

Figure 10-8   *Binding an interface element to a custom property*

CHAPTER
11

Using EOModeler

EOModeler helps you build your data model for use in a WebObjects application. You can use it in either of two ways: you can build your database tables in OpenBase and have EOModeler automatically create the model from them, or you can build only the database in OpenBase and then build your model with EOModeler and have it generate the SQL to build the OpenBase tables. This chapter describes both procedures.

Note that the terminology in EOModeler reflects data models: entities (database tables for the most part) have attributes (columns or fields). When you move the data model entities into WebObjects, they become Java classes, and their attributes become properties (or variables).

Getting Started with EOModeler

In many ways, your data model is the most important part of your WebObjects application. Located conceptually between the database and the interface elements you create in your WebObjects application, it truly is the heart of your project. It is unforgiving in some ways: for example, if a database column is not in the model, there is absolutely no way you can access it from your WebObjects application. In addition, when it comes to relationships, the model has to be correct in order for the automated WebObjects assistants to work. Direct-to-Java Client, Direct-to-Web, and even the basic display group project template in Project Builder rely on the model.

Whether you create your database tables with OpenBase or with EOModeler, you start in the same way: you create an OpenBase database (or a database in whatever database product you are using). Next, launch EOModeler, and choose New Model from the File menu. The wizard shown in Figure 11-1 appears. Select the adaptor that you want: JDBC is the correct choice for OpenBase and most other databases you will be using.

Next, you connect to the database as shown in Figure 11-2. If your database is running on your own computer, the URL is the one shown in this figure, although you can substitute the name of your host (usually `localhost`) for 127.0.0.1. You also need to specify the name of your database: SiteDemo is the database used in this book's example. If your database is not located on your own computer, you use the IP address or name of the computer on which it is located.

The OpenBase driver name is always com.openbase.jdbc.ObDriver. If you are using another database, you will use another driver, and it will be identified in that database's documentation.

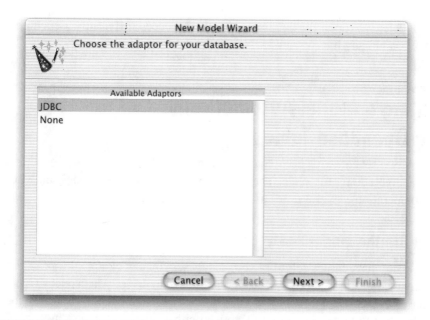

Figure 11-1   *Select an adaptor in the New Model Wizard*

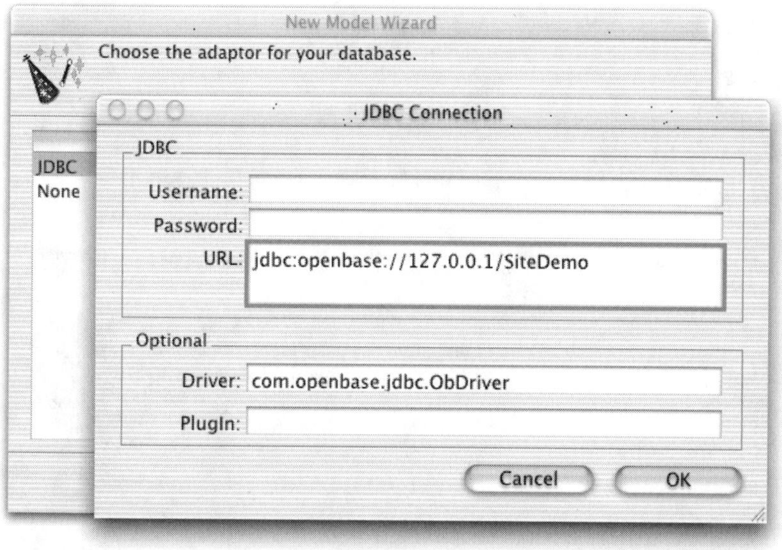

Figure 11-2   *Connect to your database*

EOModeler will open the database. You then proceed differently, depending on whether you already have created tables in the database or not.

Creating a Model Automatically from OpenBase Tables

There are two sets of steps involved in creating a model. The first set sets up the model, and you do it only once. The next set is used to edit the model, and you may do these operations several times as your project evolves.

Setting Up the Model

If you already have tables set up in your database, you can check all four of the checkboxes shown in Figure 11-3. (You do not have to do so: you can let EOModeler do some of the work for you and you can do the rest. This chapter describes the basic operations in which you let EOModeler either do everything or nothing.)

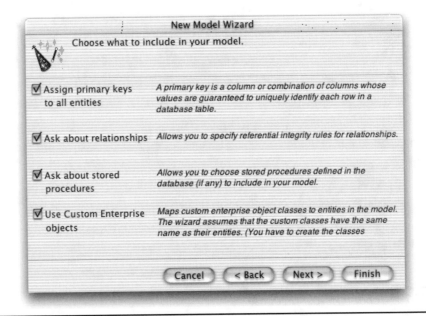

Figure 11-3   *Set up your model options*

As Figure 11-3 shows, EOModeler has four separate functions that it can perform when run against existing database tables.

▶ It can assign primary keys with unique values to rows.

▶ It lets you specify referential integrity rules. Note that referential integrity is not part of basic SQL. You can specify some relationship rules in OpenBase, but you need to refine them in EOModeler.

▶ It lets you choose whether or not to bring stored procedures into your data model from the database.

▶ It lets you use enterprise objects with the same names as the database tables.

On the next panel (shown in Figure 11-4), choose the tables from your database to include in the model. To select tables that are not next to one another, hold down the COMMAND key while you click the various tables you want.

If you have asked EOModeler to create referential integrity rules for relationships, you now will see a series of panels such as Figures 11-5 and 11-6. In Figure 11-5, the relationship between the Item table and its related Discussion table is clarified.

In this type of relationship, each Item can have zero or many Discussion records which point to it. In this case, you check the box indicating that the primary table

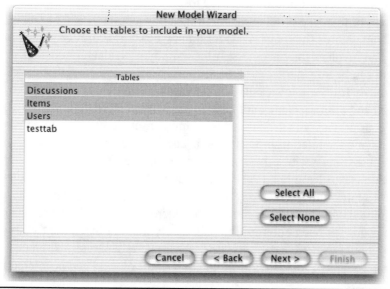

Figure 11-4   *Select your database tables*

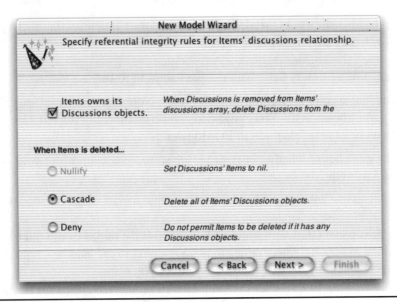

Figure 11-5   *Setting the Item-Discussion relationship*

(Item) owns its related objects. When an Item record is deleted, all of its related records should be deleted: this is the Cascade choice. No Discussion record can exist without an Item record for it to be related to.

Examples of this type of relationship in which deletions should be cascaded are payroll detail records (hours worked) for employees, test scores or grades for students, and invoices for customers. If the employee, student, or customer does not exist, there can be no payroll detail, test scores, or invoices. Note that the reverse is not necessarily true: employees may be on vacation, students may not have taken classes yet, and customers may not have made purchases. In defining the database rules for your project, you need to cross-examine users to make certain that you and they understand the relationships involved. The rules that you create here will be inviolable; users must wrack their brains for the odd cases they may remember from the past. Sometimes, you will find that although when processing is completed all of the rules apply, during processing they do not. For example, it may be the case that a payroll record of hours worked needs to be entered into a system using an employee ID that has not yet been entered; this can easily happen when the two types of data entry (hours worked and employee data) are done separately. If an employee identifier is generated separately from the data entry process and is entered both on the hours worked and employee data records, then the rule is not that related records must exist but rather that if they exist, they must be consistent.

EOModeler continues through each of the relationships you have stored in your database. Figure 11-6 lets you specify the relationship between the User table and the Item table.

The relationship here is different. Each Item record may have a User associated with it. If it is created by a logged-in user, it should have a reference to that User record. However, in a system that allows anonymous postings, you can have Item records that are created without a User reference. Thus, it is possible for Item records to have no User.

In addition, a system like that envisioned here can have users that have never posted Item records. Thus, the User table does not own its Item objects, and the checkbox at the top is not checked. If a User record is deleted, references to it in the Item table are set to null (the Nullify option); there is no reason to delete the Item record if the User is deleted.

NOTE

These choices are based on the business logic and the rules of the system being created.

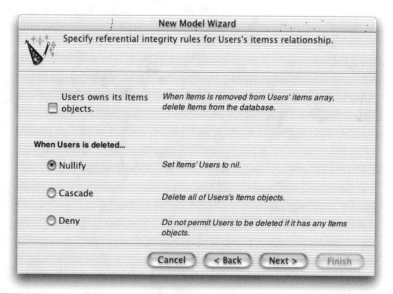

Figure 11-6   *Setting the User-Item relationship*

Editing the Model

Once you have set up the model, the wizard terminates, and you see a window like that shown in Figures 11-7, 11-8, or 11-9. Each is a different view of the same model. You select the view you want with the pop-up button at the left of the toolbar at the top of the window.

Browser View

In the Browser view shown in Figure 11-7, you can see the as-yet unnamed model at the top. Within it are the three database tables that were picked up from the OpenBase database. When a table is selected, its columns appear in the next pane of the browser. These have automatically been imported from OpenBase by EOModeler.

The Browser view emphasizes the hierarchical structure of a single element in the display at the top. It is a good way of seeing a single element and its ancestors.

Diagram View

In the view shown in Figure 11-8, you can see each of the tables, the columns within the table, and the relationships among the tables. At the left, you can expand or contract each of the model's entities. In Figure 11-8, the Discussions table is highlighted at the left, and if you look closely, you can see that it is also highlighted in the main pane of the view.

Figure 11-7 *Browser view of the model*

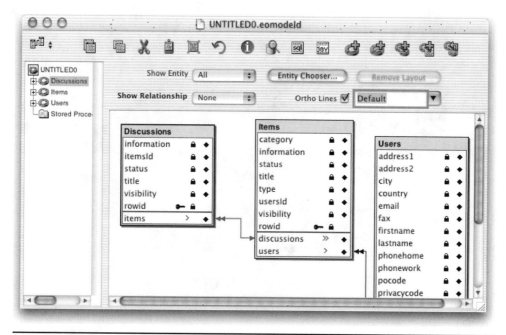

Figure 11-8 *Diagram view of the model*

Next to each column, symbols indicate its characteristics.

▶   A key indicates that the column is a primary key.

▶   A padlock indicates that the column can be used to lock the entity.

▶   A diamond indicates a class property—that is, a column name that will
    be carried forward into a class created for your WebObjects application.

You can toggle any of these symbols on or off. For example, clicking a diamond
will remove it, and that column will not be a class property: you will no longer be
able to access it from your WebObjects application.

Diagram view is a good way of looking at the overall model and seeing the
relationships among entities.

Table View

Finally, you can choose to look at the model in the Table view shown in Figure 11-9.
As with the previous view, the columns are shown along with the relationships for

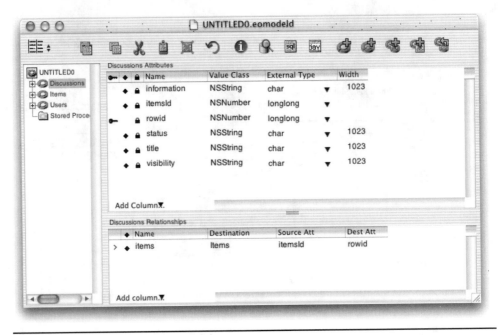

Figure 11-9   *Table view of the model*

the selected table. Only one table is shown at a time in this view, and this is the best view to use to home in on a specific table, its columns, and its relationships.

Creating Java Classes for Your Model Entities

Buttons along the toolbar let you manipulate the display and add entities, columns, and other objects. They are described in the EOModeler documentation.

One button that you should know about at this point is the Java button. It takes the information in your model and creates Java classes in your WebObjects application with the appropriate columns and tables. If you are creating a data model from an existing database, click the Java button now, and then quit EOModeler to return to Project Builder, where your classes will be waiting for you.

You need not do anything with them yet: the default implementations will work just fine with the basic WebObjects code that has been generated. However, their variables—the class properties marked with diamonds—will now be available to you in WebObjects Builder so that you can link interface elements to the data model's data.

Creating Database Tables from Your Model

If you have no tables in your OpenBase database, you can create them from EOModeler. On the wizard panel shown at the start of the process in Figure 11-3, make certain that no checkboxes are checked and click Finish. Your model will appear as shown in Figure 11-10, although it may appear in one of the other views (Table or Diagram, depending on how you have set the display). There are no tables inside the unnamed model in this view; you will create them in EOModeler, and they will be inserted into the OpenBase database using SQL generated by EOModeler.

With the model itself selected at the left (UNTITLED0), create a new entity using the third button from the right. The model will reflect the new entity, as shown in Figure 11-11.

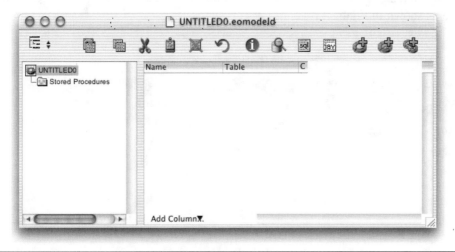

Figure 11-10 *Model with no database tables*

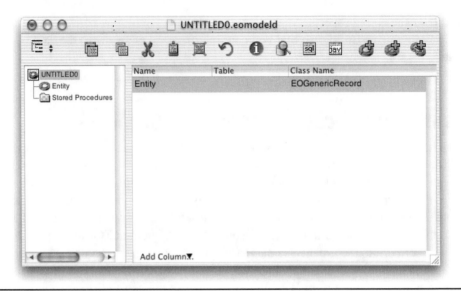

Figure 11-11   *A new entity is created*

You can rename the entity by double-clicking Entity and typing a more meaningful name as shown in Figure 11-12.

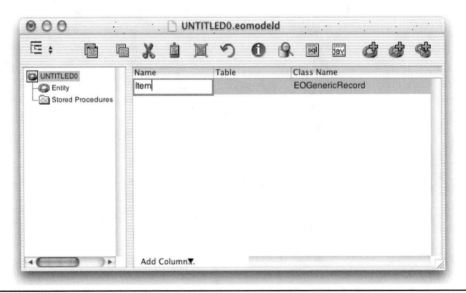

Figure 11-12   *Name the entity*

Select the renamed entity in the pane at the left. Use the New Attribute button (to the right of the New Entity button) to create a column (attribute) inside the new entity. The results are shown in Figure 11-13.

As you can see from Figure 11-14, you can create a variety of attributes; you rename them exactly as you did the entity itself—by double-clicking the name. You can set values for their type and other important values. Most important, you must specify the name of the column in the table that will be created for each attribute. Often, these names are the same as the names of the attributes.

You can use the Inspector (from the Tools menu) to examine any object in the model. Figure 11-15 shows the inspector for the Item entity. You will need to open it for each entity that represents a table and type in the name of the table you want to create. As with attributes, the table name is often the same as the name of the entity.

Other buttons at the top of the Inspector window let you add additional information to the model. The buttons change depending on whether you are inspecting a database entity (table) or an attribute (column/field). In each case, however, the right-most button opens a blank pane into which you can type documentation about the entity.

Adding documentation to the model itself means that you know where the documentation is. (It poses no run-time burden on your application.) The only point that you need to remember is that you should update this documentation if any aspects of your model change. Years from now, if someone (even you!) looks at the

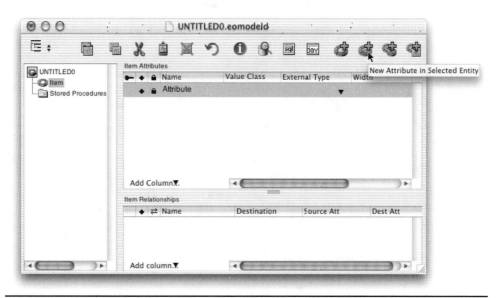

Figure 11-13 *Creating a new attribute*

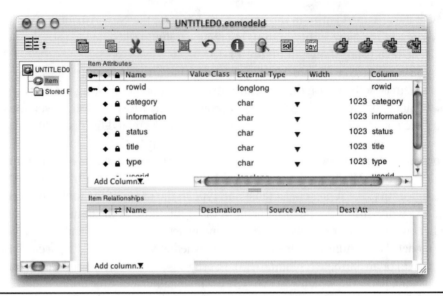

Figure 11-14 *Attributes are created for the entity and renamed*

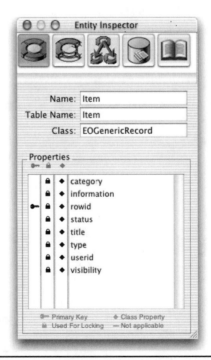

Figure 11-15 *Inspect objects in the data model with the Inspector*

documentation and sees that it is wrong, all of the documentation will become suspect, and all of that work will have been for naught.

When you have created all the entities and their attributes and specified their names using the Inspector and the model view, you can click the SQL button in the center of the toolbar. It will create the appropriate SQL for you as shown in Figure 11-16. Note that not only does it create the tables you have described, but it also will create an internally used table of primary keys (EO_PK_TABLE). Leave that table alone, since it belongs to EOModeler.

If you are updating a model, you may want to drop existing tables—but beware, the data in them will be lost. You can either save this SQL to a file or execute it directly with the button at the lower left. If you choose to execute it, the tables will be created. Figure 11-17 shows the Data Viewer in OpenBaseManager after the SQL has been executed. There is no data yet, but as you can see, the columns in the table have all been created.

In EOModeler, you can add a relationship with a menu command (Add Relationship from the Property menu) or with the button to the right of the toolbar.

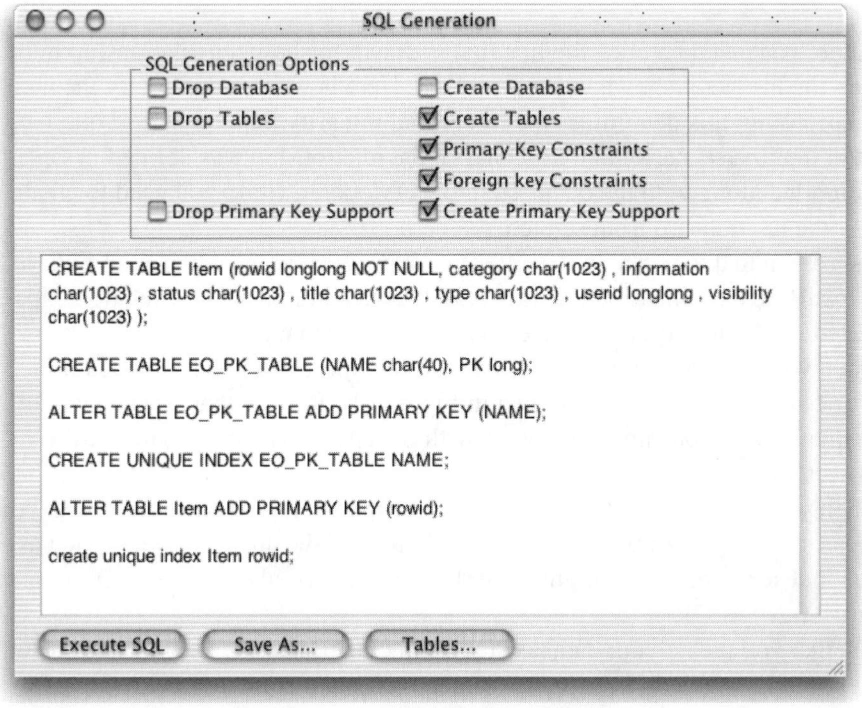

Figure 11-16 *Create SQL automatically with EOModeler*

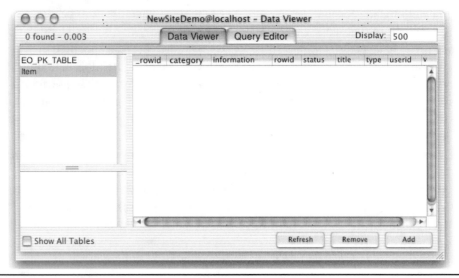

Figure 11-17 *Tables are created in OpenBase*

If you do, you can then click the line that is drawn to show the relationship in order to open the Inspector shown in Figure 11-18. Here is where you specify the nature of the relationship; this determines the referential integrity that the wizard queried you about in the first scenario. In that scenario, the relationship was defined in OpenBase and imported along with the database into EOModeler. Here, you need to create and specify the relationship from scratch.

The reason that you can do this after you have created the tables with SQL is that OpenBase (like most SQL databases) does not store details of relationships and referential integrity: these are elements of the data model.

When you have completed specifying the relationship and have named it in the Inspector, it will appear as shown in Figure 11-19. Note that you can control the display of relationship information with the additional controls below the standard toolbar.

When you have finished, you can return to OpenBaseManager and look at your database schema. All of the tables will be there, and the characteristics (such as unique indexes, types, and lengths) will have been carried over from EOModeler (Figure 11-20).

Whether you create your database tables in OpenBase or through EOModeler scarcely makes much difference; use whichever tool and interface you prefer.

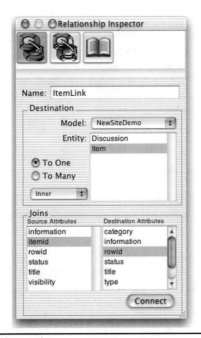

Figure 11-18   *Specify a relationship*

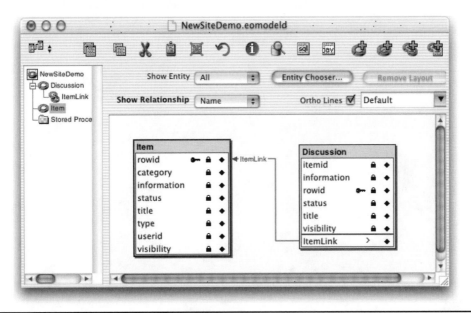

Figure 11-19   *Relationship named in the view*

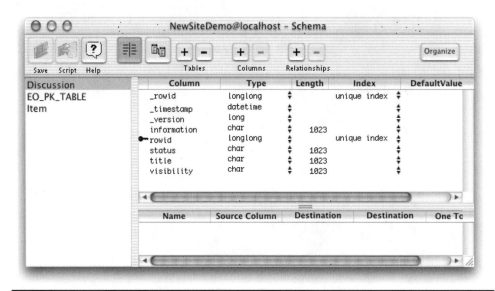

Figure 11-20   *Database schema in OpenBaseManager*

Working with the Model and the Database

IN THIS CHAPTER:

Creating Java Classes from EOModeler

Using EOGenericRecord

EOEnterpriseObject

As is so often the case in WebObjects, the default behavior works just fine in a wide variety of cases. This chapter shows you how to work with Java classes you create from EOModeler as well as with EOGenericRecord, the object that frequently represents your Enterprise Objects Framework objects. It shows you how to create such objects on demand in your WebObjects code and how to access their attributes (data).

Creating Java Classes from EOModeler

As was mentioned in the previous chapter, you can create Java classes for your Enterprise Objects Framework entities from EOModeler. Select the entity for which you want to create a Java class, and then click the Java class button as shown in Figure 12-1.

EOModeler will create the appropriate classes and place them in your project, where you can then edit them with Project Builder. The name of the class will be the

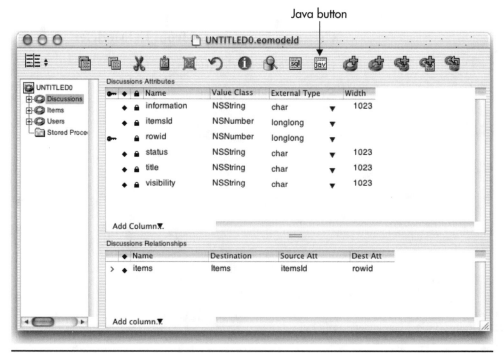

Figure 12-1 *Create Java classes from EOModeler*

same as the name of the entity in EOModeler. In many cases, the name of the database, the EOModeler entity, and the class are all the same. However, you can differentiate them. With an entity selected in EOModeler, open the Inspector from the Tools menu as shown in Figure 12-2. This will let you enter both the entity name and the database table. (This is also the tool you use to specify the data elements that you want included in the Java class.)

When you create the Java class, you will be prompted to name the file and to choose a location on disk for it. The name should be the name of the class inside the file (this is the default), and the initial location will be within your project folder where your EOModel file resides. This, too, is appropriate.

When the file is created, you must manually add it to your project in Project Builder. First, select the group to which you wish to add it. Normally that is the Classes group that is created for you when you first create a WebObjects application. (Application.java, Session.java, and DirectAction.java are already there in most cases.) Choose Add Files from the Project menu, and then select the file you have just created. You will be prompted as shown in Figure 12-3. You normally copy the

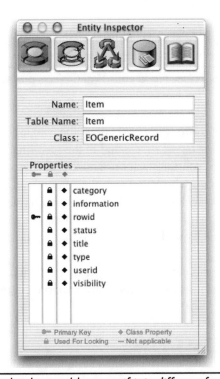

Figure 12-2   *Specify the database table name if it is different from the entity name.*

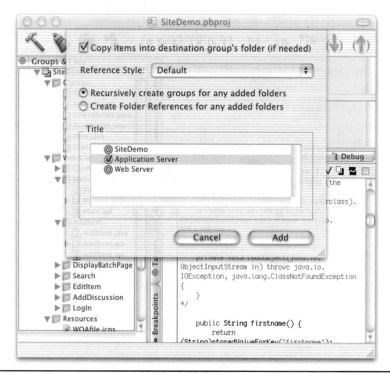

Figure 12-3   *Add your Java class file to your WebObjects project.*

item into the destination group (the checkbox at the top), and you make certain that the Application Server target is selected in the scrolling list at the bottom.

If your project is large, you may want to create a new group such as Custom Classes or EOF Classes into which you can place your Java classes that manipulate Enterprise Objects Framework entities. As long as you have added the files to your project in the manner shown here (that is, by checking the Copy Items checkbox at the top of the sheet, and by adding the files to the Application Server target), you should be okay.

By default, the class that is created for you is a descendant of the EOGenericRecord class. Like most of the other default values, it is appropriate in most cases. It is described in the following section.

Using EOGenericRecord

EOGenericRecord is a descendant of EOCustomObject, which in turn is derived
from EOEnterpriseObject. Your class descends in turn from EOGenericRecord. This
section walks you through the class that is created for you, and then it shows you
how to instantiate an object of your own custom class.

A Walk-Through of the Default Implementation

The default implementation may be sufficient for many purposes. This section
shows you what is in it. You can extend it if necessary, and you can modify its
behavior—but that is usually not a good idea.

There are four sets of methods in the default implementation:

▶ Constructor

▶ Accessors

▶ Relationship management

▶ Other methods

Constructor

As you would expect, the class begins with a constructor which, by default, does
nothing but call `super`. If you need to do something special in your class
implementation, you can modify the constructor.

```
public class Discussion extends EOGenericRecord {

    public Discussion() {
        super();
    }
}
```

Remember, however, that this class represents the WebObjects entity. If you want
to set a default value for fields in new database records, you cannot do so in this way
if some of your users access the database other than through WebObjects.

Accessors

Following the constructor, you will find accessors for each of the entity's attributes (normally they are the database table columns). Here are two sets of accessors that were generated automatically by EOModeler:

```
public Number postedby() {
   return (Number)storedValueForKey("postedby");
}

public void setPostedby(Number value) {
   takeStoredValueForKey(value, "postedby");
}

public String status() {
   return (String)storedValueForKey("status");
}

public void setStatus(String value) {
   takeStoredValueForKey(value, "status");
}
```

You might expect accessors to deal with local, private variables; in fact, you probably would expect to find such variables defined within your custom class. You can declare such variables, and WebObjects can access them (if you write your own accessors), but the default behavior uses the key/value encoding that is used in dictionary objects.

This is implemented in EOCustomObject (described next). What is implemented in EOGenericRecord are the two methods used in these accessors—`takeStoredValueForKey` and `storedValueForKey`. They call underlying methods named `takeValueForKey` and `valueForKey`. (Of course, you can override any of these methods, but the default behavior is usually correct.) It is important to know that `takeValueForKey` and `valueForKey` have the side effect of calling `willChange` and `willRead`, respectively. As you might expect, those methods manage persistence and change.

Relationship Management

When you have created a relationship in EOModeler, it is implemented in your Java classes using the same style of accessors. Both the Item and Discussion entities have a one-to-one relationship to the User entity (each Item or Discussion record may have a link to the User record that created it).

The accessors use a custom type—User—to implement the reference. Here are the accessors from Item and Discussion that return and set the User object.

```
public User user() {
  return (User)storedValueForKey("postedby");
}

public void setUser(User value) {
  takeStoredValueForKey(value, "postedby");
}
```

Item records have a one-to-many relationship with Discussion records: each item can have any number of Discussion records (or none). The accessors in Item therefore return arrays of Discussion records, as you can see here:

```
public NSArray discussion() {
  return (NSArray)storedValueForKey("discussions");
}

public void setDiscussion(NSMutableArray value) {
  takeStoredValueForKey(value, "discussions");
}
```

In the case of a one-to-many relationship, the object needs to be able to insert new records into the array of related records. The default implementation provides this functionality. Note that `willChange` is called in these implementations. It is called automatically in `takeValueForKey`, so there is no reason for it to be called explicitly in the other accessors.

```
public void addToDiscussions(Discussion object) {
  NSMutableArray array = (NSMutableArray)discussion();

  willChange();
  array.addObject(object);
}

public void removeFromDiscussions(Discussion object) {
  NSMutableArray array = (NSMutableArray)discussion();

  willChange();
  array.removeObject(object);
}
```

Other Methods

For the sake of completeness, you may want to know that in addition to its constructor, EOGenericRecord also has a function that returns its EOClassDescription; additionally, it has a method called `usesDeferredFaultCreation` that returns true. You can override this to use the regular faulting mechanism, but it is not usual to do so.

Thus, the EOGenericRecord-based class that is created for you can handle all of your entity's persistence and access needs. If you choose to add or delete attributes (columns) to or from your entity, you need only add or delete accessors in this style: there is no need to add or remove instance variables from the Java class.

Instantiating an Enterprise Objects Framework Object

When you write your application, you will find that you do not often need to instantiate your EOModeler entities. They are automatically instantiated for you when they are fetched from the database, and you access their attributes in your code or using the interface elements of Interface Builder or WebObjects Builder.

There is one time when you do need to instantiate these entities: that is when you are creating a new one. The code snippet shown here takes data from user input (in an HTTP request that is part of the request-response loop), creates an object, and stores that data in it.

You will find this code in many WebObjects applications. You merely need to customize it for your own object and its attributes. First, you will need to declare a key to use in key/value encoding for each data field that you will access in your interface (that is, in the request) and in the data entity. It is often easiest to use the same key in both places to refer to the data, whether it be in the interface or in the database.

```
private String informationKey = "information";
```

The actual method to instantiate the object will look like this. The underlined items need to be customized. First, you need a reference to your WebObjects application. Next you obtain the class description for the class that you are going to instantiate:

```
public EOEnterpriseObject discussionFromRequest( WORequest aRequest ) {
  Application anApp = Application.myApplication();
  EOClassDescription aCD =
    EOClassDescription.classDescriptionForEntityName( "Discussion" );
```

You next declare your object. The try block that follows the declaration is used as is in almost every case. Notice that although the object you have declared is general (EOEnterpriseObject), the class description that you have obtained and stored in the aCD variable means that the `createInstanceWithEditingContext` method will create a correctly typed object for you.

```
EOEnterpriseObject aDiscussion;
try {
  EOEditingContext anEC = anApp.lockEC();
  aDiscussion =
    (EOEnterpriseObject)aCD.createInstanceWithEditingContext
      ( anEC, null );
} finally {
  anApp.unlockEC();
}
```

Once you have your object, it is a simple matter to retrieve data from the request and to place it into the just-created object. If you use the same constant as a key for both the request and the entity, each transfer of data will consist of pairs of lines such as these:

```
String theData = (String)aRequest.formValueForKey (informationKey);
aDiscussion.takeValueForKey( theData), informationKey );
```

Finally, you return the object you have just created.

```
return aDiscussion;
}
```

Although that code is correct, there is one aspect to it that may be wrong in your implementation. The string value retrieved from the request may be a zero-length string; in that case, it should be passed through as null, rather than as a zero-length string. Accordingly, many WebObjects applications use a utility function such as this (it is from the Movies example). It treats zero-length strings as nulls when it extracts them from a request with a given key value:

```
public String nullEnabledFormValueForKey( WORequest aRequest, String aKey ) {

  String temp = (String)aRequest.formValueForKey( aKey );
  if ( (temp != null) && (temp.length() == 0) ) {
    return null;
  }
  return temp;
}
```

You can then replace the pair of lines that retrieve data and store them in the newly created object with the following single line:

```
aDiscussion.takeValueForKey(
    nullEnabledFormValueForKey( aRequest, informationKey ), informationKey );
```

EOEnterpriseObject

EOGenericRecord provides default functionality that is satisfactory and complete for many purposes. However, if you need to customize it, you can override methods of its immediate ancestor, EOCustomObject, and of EOEnterpriseObject. The areas that most frequently need to be addressed are:

▶ Extra processing on creation or retrieval of the object

▶ Validation

Extra Processing

Two methods, `awakeFromFetch` and `awakeFromInsertion`, are called when the object is fetched or inserted into the database table. If you need to do processing after the data is retrieved but before it is used, override `awakeFromFetch`. Be aware that this method is called as database accesses are going on: related objects may not yet be completed; however, you can do any adjustments to your own object as you see fit.

It is more common to override `awakeFromInsertion`. This method is called when an object is created for insertion into the database. Overriding this method lets you set default values (such as a timestamp for record creation).

Validation

A great deal of code in database systems revolves around validation of data. If you validate the data properly before storing it, then you need have no qualms about its retrieval. WebObjects provides default validation routines that you can override as necessary. They let you validate individual properties as well as objects as a whole.

Validation for properties is handled by methods that incorporate the property name. If your object has a city property, a validateCity method will be looked for and invoked as needed if it is found. (Note that depending on where in the processing cycle you are, this method may be called to validate data from an object in the interface or from an object about to be stored in the database.)

The form of a property validation routine is simple. Simply replace the underlined text with the name of your property, the test (or tests) you want to perform, and the message to be returned in the case of an error.

```
public void validateCity(String city)

   throws EOValidation.Exception

{

  if (/*your test here*/)

    throw new EOValidation.Exception("Error Message.");

}
```

To validate the entire object, override `validateForSave`, `validateForUpdate`, `validateForInsert`, or `validateForDelete` (or as many of them as you need). Each has the same structure. You can use the following boilerplate code and replace just the test and the error message. Note that the call to `super.validateForSave` will invoke property validation methods if they exist for each of the properties in the object. The same holds true for both `validateForInsert` and `validateForUpdate`.

```
public void validateForSave) throws EOValidation.Exception
{

  EOValidation.Exception superException = null;
  EOValidation.Exception myException = null;

  try {
    super.validateForDelete()
  } catch (EOValidation.Exception s) {
    superException = s;
  }
```

```
    if (/*your test here*/)
      myException = new EOValidation.Exception("Error Message.");

    if (superException && myException) {
      NSMutableArray exceptions = new NSMutableArray();
      exceptions.addObject(superException);
      exceptions.addObject(myException);
      throw
        EOValidation.Exception.aggregateExceptionWithExceptions(
          exceptions);
    } else if (superException) {
      throw(superException);
    } else if (myException) {
      throw(myException);
    }
}
```

The default behavior of Enterprise Objects Framework is remarkably complete. Because of the nature of relational databases, much of the processing adheres to a common architecture. As a result, you have little code to write, and you write it in very clearly delineated methods. The trafficking of calls to validation and creation routines, for example, is handled for you: you merely write your own specific validations and implement your customized initializations. This makes for rapid development and enormous savings in maintenance costs when compared to other ways of developing databases and implementing applications.

Creating Dynamic Web Sites with WebObjects

OBJECTIVES

▶ See how WebObjects does its work

▶ Learn how to use WebObjects Builder and Project Builder to create your applications

▶ Explore the key features of WebObjects applications: dynamic elements, the request-response loop, direct and component actions

▶ Find out how to manage state and sessions

▶ Use XML with WebObjects

WebObjects at Work

IN THIS CHAPTER:

Thisﾠpart of the book provides you with the information you need to design and implement WebObjects sites. This chapter covers the processes involved in running a WebObjects application. The following chapters show you how to actually create such applications.

This chapter begins with a walkthrough of the example WebObjects site used in this book that you can use as a basis for your own sites. (All of the code can be downloaded from www.philmontmill.com.) Then you'll see how to create dynamic pages and how WebObjects interacts with legacy systems and databases. WebObjects uses adaptors for its interactions; it also implements state management and its own request-response loop. You'll learn about how clients and servers interact in dynamic Web sites.

Looking at a WebObjects Site

Even the most complex Web sites are variations on the simple pages shown here. You can use them to build an interactive bulletin board, and you can also use them to build an e-commerce site. Here is what you can do with these pages:

▶ The home page welcomes you to the site and automatically displays some information from the database.

▶ You can search the database for information.

▶ You can add new items to the database.

▶ You can edit items in the database.

▶ Having located an item in the database, you can add subsidiary items to it. In this example, you add discussion items to a basic item of information. In an e-commerce application you would add individual products to a shopping cart item; the logic is exactly the same.

▶ You can delete items in the database.

▶ Later in the book, you will see how to use the database to provide a certain level of security.

▶ Although not part of this example, you can easily implement editing and deletion of discussion items: they follow exactly the same steps as editing and deletion of information items.

Figure 13-1 shows the home page for the example WebObjects site. You can download the site from www.philmontmill.com and use it as the basis for your own site.

Figure 13-1   *Example home page*

The Home Page

If you are used to creating HTML pages manually, you can probably create these
pages easily yourself. However, with WebObjects, these pages are created dynamically
using both HTML and data generated on the fly. This section describes each page and
shows you the WebObjects dynamic features that are included.

The home page is straightforward. What may not be immediately apparent,
however, is the dynamic element—the notice of the meeting towards the top of the
page. This item is pulled from a database using a query that retrieves items marked
with a status of Public and a visibility value of 0 in the database. (Visibility controls
on which page an item appears.) Such a dynamic field is useful on a home page; it
keeps the page fresh, and it provides varying information for users.

TIP

*All too often, home pages are designed as if they were book covers or facades of buildings that
are set in stone—they never vary. As a result, frequent users skip them or ignore their contents.
Having changing information can make a home page usable.*

Static Pages: Privacy Statement

Links on the home page provide a variety of additional information. The privacy policy, for example, is the page shown in Figure 13-2.

This is a typical HTML page; it can be generated by WebObjects or it can be created manually. It contains nothing but formatted text. It is the most basic type of Web page—a static page.

Form Submission Pages for Data Entry

Web sites frequently include forms to structure information that users request. The data is often edited by WebObjects and then stored in a database. Figure 13-3 shows a typical form. This one is used to enter information into the database.

HTML pages can contain multiple forms; however, each form contains one set of data fields and one Submit button. WebObjects extends HTML to allow multiple Submit buttons in a single form. WebObjects form elements can perform error-checking and complex operations on the data that users provide.

Static Response Pages

It is good interface design to provide some type of feedback to users after they have submitted data. Figure 13-4 shows a typical static response page.

Figure 13-2 *Privacy policy*

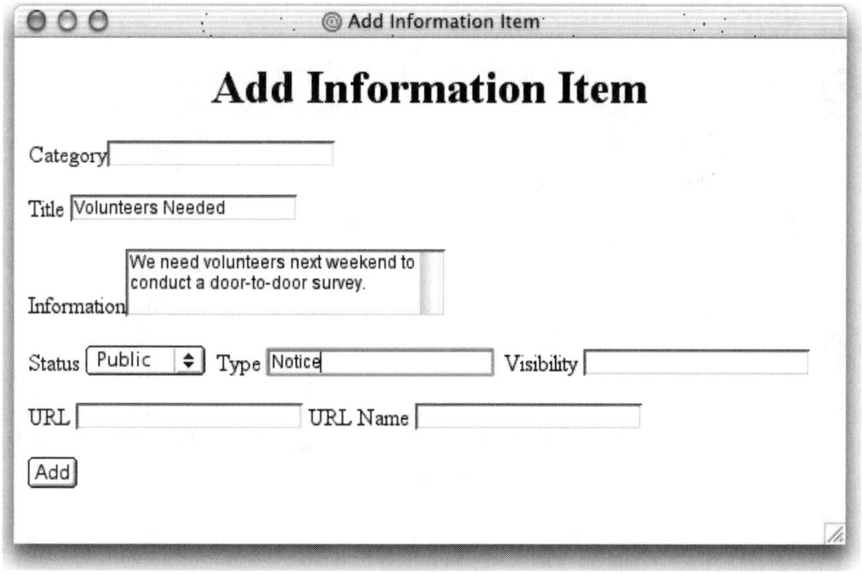

Figure 13-3   *Form page to add information*

This is a simple HTML page with no variable data.

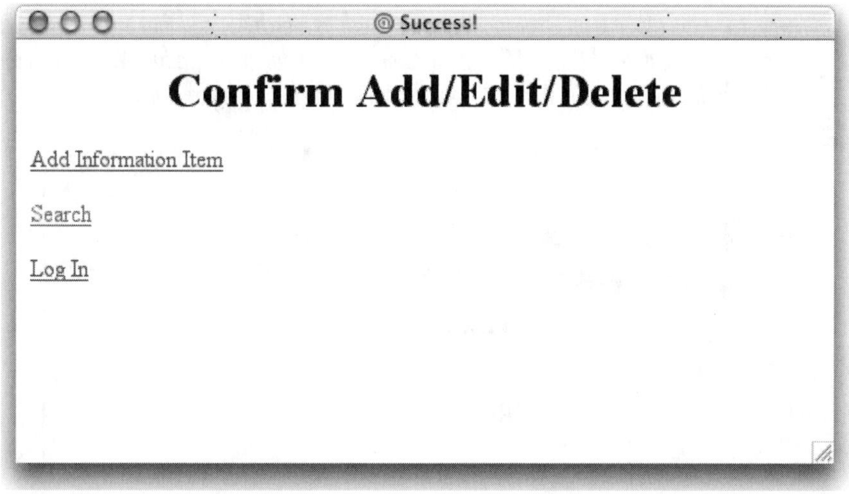

Figure 13-4   *Static response page*

NOTE

Response pages should not be dead ends—they should always provide some type of link onward or back to a known location on the site. "Use your browser's Back button" often appears, but when it follows a form that has been submitted, the user may need to click Back several times; a link is much simpler.

Dynamic Response Pages

Figure 13-5 shows a dynamic response page: it contains some of the information that the user provided on the form (the user's name in this case).

A dynamic response page requires WebObjects to pass data from the form page onto the response page (which is very easy to do). In many cases, the dynamic response page includes all of the entered data; users may even be invited to print the page as a copy of an order or other data entry.

Form Submission Pages for Searching

Figure 13-6 shows another form; this one is used to control a search of a database rather than providing data to be stored in it.

NOTE

In practice, a form that is used to submit a search differs from one used for data entry in the error-checking that you implement in WebObjects. Data that is entered into a database can be edited to prevent errors; on the other hand, data that is used for a search cannot be edited in that way. For example, it is an error to enter a date such as March 45, and that error must be caught. Searching for a date of March 45 does no damage to the database. (In fact, WebObjects converts a date such as March 45 to April 14—45 days from the beginning of March.)

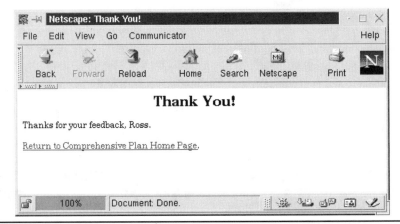

Figure 13-5   *Dynamic response page*

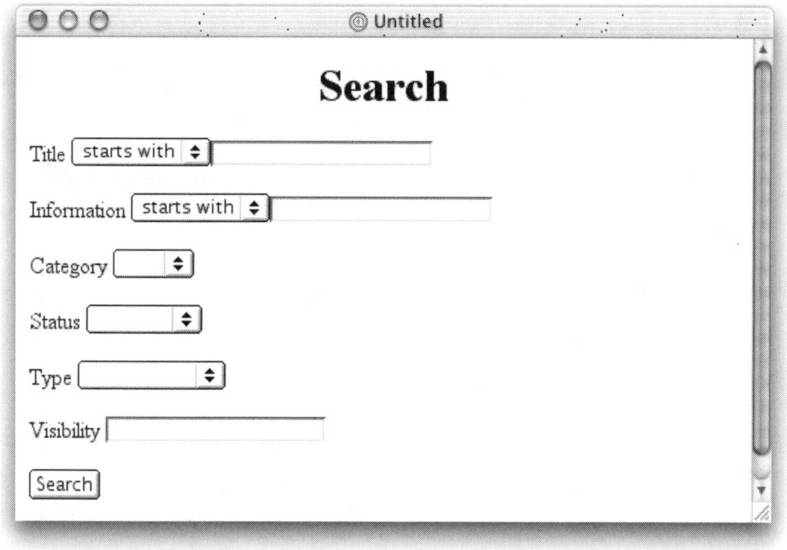

Figure 13-6   *Search form*

Search Response Page

The response to a search request is always a dynamic response page such as the one shown in Figure 13-7.

The page title and graphics may consist of static HTML. WebObjects combines it with the dynamic results of the search that was requested. These results are almost always presented in a repeating section of HTML: each entry is formatted similarly and the loop is repeated for each item returned from the database. (WebObjects automatically handles all this for you.)

Search response pages may also include additional control or navigational features. In the example shown here, you can edit or add discussions to the items that are displayed.

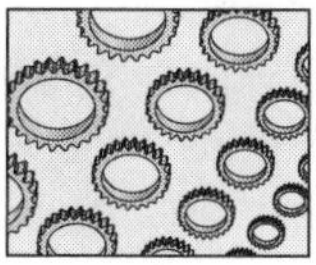

NOTE

A search response page can present the results of a user-defined search or of a prepared search by the WebObjects programmer. In this case, for example, clicking Upcoming Events on the home page (Figure 13-1) automatically executes a search for events scheduled after the current date and time; the results are presented as shown in Figure 13-7.

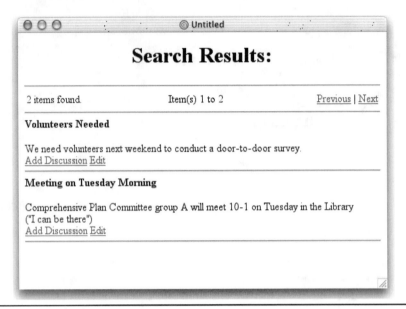

Figure 13-7 *Search response page*

Other Pages on the Site

The pages described so far are the basic HTML pages for almost all sites. Three additional pages are used in the example, but they repeat the basic structure and coding of those shown so far.

Figure 13-8 is the page that you use to add a discussion to an information item.

You can also edit information. Figure 13-9 shows the form that is used for this. It differs from the forms shown previously in that when it first appears it contains the current information from the database: forms you use to add data normally appear with no data filled in at the beginning.

Finally, in Figure 13-10, you see another variation on forms. This page allows you to log in to the application. It contains two separate forms, each with its own Submit button. (The Submit button in the first form is titled "Log In," and the Submit button in the second form is below the bottom of the window and not visible in the figure.)

What Happens

It starts when a user requests a WebObjects page. Typically, the URL is something like this:

```
http://www.philmontmill.com/cgi-bin/WebObjects/SiteDemo
```

Figure 13-8 *Adding a discussion to an information item*

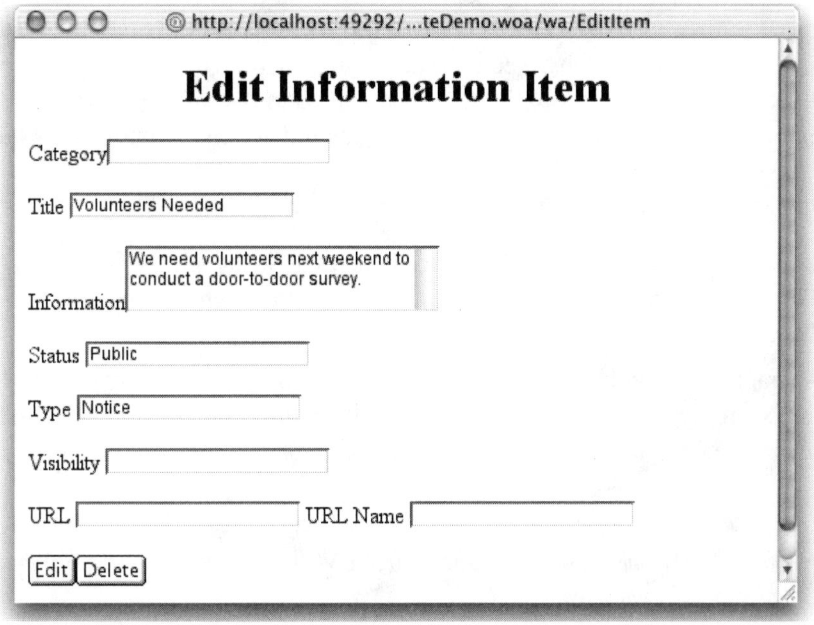

Figure 13-9 *Editing information*

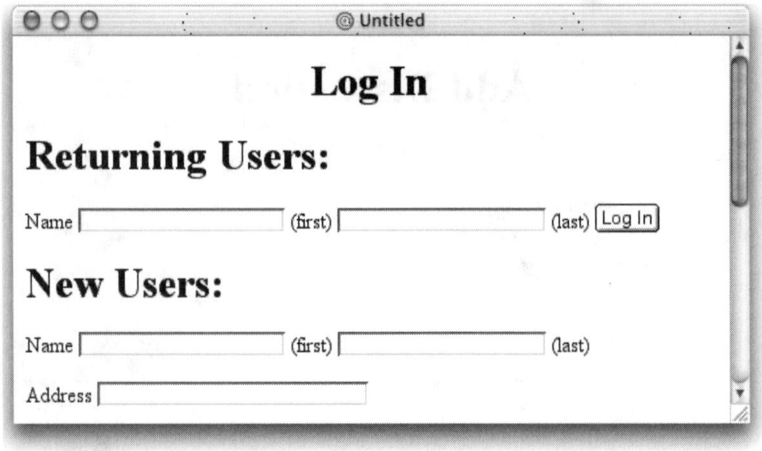

Log In

Returning Users:

Name [   ] (first) [   ] (last) [Log In]

New Users:

Name [   ] (first) [   ] (last)

Address [   ]

Figure 13-10   *Logging in*

The HTTP server requests WebObjects—in the cgi-bin directory—to launch the SiteDemo application; without further qualification in the URL, the home page is created and returned to the user. (This oversimplification is explained in greater detail in the "How It Happens" section later in this chapter.)

This section walks you through the files involved in two of the components of SiteDemo. You will learn how to create this code in later chapters; for now, just follow along with the examples.

There are two sets of files:

1. A file with the suffix .java contains the boilerplate Java code for your component. You may not need to modify it, but if you do, here is where you do so (using Project Builder).

2. A wrapped file with the suffix .wo contains the HTML-related code. (A wrapped file is simply a folder: the .wo folder contains three subsidiary files with the suffixes .html, .woo, and .wod.)

NOTE

The full text of this WebObjects application (called SiteDemo) is available in the WebObjects section of www.philmontmill.com.

As noted in Chapter 2, an HTTP server returns HTML pages in response to requests; these can be prepared (static) HTML pages stored as files on the server, or they can be created dynamically as needed. WebObjects is all about creating those pages dynamically.

ConfirmAddEdit

The component used in this section is the one shown previously in Figure 13-4 since it is one of the simplest. When you create it in Project Builder, all of the files shown here are created for you. The listings in this section show what they look like after you have made your enhancements. (The step-by-step process is described in Chapters 14 and 15.)

ConfirmAddEdit.java

The basic Java code for a component is shown here.

```java
import com.webobjects.foundation.*;
import com.webobjects.appserver.*;
import com.webobjects.eocontrol.*;
import com.webobjects.eoaccess.*;

public class ConfirmAddEdit extends WOComponent {

  protected String userFirstname;
  protected String userLastname;

  public ConfirmAddEdit(WOContext context) {
    super(context);
  }

  public boolean hasUserName () {
    String userName = userFirstname + userLastname;
    return ((userName != null) && (userName.length() == 0));
  }

}
```

The boldface code is essential in all components: you need to import the appropriate frameworks and to declare a constructor for your component. This is the code the Project Builder automatically generates for you. The rest of this code is described later on.

ConfirmAddEdit.wo

The wrapped ConfirmAddEdit.wo file (actually a folder) is created by Project Builder. Together with the .java file, it provides the functionality and appearance of your component.

In general, a WebObjects component is responsible for generating an HTML page to satisfy a user's HTTP request to an HTTP server. (Components may sometimes generate only part of a page and, in some cases, may generate nothing at all; however, in most cases, a one-to-one relationship exists between components and pages.)

ConfirmAddEdit.woo

Within the wrapped Main.wo folder, Main.woo is automatically created for you. It contains information that WebObjects uses internally, including version information, text encoding, and the like. You can view it, but you should not change it.

Here is Main.woo from a WebObjects application.

```
{
    "WebObjects Release" = "WebObjects 5.0";
    encoding = NSMacOSRomanStringEncoding;
}
```

ConfirmAddEdit.html

This file contains the template HTML code that is used to generate the HTML to be returned to the HTTP server (and thus, to the user). It is standard HTML with certain additions unique to WebObjects. You can create this code by using a standard HTML editor, but most commonly, you will use WebObjects Builder to create it.

The WebObjects additions are handled by WebObjects as it actually creates the page. For that purpose, it uses the .wod file (described in the next section). As you will see, each WebObjects addition has a unique name—and a counterpart in the .wod file. The WebObjects elements in the .html file are said to be *bound* to the WebObjects declarations in the .wod file using the name. (With WebObjects Builder, you can create these bindings by using unique names or by using the mouse to attach two objects.)

The template code in ConfirmAddEdit.html consists primarily of HTML. That code is annotated. Only when you get to the WebObjects element will you be in the sphere of WebObjects—that point is clearly indicated in the description.

The code for the ConfirmAddEdit page shown in Figure 13-4 is shown in its entirety in this section, together with some brief annotations.

NOTE

If you are not familiar with HTML, this can serve as a brief introduction. When you use WebObjects Builder, you can easily create template HTML pages without worrying about the underlying code.

HTML documents consist of elements that are enclosed in a left angle bracket (<) and a right angle bracket (>). Each type of element has a name such as P (for paragraph) or TABLE (for table). Elements may contain data that follows the initial tag; they may be terminated by tags that start with a forward slash (/). Thus, a paragraph can be written as follows:

```
<P>
This is a paragraph.
</P>
```

Those three lines are one element: a start tag on the first line, data on the second line, and a closing tag on the third line.

NOTE

In HTML, capitalization and spacing generally do not matter. However, they do matter in XML. In this book, reserved words in HTML that are not case sensitive are capitalized for clarity. Reserved words in WebObjects (where capitalization does matter) are presented as they are in WebObjects—generally lowercase. Thus, HREF is an HTML attribute and href—which has the same meaning—is a WebObjects property. User identifiers are in upper- and lowercase. Note, too, that one-word attributes in HTML— such as CENTER—need not be quoted. Recommended use, however, is to use quotes around such attributes, as they are in the examples in this book.

Each HTML document starts with a comment describing the version of HTML that it uses. Following that, an HTML element appears in which the entire document is placed. (Note that the last line of this listing is the closing tag for the HTML element—</HTML>.) The HTML element consists of a HEAD element followed by a BODY element. In the HEAD element, the title of the page is what you usually care about—it is displayed at the top of a browser window:

```
<!DOCTYPE HTML PUBLIC "-//W3C//DTD HTML 3.2//EN">
<HTML>
<HEAD>
  <META NAME="generator" CONTENT="WebObjects 5">
  <TITLE>Success!</TITLE>
</HEAD>
```

Following the HEAD element, the BODY element is placed in the HTML element. Note that elements—such as BODY—can have attributes within them. In this case, the BGCOLOR (background color) attribute for the page is set to a value (white).

```
  <BODY BGCOLOR=#FFFFFF>
  <H1 ALIGN=CENTER>Confirm Add/Edit/Delete</H1>
```

The pattern of HTML elements should be clear now, even if you are not that familiar with HTML itself. In the previous code, a header 1 element—the largest headline type—is created; it is aligned in the center of the page and contains the text "Confirm Add/Edit/Delete."

Attributes—such as ALIGN—are specified for each type of HTML element. You need not use each of the possible attributes for a given element; defaults are declared for each one. The text of an element is typed into the HTML file just as you see it here.

As you will see, WebObjects declares elements that are similar to HTML elements and often extends those elements. This strategy is an easy way to provide additional attributes over and above those that are part of the HTML standard. As it runs, WebObjects applies its own rules to the data you provide and translates it all into standard HTML.

TIP

The code in this example does not use custom fonts and formatting. While there is much dispute over this decision, many people agree that allowing users and their browsers to set default fonts for different styles is more efficient than specifying fonts that may not be present on each user's computer. The flipside of this, of course, is that your pages vary more in appearance from one user's browser to another than if you specify more of the details of their appearance.

Next, hyperlinks are provided to the three pages you can select:

```
<P><WEBOBJECT NAME=Hyperlink1>Add Information Item
</ WEBOBJECT></P>

<P><WEBOBJECT NAME=Hyperlink2>Search</WEBOBJECT></P>

<P><WEBOBJECT NAME=Hyperlink4>Log In</WEBOBJECT></P>
```

These are not standard hyperlinks; rather, they are special WebObject elements that are interpreted by WebObjects as it generates the page. Each is named (although the names are not used), and each has the text string (such as Add Information Item) that you see in Figure 13-3. To function properly, these WebObject elements need further information: it is provided in the .wod file described in the next section.

The following tags close elements that were opened much earlier in the file. Note that they must be used in the right order: the table is inside the body of the document, which, in turn, is inside the HTML element.

```
</BODY>
</HTML>
```

ConfirmAddEdit.wod

The WebObjects declarations file—with suffix .wod—provides the bindings for the WebObjects elements in the HTML file. Those bindings are accomplished by using the name of each WebObject. For example, the first WebObject element in the HTML file was referenced as follows using the name Hyperlink1:

> <P><WEBOBJECT NAME=Hyperlink1>Add Information Item
> </WEBOBJECT></P>

Its name (Hyperlink1) is used to bind it to the first declaration in Main.wod, as shown here:

```
Hyperlink1: WOHyperlink {
 actionClass = "DirectAction";
 directActionName = "AddItem";
}
```

This link uses the direct action technology of WebObjects. In the case of direct actions, a Java method that you write is called to process the command and return the page to the user. The Java method name has the word Action appended to its name; thus, the Java method you would write to process this link would be called AddItemAction.

Older WebObjects technology lets you simply specify the component page to be generated. In such a case, your binding would look like this:

```
Hyperlink1: WOHyperlink {
 pageName = "AddItem";
}
```

Instead of invoking a method called AddItemAction, the page with the name AddItem would be created and returned to the user. You can write code in AddItem.java just as you can in AddItemAction.

Each declaration is of the same format. It consists of the binding name, a colon, and then the class name of the WebObject element to which it refers. In this case, the WebObject is a standard class—WOHyperlink. However, as you will see later, you can create your own WebObject classes.

Each WebObject has certain attributes that you can set in the .wod file (or graphically by using WebObjects Builder). The attributes that you can set depend on the specific WebObject link.

Many of the WebObjects elements are analogous to standard HTML constructs (such as links). Others expand standard HTML constructs, and still others provide services not provided in HTML. For those elements that expand HTML constructs, you will find many HTML attributes in the WebObjects elements. For example, WOHyperlink contains a target attribute that lets you specify the frame into which the WebObjects component will be placed; it is exactly the same as the target attribute of an anchor in HTML.

The balance of Main.wod is shown here. As you can see, each WebObjects element in the HTML page is bound using its name.

```
Hyperlink1: WOHyperlink {
     actionClass = "DirectAction";
     directActionName = "AddItem";
}

Hyperlink2: WOHyperlink {
     actionClass = "DirectAction";
     directActionName = "Search";
}

Hyperlink3: WOHyperlink {
     actionClass = "DirectAction";
     directActionName = "LogIn";
}

Hyperlink4: WOHyperlink {
     actionClass = "DirectAction";
     directActionName = "LogIn";
}
```

AddDiscussion

The AddDiscussion form (shown previously in Figure 13-8) is a simple HTML form that lets users enter data.

AddDiscussion.java

The basic Java code is provided for you and is in bold here:

```
import com.webobjects.foundation.*;
import com.webobjects.appserver.*;
import com.webobjects.eocontrol.*;
```

```
import com.webobjects.eoaccess.*;

public class AddDiscussion extends WOComponent {

protected String information;
Item theItem;

  public AddDiscussion(WOContext context) {
    super(context);
  }
}
```

The two lines that you will add declare data fields that you will use in processing.

AddDiscussion.html

As always, you start with a standard document header:

```
<!DOCTYPE HTML PUBLIC "-//W3C//DTD HTML 3.2//EN">
<HTML>
  <HEAD>
  <META NAME="generator" CONTENT="WebObjects 5">
  <TITLE>Untitled</TITLE>
  </HEAD>
```

Following the header, the body of the HTML document is declared.

```
<BODY BGCOLOR=#FFFFFF>
  <H1 ALIGN=CENTER>Add Discussion</H1>
</HTML>
```

If you are used to HTML, you would expect to see a FORM element with two text boxes (INPUT elements of type text), a Submit button (INPUT element of type submit), and a Reset button (INPUT element of type reset). Instead, all of those elements are replaced with WebObjects elements, as the following code makes clear:

```
<WEBOBJECT NAME=Form1>
     <P><WEBOBJECT NAME=TextField1></WEBOBJECT></P>
     <P>Discussion:</P>
     <P> <WEBOBJECT NAME=Text1></WEBOBJECT></P>
     <P><WEBOBJECT NAME=SubmitButton1></WEBOBJECT></P>
   </WEBOBJECT><P></P>
</BODY>
```

AddDiscussion.wod

Once again, the WebObjects elements are bound to declarations using their names.

The form as well as its submit button are bound to a direct action (ConfirmAdd Discussion, which is implemented in Java by ConfirmAddDiscussionAction). Because WebObjects allows you to have multiple submit buttons, you can have a separate action for each one of them. If you do not have multiple submit buttons, the form's action is used.

```
Form1: WOForm {
  actionClass = "DirectAction";
  directActionName = "ConfirmAddDiscussion";
}

SubmitButton1: WOSubmitButton {
  actionClass = "DirectAction";
  directActionName = "ConfirmAddDiscussion";
}
```

The text area on the page is bound to the information variable that was declared in the .java file: that ensures that the value of that variable is used to set the field—and that when the user clicks the Submit button that the value in the field is placed in the variable in the Java code. This is how you communicate back and forth. The name variable is bound to the string "information." Using this string, the Java code can find the appropriate text field and manipulate its data.

The reason you may need to access the data both by field name and by variable name is that you may not have both of them available to you at the same time. Or, you may use one mechanism for setting a field and another for retrieving its data.

```
Text1: WOText {
  name = "information";
  value = information;
  cols = 40;
}
```

Finally, there is a hidden field on the form that contains the unique identifier of the item in the Item table to which this discussion is to be added. This was the other variable declared in the .java file. The variable in the .java file is of type Item, and it is named theItem. The value of this hidden field is the rowid variable within Item.

```
TextField1: WOHiddenField {
  name = "itemid";
  value = theItem.rowid;
}
```

How It Happens

The previous section demonstrated how WebObjects components combine HTML with declarations to generate dynamic pages in response to users' HTTP requests. However, WebObjects applications typically function in a world in which more than one user is accessing the application at a time. Three concepts—adaptors, state management, and the request/response loop—help implement that functionality.

Adaptors

The URL that started the compplan application was shown previously:

```
http://www.philmontmill.com/cgi-bin/WebObjects/SiteDemo
```

A WebObjects adaptor, located in the cgi-bin directory, passes HTTP requests from the HTTP server to the WebObjects application. Several WebObjects adaptors are available: each is customized to work with a specific HTTP server. (Adaptors are currently available for Apache, ISAPI, NSAPI, CGI, and WAI.) Use the adaptor that matches your HTTP server; all current WebObjects adaptors match current and prior versions (back to version 3) of WebObjects.

Adaptors let WebObjects take advantage of specific features of different HTTP server APIs without letting those specific features interfere with the performance of WebObjects in other environments. For example, Enterprise Objects Framework uses adaptors to communicate with Oracle, LDAP, Sybase, Informix, OpenBase, or any ODBC database. Again, WebObjects (and your code) is insulated from the idiosyncrasies of other products' APIs.

State Management

HTML is a stateless protocol. Therefore, when you develop an interactive Web site, you need to pass all of the information that you accumulate back and forth (often in hidden fields) so that when the time comes to process a transaction or to store data, all of the data—perhaps entered by the user over the span of half a dozen Web pages— is available.

State management is the ability to store an object's state—that is, its data as of a certain moment—for future use. That future use might be a minute or two later when the user clicks an OK button; it also might be days later when a user returns to your site and wants to continue shopping with a half-full shopping basket or wishes to pursue some research that was partially completed.

Because state management is needed so frequently in interactive applications, WebObjects implements it in a variety of ways—and you can expand and extend those implementations further. State management can apply to a WebObjects application, to an individual session—that is one user's interaction with the application, or to a specific page (component).

Application

Your WebObjects application can store information that all users need. Some examples of application state information include highest score (for a multi-user game), total number of satisfied customers (for an e-commerce site), and so on. State information is normally stored in variables; state information can also be stored in a database. Storing state information in a database is smart—and may even be necessary—when the information in the database is manipulated both by WebObjects and by other applications. Furthermore, do not confuse state information with information that is generated by or provided by the application. While at first glance, today's date might seem to be an application state item, in fact, today's date is an item that the application itself should normally generate on request from any of its components. (In other words, the date is not stored because it can change in the Web's 24 x 7 environment.)

Session

WebObjects creates sessions that are specific to an individual user's interaction with your application. Sessions time out (according to parameters that WebObjects allows you to set) or you can use the defaults, and they can be terminated by users if you allow users to explicitly log off. State information that is appropriate for a session includes an individual's score (in a game) and a shopper's shopping cart (in an e-commerce site). Note that in each case, multiple sessions—representing multiple users—may coexist within a single WebObjects application.

Sessions and direct actions do not mix. Direct actions do not take advantage of sessions: each component and its actions manages to encapsulate all the state information that is needed. This means that users can bookmark pages created by direct actions and return to them: when sessions are involved, the bookmarked pages cannot be gone back to since the bookmark contains a session identifier that is transient.

Component

WebObjects can store components—including those that you create—for future use. A shopping cart component or a database search component can be stored; a user's session might contain a reference to such a component. Through the sessions and, thus, the shopping cart, individual items can be found.

Request-Response Loop

The *request-response loop* is the continuous process whereby a user sends a request to an HTTP server and gets back a response—usually an HTML page. The request can be a hyperlink or it can be the Submit button on a form. It can be sent with a lot of data or it can be the simplest possible request.

WebObjects keeps track of each user's requests and responses; a great deal of processing (including database accesses) may happen on the way to a response. However, everything is part of the request-response loop. (This is not just specific to WebObjects; it is the way the Web works.)

This structure has important implications. Perhaps the most significant implication is that you normally cannot have a response without a request, and you actually cannot have a request without some response (although the user may not see the response).

An example of the request-response loop and the design choices that it implies can be shown in a simple case of a notification system. If a user wants to be notified at a certain time, for example, it is easy to create a form in which the time is specified. When the user clicks Submit, the response is returned:

```
OK. You will be notified at 4:15 PM today.
```

And that is the end of the request-response loop. At 4:15, how is it possible to send a message—a response—to a user who may not be logged on? There is certainly no outstanding request to be answered—the OK message was the response. This is a classic problem of the HTTP request-response loop structure; it can be overcome, worked around, and even taken advantage of, but it must be recognized.

Using WebObjects Builder

IN THIS CHAPTER:

Using WebObjects Builder

Binding Keys and Actions to Properties

Creating New Bindings

W ebObjects Builder is the tool you use to construct your WebObjects component pages. It combines a graphical user interface to HTML development with the graphical tools you need to create and manipulate WebObject elements. It interacts with your components' Java source code so that you can create bindings—the linkages between the methods and variables in your Java code and the WebObjects properties that use them.

WebObjects Builder manipulates the .wo folder (actually a wrapped file) in your WebObjects component folders. (In addition to the .wo folder, there is normally a .java file and a .api file.) As you saw in the previous chapter, the .wo folder contains three files: a .html file with standard HTML, a .wod file with the declarations of the component, and a .woo file containing the bindings. All three of these files are read and written by WebObjects Builder. Although the contents of the wrapped files have been explained in the previous chapter, in practice, you normally stick with WebObjects Builder and never see those files at all.

This chapter provides an overview of WebObjects Builder and how to use it. It then focuses on interacting with your WebObjects code: adding keys (variables) and actions (methods) to it from WebObjects Builder and accessing existing keys and variables in WebObjects Builder from the code you have written in Project Builder. Finally, it provides a step-by-step guide to creating bindings for your WebObjects elements' properties.

Using WebObjects Builder

You can launch WebObjects Builder by itself, or you can open it by double-clicking a .wo file from Project Builder as described in the next chapter. The main WebObjects window is shown in Figure 14-1. It is called the *Component window*.

At the top of the window, buttons let you quickly access editing features. In general, the buttons toward the left of the top row let you edit text and other interface elements; those at the top right let you edit HTML elements. The second row of buttons lets you create and edit WebObjects elements. Several buttons at the left of both rows let you control the appearance of the Component window and the display of other windows.

NOTE

The buttons described in this section are those that appear in Figure 14-1. Your version of WebObjects Builder may look different.

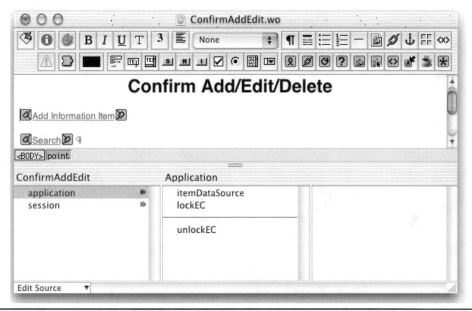

Figure 14-1   *Working in WebObjects Builder*

The window shown in Figure 14-1 contains two resizable panes below the buttons. At the top there is an editor for the HTML; below that is an object browser (it contains entries for the application and session objects in Figure 14-1). The top pane reflects the contents of the .html file, and the bottom pane reflects the contents of the .wod file.

Window Controls

The first buttons at the left of each row control window appearance. As you can see in Figure 14-2, the first one lets you switch among three different displays: a layout display (shown), a preview display, and an HTML source display. In the layout display, the page is shown much as it will appear; WebObjects elements such as links are shown so that you can click them and edit them. The preview display shows no such WebObjects elements.

The second button lets you open the Inspector window; it is shown in Figure 14-3. The Inspector window can be used for any selected entity in a WebObjects Builder window. Many people leave it open at the side of their display at all times: its contents change depending on the object that you have selected.

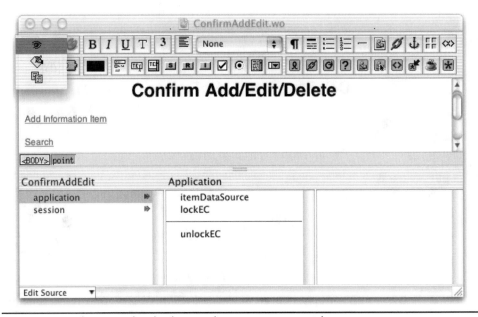

Figure 14-2   *Changing the displays in the Component window*

The third button in the first row opens the palettes window in which your reusable WebObjects components are displayed. These are described in Chapter 28.

In the second row, the first button on the left opens the HTML validation window. Here you can see if the WebObjects HTML parser has detected problems with your

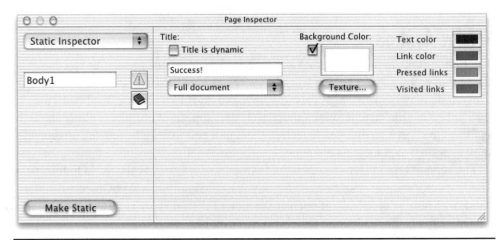

Figure 14-3   *Inspector window*

code. The second button displays the contents of your component's .api file in a graphical interface.

Text and Image Editing Controls

In the first row, the text buttons control standard editing controls:

▶ Boldface

▶ Italics

▶ Underlining

▶ Typewriter (fixed-width) font

▶ Font size

▶ Alignment

▶ Font

In the second row, the third button from the left opens the Color Picker.

The general cautions about HTML pages apply. These include a warning to avoid underlining (users will think underlined text is a link), and an awareness that not all fonts are available on all users' computers. Leaving the font set to None (as shown in Figure 14-2) allows the user's text preference for the browser to be used.

HTML Controls

The HTML controls appear at the right side of the top row, beginning after the pop-up button that lets you select a font. In order, these controls let you insert the following HTML elements:

▶ An HTML paragraph

▶ A heading

▶ A bulleted list

▶ A numbered list

▶ A horizontal rule

▶ An image

▶ A link

▶ An anchor

- ▶ A table
- ▶ An element with a tag name that you provide

Many of these elements require additional information. You use the Inspector window to supply that information. Figure 14-3 shows the Inspector window when the body element is selected: you can specify a title as well as various colors.

WebObject Element Controls

On the second row, buttons let you insert WebObjects elements. The first set (starting with the fourth button from the left) inserts form elements; the second set inserts other WebObjects elements. (There is more information on these elements in Chapter 16. This chapter focuses on WebObjects Builder and how to put the elements into your pages.)

The form elements you can insert are:

- ▶ A WOForm
- ▶ A WOTextField (one line)
- ▶ A WOText (multi-line)
- ▶ A WOSubmitButton
- ▶ A WOResetButton
- ▶ A WOImageButton
- ▶ A WOCheckBox
- ▶ A WORadioButton
- ▶ A WOBrowser (similar to a SELECT element in HTML)
- ▶ A WOPopUpButton

Note that each of these elements has a counterpart in HTML; their WebObjects equivalents provide additional functionality.

The final set of buttons follows the form element buttons. They let you insert:

- ▶ A WOString
- ▶ A WOHyperlink
- ▶ A WORepetition

▶   A WOConditional

▶   A WOImage

▶   A WOActiveImage

▶   A generic WebObject element (which can be any WebObject element at all)

▶   A WOComponentContent

▶   A WOApplet

▶   A custom WebObject

Beneath the HTML editor, a single line of text identifies the path of the selected element. In Figure 14-4, for example, the HTML editor is set to Preview mode, and the selected element is the text within a WOHyperlink element, which in turn is inside a paragraph that is inside a WOBody element.

If multiple elements are selected, and the path display shows this, WebObjects Builder will make the path description as accurate as it can: multiple selections may be able to be identified as being within a given paragraph, for example.

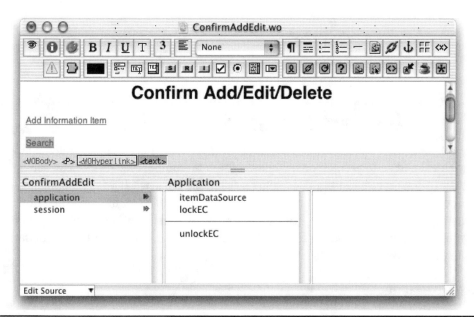

Figure 14-4   *Viewing an element's path*

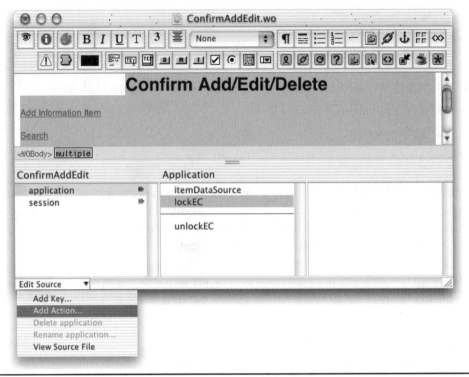

Figure 14-5 *Multiple selected elements in the path display*

Binding Keys and Actions to Properties

The object browser at the lower part of the Component window shows you the keys (variables) and actions (methods) declared for your component. As you can see in Figure 14-5, you can add keys and actions from this window. If you do so, the source file (.java) will be updated appropriately. You can work in either direction: declaring keys and actions in .java and letting WebObjects Builder import them or adding keys and actions in WebObjects Builder and letting the .java files be updated. More likely, you will work in both ways.

Binding Attributes with Text

When a WebObjects element is selected, the Inspector window shows its bindings as in Figure 14-6.

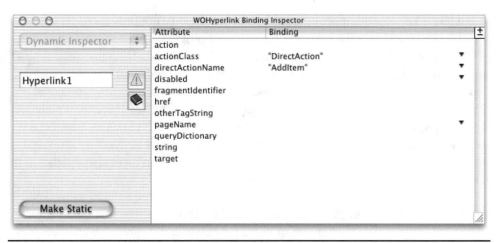

Figure 14-6   *WebObjects element bindings*

You can type in the value of any of the attributes; you can also use the arrows to select from appropriate scrolling lists. (You will later see how to graphically bind keys and actions to attributes.)

Note that many bindings are to strings, which are quoted as in Figure 14-6. Other bindings are to the names of keys and actions, which are not quoted. If you bind an attribute to an unquoted string, it expects to find a key or action with that name at run time.

If you add an action to a component, you will be asked to name it as shown in Figure 14-7. You also must select or type in the name of the page that will be returned. This frequently is left as null so that the Java code you write can dynamically decide which page to return. If the returned page is not otherwise set and is left as null, the same page as the component is returned. In other words, if you want to keep a single page in front of the user and modify its contents, simply return null each time.

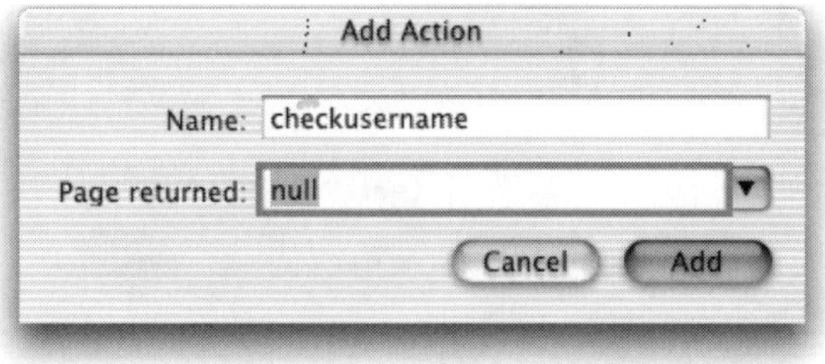

Figure 14-7   *Adding an action to a component*

Adding a key to a component requires that you specify not only its name but what it is. Figure 14-8 shows the information you must provide. There are three basic sets of data you specify. First, you must name the key. As always, the name should be meaningful and should be consistent with whatever standards you impose. Frequently, key names are lowercase, and method or class names are capitalized.

The next section lets you specify not only the type of the key, but also whether it is a single value, an array, or a mutable array. Mutable objects such as arrays can be modified at run time. Thus, if you have a variable number of items in an array and add or delete from it, it must be declared as mutable. If it can be read-only, then it is not mutable.

Finally, you specify how the Java code will be created. You can have this new key be a variable, or you can have it referenced by accessors that will automatically be created for you. The best object-oriented programming technique uses accessors, but some people prefer simple variables that are private to the Java class; that method hides the variables as effectively as using accessors.

The source file is updated with the information that you provide here.

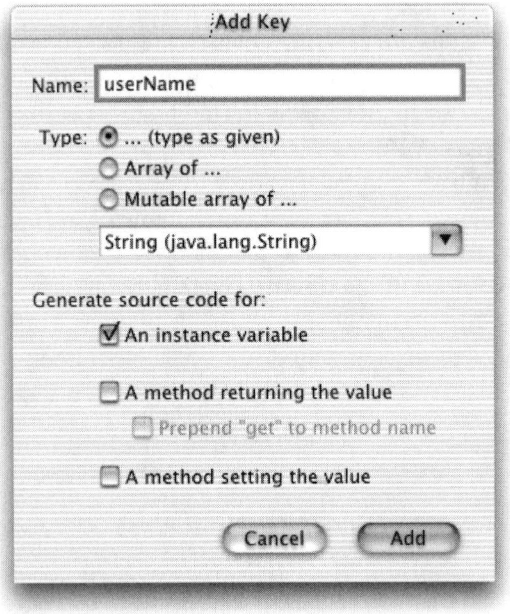

Figure 14-8   *Adding a key to a component*

Binding Attributes Graphically

If you are using the layout view, you can see WebObjects element icons. In that case, you can bind keys or actions to the element by dragging from the appropriate name in the object browser to the WebObjects element as shown in Figure 14-9. Here, the `userName` key is being bound to a WOString element.

When you release the mouse, WebObjects Builder will display a menu of the various attributes that can be bound. Select the one you want to bind the key or action to as shown in Figure 14-10. To set the WOString element's value to `userName`, you would select `value` from the menu.

The result of the two previous steps is to set the value attribute to the `userName` key as shown in Figure 14-11. Working in this way not only saves typing but prevents you from introducing mistakes due to misspellings. When you are binding a string value (a quoted string) to a key, of course, you must type it.

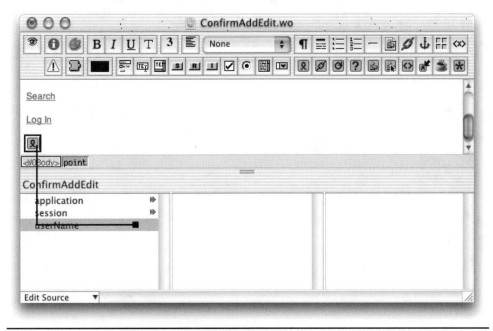

Figure 14-9   *Graphically binding attributes*

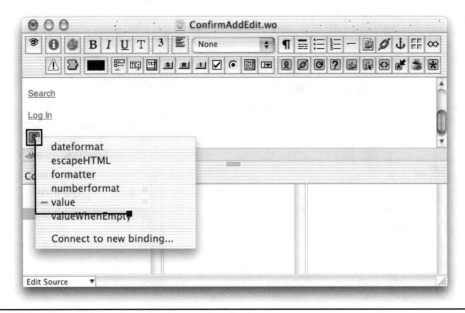

Figure 14-10   *Selecting an attribute to bind a key or action to*

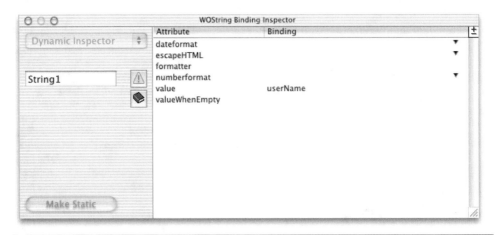

Figure 14-11   *WOString Inspector*

Creating New Bindings

Sometimes you need to create new bindings for a component. The small +– button at the upper right of the window opens a menu to do so; it is shown in Figure 14-12.

You need to add a binding to a component if you need to be able to pass data into the component from the interface and retrieve it in your Java code. Name the binding anything you want, but be sure to use that name in your Java code.

If you are used to working with traditional HTML applications, you may be accustomed to creating large numbers of hidden fields inside forms. They are an easy way to pass data back and forth from one page to another. In WebObjects, you can often accomplish the same objective by adding a number of bindings to a component (such as the form itself). You then set the various bindings to the values you would otherwise have put into hidden fields.

The names of bindings are passed through to WebObjects. Some bindings may be used to set values of variables used in display groups to retrieve data from Enterprise Objects fetch elements. The names of these bindings start with question marks. Very commonly, an added key will be set to the value of the unique key for a data record. In that way, when someone clicks a button or link to do something further with that record (add or delete it, for instance), the action that is invoked can retrieve the value of the unique key from the binding and use it for database access.

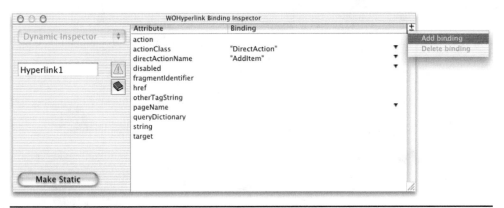

Figure 14-12   *Adding a new binding*

Using Project Builder

IN THIS CHAPTER:

Creating Projects

Editing Projects

Editing Components

Building and Launching WebObjects Applications

The Project Builder tools provide an integrated development environment (IDE) to assist you in creating WebObjects applications. This chapter provides an overview of Project Builder capabilities. A variety of tools exist: WOProjectBuilder runs on Windows and Mac OS X Server 1.0. The later Project Builder tool is based on that code, but it runs on Mac OS X. Your WebObjects documentation provides you with details on how to use the specific tool for your development environment: this chapter focuses on the functionality that is provided in the most recent tool, Project Builder for Mac OS X.

Creating Projects

You start by creating a project from the New Project command in the File menu. The assistant shown in Figure 15-1 opens for you.

In most cases, you choose to create a WebObjects application as shown in the figure. Other possibilities apply to WebObjects and to the various types of projects that you can create on Mac OS X. You will be asked to name the project, and when

Figure 15-1   *Create a project in Project Builder*

you have done so, the main editing window opens as shown in Figure 15-2. (Note that revisions to Project Builder continue at Apple; as a result, your window may look somewhat different from this one.)

At the left, the files in your project are shown; they are combined into groups that you can open or close using the disclosure triangles. This grouping relates to Project Builder itself, not to the stored locations of the files on disk. When you add files to a project (using the Add Files command from the Project menu), you locate the file, and it is added into whatever group is currently highlighted. As you add the file, you specify whether or not it is to be copied into your project. If it is copied, it normally is placed at the highest level of the project's directory on disk regardless of how embedded it is in groups in this display.

The project shown here contains a number of classes and components that have been added to the basic project. Inside the Classes folder, the Java class files are shown; inside the Web Components folder, each of the components described in the previous chapter is located. Thus, within the Main group you will find the .wo

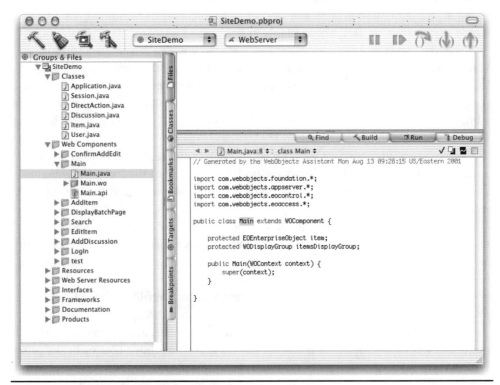

Figure 15-2   *Project Builder editing window*

folder containing .wod, .woo, and .html files; you will also find the .api and .java files for ConfirmAddEdit.

The organization that you see in this window relates to the project: Project Builder keeps track of where files are within your project. Thus, you will normally not see a Web Components folder inside your project; neither will you see a Classes folder (neither exists). Because Project Builder keeps track of where files are, you should be careful about moving or renaming files. Use the Rename command from the Project menu to handle your renaming; in that way, Project Builder will update its internal tables.

Editing Projects

You edit projects in a variety of ways. You can double-click a filename to open it in its own window. If you double-click a .wo wrapped file, you will open its three constituent files in WebObjects Builder.

A single click on a file will display its contents in the editing pane at the bottom of the main editing window, as you can see in Figure 15-2. The normal features you would expect from an IDE are available to you.

All of the panes in this window are resizable, so you can move things around as you are working and need more or less space. At the top of the editing pane (the lower right of this figure), a number of controls can help you navigate quickly. At the left, arrows let you move to the next and previous displays just as the arrows in a browser do. Thus, if you move from looking at Main.java to ConfirmAddEdit.java, the back arrow will take you back to Main.java.

The next pop-up menu (set to Main.java:8) in this figure, lets you quickly go to each of the files that you have looked at in the editing pane. Whereas the previous and next arrows take you through the entire sequence you have created, this pop-up menu lists each file only once.

The next pop-up menu lets you quickly move to each of the classes and methods in the file. In this case, there is only one—the class Main. However, in a class such as DirectAction.java, all of your direct action methods may be present, and this can easily let you move among them.

At the right, four buttons let you check the syntax of the file, split the browser into two panes and reunite it, and go to headers for your classes.

You can drag the files and folders in the Files tab around to reorganize them. This does not change their location on disk. In this way, you can move files from one group to another.

In addition to editing the code files within a project, you can edit the project's settings. You do so by clicking the Targets tab as shown in Figure 15-3.

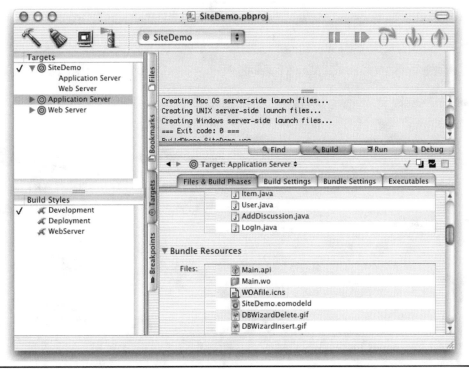

Figure 15-3   *Editing target and build settings*

A single target can contain other targets: in Figure 15-3, the SiteDemo target contains both the Application Server and Web Server targets. By default, SiteDemo—the application itself—builds both of the other targets. This is the default mechanism set up for you by Project Builder when you create a new project. As a result, you rarely have to manipulate these settings.

For any given target, you can specify a variety of settings. Figure 15-3 shows some of the files that are automatically part of a WebObjects project if you have used Project Builder. These are among the settings that Project Builder keeps track of as you add or remove files from a project. You do not need to manually adjust these settings.

Within a single project, a variety of build styles can exist. These are listed at the bottom left of the main window. The three shown here—development, deployment, and WebServer are all created automatically for you.

You can customize the toolbar as shown in Figure 15-4. If you move the Active build style pop-up button into the toolbar (as shown), you can switch easily between development and deployment build styles.

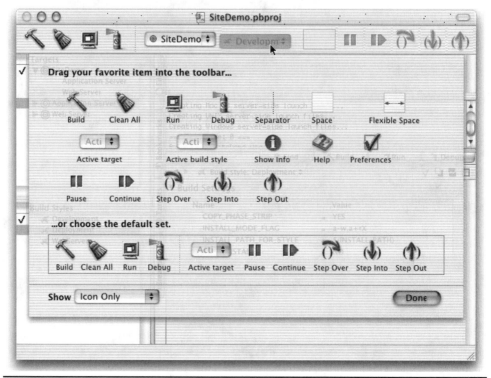

Figure 15-4   *Adding build styles to the toolbar*

Editing Components

Use the New File command in the File menu to add new files to the project. This section walks you through two such processes: the creation of a simple component and then the creation of a display group component.

Creating a Simple Component

The assistant window shown in Figure 15-5 lets you select the type of file to add.

It is important to use the New File command to add files because in some cases—such as Web components—several subsidiary files need to be created and named appropriately. Before creating the file, select the group in which you want it to be placed in the Files tab. For Java classes, you normally select the Classes group; for components, you select the Web Components group.

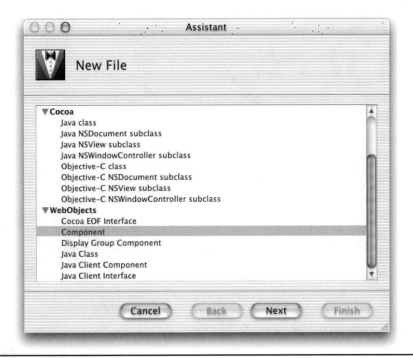

Figure 15-5   *Adding a file to a project*

NOTE

You can create Java classes for both WebObjects and Cocoa (as Figure 15-5 shows). Make certain that you are working within the WebObjects section of the assistant.

After you select the type of file to add, you need to specify its name. You also may need to add other information as shown in Figure 15-6.

By default, files are added to the Application Server target as shown here. This is normally the correct behavior. Project Builder will automatically update its tables and the target settings that it needs.

If you have an existing file that you want to add to your project, use the Add Files command in the Project menu; this will properly copy the file (or folder and its contents) into the project. A common example of a file that you add to the project (rather than creating from scratch within it) is your Enterprise Objects Framework model. Select the group into which you want to place it (usually Resources), and then choose Add Files from the Project menu.

Figure 15-6   *Naming a new Project Builder file*

Creating a Display Group Component

A display group component provides a powerful view of a database. The Project Builder assistant is capable of automatically preparing a very powerful display group with a minimum of your effort.

First, you need to associate an Enterprise Objects Framework model with your project. Do this by using EOModeler to create the model. Then, select the Resources folder in your project and use Add File from the Project menu to add the model to your project. After that, you can build a display group component. Choose New File from the File menu, and then select a Display Group Component. Project Builder will open your model and will list the entities it finds there. As shown in Figure 15-7, you must choose the primary entity for your component.

A variety of layouts can be created by default, as shown in Figure 15-8. The best way to become familiar with them is to experiment with each one in turn. (At this point, you may want to jump ahead to Figure 15-12: that is the final component that is built with the choices that follow in this chapter. You can refer to the finished display to see what choices wind up where.)

Next, select the data to display from each record, as shown in Figure 15-9. Note that you can include not only attributes of the object itself but also attributes of

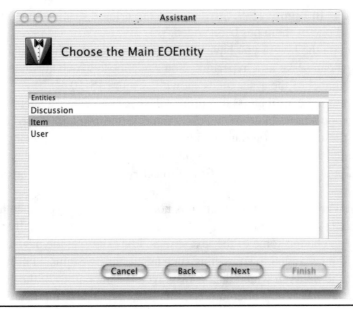

Figure 15-7   *Choose the main EOEntity*

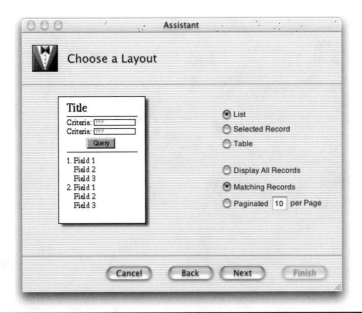

Figure 15-8   *Select the layout for your component*

related objects. In Figure 15-9, attributes of the related discussions object are displayed, and one of them has been added.

Depending on the layout you have chosen, one of the attributes may be able to be hot—that is, it can serve as a hyperlink. You can choose which attribute (if any) that is on the next panel of the assistant as shown in Figure 15-10.

Finally, choose the attribute(s) that users will specify to create a query. In Figure 15-11, the component is set up so that users can select information based on its status.

Based on these choices (and using the Enterprise Objects Framework model that was created for SiteDemo), the display group component is created. You can compile and build it and then run it from Project Builder: the results are shown in Figure 15-12.

The display group is functional, but it is not yet finished. If you open it in WebObjects Builder, you can modify the format. The spacing is usually all right, but you need to change some of the text strings. For example, the page title ("Page Title") should be changed to something such as "Items by Status." Furthermore, the names of the fields in which data is displayed are the names of the attributes; in turn, these are the names of columns in the database. The string that is used in WebObjects Builder to identify the postedby attribute should be changed to "Posted By" or "Author."

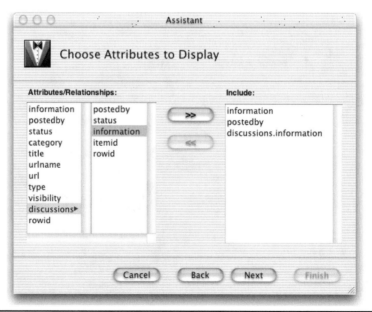

Figure 15-9 *Select data to display*

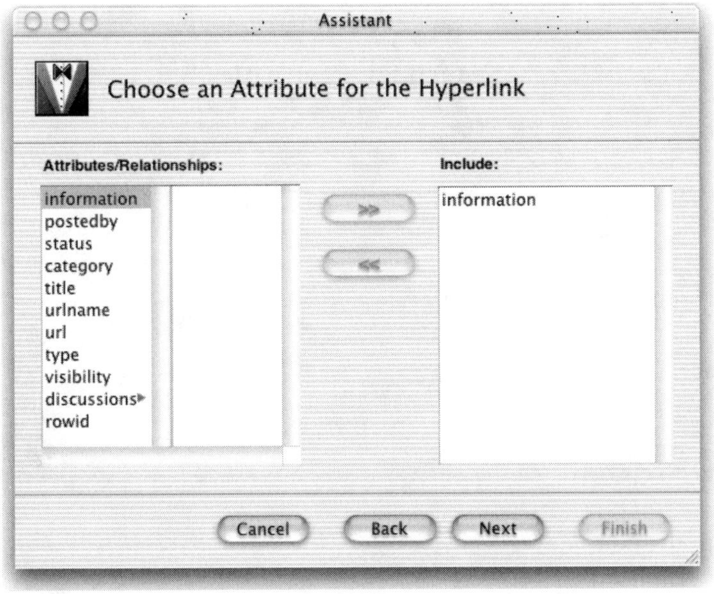

Figure 15-10   *Choose a hyperlink*

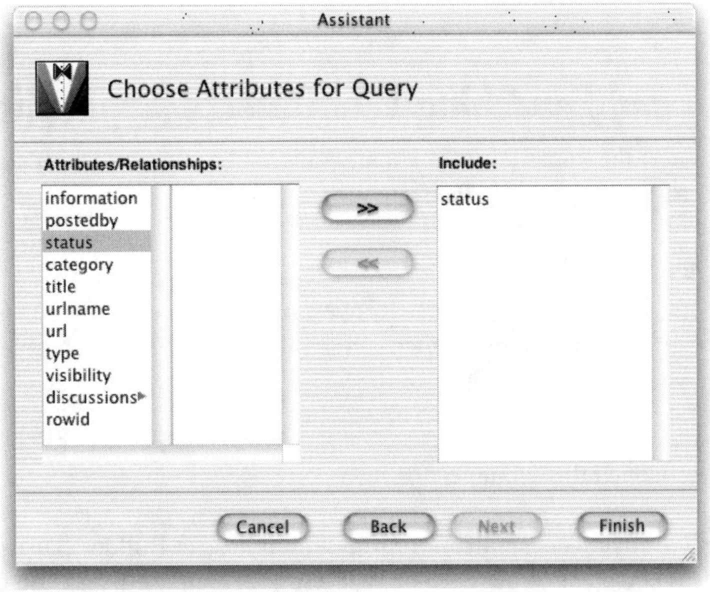

Figure 15-11   *Choose a query attribute*

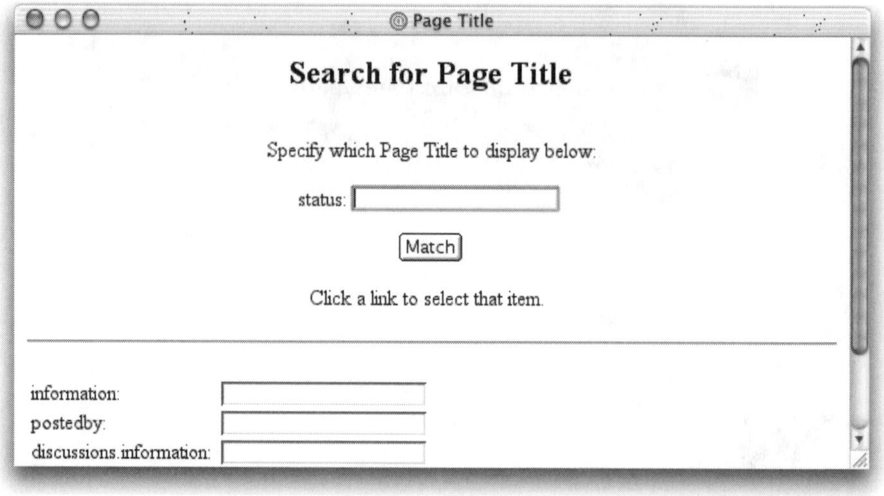

Figure 15-12   *The display group component in action*

These are the clean-ups you need to do; the basic functionality is all done automatically. In this way, it is very easy to create small WebObjects applications that interact with databases through Enterprise Objects Framework models.

Building and Launching WebObjects Applications

The four icons at the upper left of the main window let you work with your project. From left to right, they provide the following functionality:

▶ You can build the project.

▶ You can clean the project. This removes all of the object code and forces everything to be recompiled. Occasionally, this may clear up problems when files have become unsynchronized.

▶ You can run the project.

▶ You can launch the debugger for Java.

Running a WebObjects application from within Project Builder causes it to be launched by WebObjects; your default Web browser is opened, and you can use it just as a Web user would. This is not the normal way in which WebObjects applications are launched, so you may need to be aware of how Project Builder and WebObjects interact.

Most important, Project Builder assumes that the computer on which you are running is called `localhost` and has an IP address for `localhost` of 127.0.0.1. This is normally the case. However, in some environments, your computer may have a different name assigned to it. (This frequently happens with some DHCP setups.) If WebObjects cannot be launched, check to see what your computer's name is. On Mac OS X, you can do this by launching Terminal. The default prompt for Terminal shows your computer's name. If, for example, it is dhcppc1, WebObjects will not run. The solution is simply to change the computer's name. In Terminal, type the following:

```
sudo hostname localhost
```

You will be prompted to enter an administrator password, and the change will then take place. (You need not restart.)

It is a good idea to start by compiling one of the WebObjects examples (such as Hello World) and testing that you can run it from Project Builder. If you cannot, you are not likely to be able to run anything else.

Before attempting this test, remember to copy the example you choose into your own directory. The default security settings do not allow users—even administrator users—write access to the folder in which the WebObjects examples are placed during installation. It is better to copy them to another location than to change the security of the folder in which they are placed. By copying them, you can easily revert to the original versions without having to reinstall WebObjects.

Using Dynamic Elements

IN THIS CHAPTER:

How Dynamic Elements Work

Syntax for WebObjects Dynamic Elements

D ynamic elements do most of the work of WebObjects applications. You create components (including HTML templates), and you may write code for your component classes; but the routine process of handling users' HTTP requests and creating HTML responses is done using dynamic elements.

This chapter explains how dynamic elements work. Following that, the syntax is provided for all of the WebObjects dynamic elements. These dynamic elements fall into three general categories:

▶ HTML dynamic elements implement and extend basic HTML functionality—hyperlinks, for example.

▶ Form dynamic elements implement and extend the HTML form elements that are used when users submit data—Submit buttons and text fields, for example. (Form elements are also sometimes used to present data, but their primary use is in collecting data from users.)

▶ Programming elements implement concepts such as conditions (if/then statements) and repetitions that are not present in HTML. They also provide gateways to JavaScript and VBScript.

NOTE

You rarely override or modify the existing dynamic elements in WebObjects. You can create new ones if necessary, but because one of the purposes of dynamic elements is to create HTML as part of the response to a user, moving beyond standard HTML is dicey. Note, too, that Java client WebObjects applications use dynamic objects in a similar but simpler way than is described in this chapter. Java client design is covered in Chapter 23.

How Dynamic Elements Work

Like all objects, dynamic elements consist of functionality (methods) and data. This section describes each of those aspects in turn.

What Dynamic Elements Do (Methods)

Dynamic elements have three basic functions:

▶ They take values from an HTTP request and place them into themselves (and therefore into a WebObjects component or class where they can be acted on). This is done by a method called `takeValuesFromRequest` that is present in all dynamic elements. (Remember that WebObjects components create pages or parts of pages; WebObjects classes include components, the application and session class, as well as other nonpage classes you may create.)

▶ They can cause actions to be invoked—as is the case when a user clicks the Submit button or a hyperlink. This is done by a method called `invokeActionForRequest`.

▶ They can generate HTML. Dynamic elements typically generate a part of the HTML page that winds up being returned to the user; each dynamic element appends its part of the HTML code to the page in progress, which is ultimately returned to the user. This is done by a method called `appendToResponse`.

Each of the three methods mentioned here takes a pair of arguments: the first is either a request (WORequest in the first two methods) or a response (WOResponse in the last method). The second argument in all cases is a WOContext object. That object enables the dynamic element to access the appropriate application and session (and thus, their data).

What Dynamic Elements Know (Properties)

Each dynamic element has a group of properties. You can set these properties by using WebObjects Builder—frequently they are bound to data elements in WebObjects components or classes.

NOTE

HTML elements have attributes for their data. Dynamic elements in WebObjects have properties; these properties are bound to values in WebObjects components, and sometimes they are referred to as bindings. Sometimes these attributes and properties have the same names and are exactly the same item: the `target` attribute, for example, is of the FORM HTML element and a property or binding of the WOForm dynamic element in WebObjects.

How It Works

Dynamic elements do not contain their properties until run time; as a result, they function more dynamically than static HTML. Take hyperlinks, for example. In HTML, they are specified using either anchor (A) or link (LINK) elements.

NOTE

Anchors are the freeform links that appear throughout HTML pages. The LINK element describes types of links where those types are specified document relationships—next or previous pages, a link to help, and so forth.

An essential part of an anchor or link element is the HREF attribute—the address of the hyperlink (or its name if it is in the same document). A typical hyperlink looks like this:

```
<A NAME = "demoLink" HREF="http://www.philmontmill.com/index.html">
See what's new at Philmont Software Mill.
</A>
```

The starting tag contains the anchor element's name (optional, but a good idea) and the URL to which the hyperlink points. Following the starting tag, the text of the link appears; the element closes with the ending tag.

NOTE

Of course, instead of text for the link, you could insert an image by using the IMG element.

Compare the HTML hyperlink to the WebObjects WOHyperlink dynamic element. Among its properties, you will find `href`—exactly the same attribute as in the HTML anchor element; and you will find `pageName`—the name of a WebObjects page (component) to be displayed. If you use `pageName`, your WebObjects component can create the page as needed; in that page, you can insert dynamic data (such as a name to follow "Thank you,").

Further, you can specify an action method in the component or in a direct action that will return a WebObjects element. (Action methods and classes are discussed in Chapter 18.) Any of these approaches will cause WebObjects to generate an HTML page on the fly; that dynamically created page will have the URL that appears in the HTML anchor element. All of this is done for you; you need merely specify how you will create the dynamic page, and WebObjects takes care of the rest.

NOTE

If you have ever tried to explain to someone—or even yourself—why it is so difficult to construct an HTML page that says, "Thank you, Simone," you will understand how important this feature of being able to insert dynamic data into pages as you create them is. And if you have ever attempted to use HTML to extract even the most basic data from a database, you will also appreciate this critically important feature of WebObjects.

Syntax for WebObjects Dynamic Elements

In this section, each of the WebObjects dynamic elements is listed. The dynamic elements are divided into three groups:

▶ Dynamic elements that generally correspond to HTML elements you use
to display information on Web pages

▶ Dynamic elements that generally correspond to HTML elements you use
for data entry in forms

▶ Dynamic elements that provide programmer services such as conditional
statements and repeat loops, as well as gateways to JavaScript, applets,
and VBScript

For each dynamic element, the HTML equivalent is provided; in addition, the
essential properties are listed for each dynamic element. WebObjects Builder flags
essential properties in red. You must provide these properties—sometimes all of them
or sometimes one or several of them. (For example, a WOHyperlink element must be
able to construct a standard HTML HREF attribute with a URL for a page to which
it is linked.) You can provide that URL in the HREF property. WebObjects can also
create it dynamically based on a page that is created dynamically by a component
identified in the `pageName` property, by an action in the component identified in the
`action` property, or by a direct action identified by a `directActionName`
property and an `actionClass` property.

NOTE

*For complete syntax, see WebObjects Dynamic Elements—you can download it in PDF or browse
it online in HTML. It is located on Apple's Developer site under the name "Dynamic Element
Specifications," but you can search for it using that title on Apple's home page (www.apple.com).
For more documentation on WebObjects, click the Developer tab on Apple's home page and follow
links to documentation and developer resources.*

Programming Support for Dynamic Elements

In many cases, you can use dynamic elements without additional programming.
You bind their properties to other WebObjects entities in WebObjects Builder and
everything works fine.

However, some dynamic elements do require certain programming support. A
WOBrowser element, for example, requires its choices to be set programmatically.
(A WOBrowser element is equivalent to the HTML SELECT element: it presents
a scrolling menu list of choices, one or more of which can be selected.)

HTML Elements

You use HTML elements to display data. Many HTML elements have no corresponding
WebObjects dynamic elements because there is no need to incur the overhead of a

dynamic element to do something that is not dynamic, such as inserting a horizontal rule. Because of the parallels between these dynamic elements and HTML elements, you can use HTML elements and convert them to WebObjects dynamic elements later, as your project becomes more complex.

otherTagString

All dynamic elements have an optional property named otherTagString. You can use it to specify a string that will be emitted inside the WebObjects dynamic element's HTML element. This way, you can include HTML attributes directly into any dynamic element.

WOBody

Use WOBody to specify the background image for a page.

HTML Comparison   WOBody elements are the counterpart to the BODY element. You can specify the background color as well as colors for links (visited and not). You use WOBody rather than the HTML BODY tag to be able to use a dynamically created image as the background of a page. (With the HTML BODY element, the image must be in a file that can be identified when you code the HTML.)

Essential Properties   You must specify where the image can be found. Use the src, filename, data, or value properties to specify where the image is located:

▶ The src property is a URL for the image. It is the same as the HTML SRC attribute.

▶ The filename property is a relative filename identifying the file within the WebObjects resources that you have identified for your application. Use the framework property if the image and component are in separate locations.

▶ The data property is an image retrieved (or created) dynamically by a program; its type is NSData, and you must specify a MIME type in the mimeType property.

▶ The value property is a WOElement object that contains the data for the image.

WOString

You either type static text on an HTML page into the HTML template or insert it dynamically using a WOString element. (See the "WOText" and "WOTextField" sections later in this chapter for elements that display text and that also allow user changes to the text.)

HTML Comparison   Text can be typed inside many HTML elements, notably the paragraph (<P>) element.

Essential Properties   You must bind the `value` property so that a string is inserted there. Typically, you bind `value` to a method that returns a string based on changing data or you bind it to a variable in your .java file.

WOHyperlink

Use the WOHyperlink element to create a hypertext reference based on text. Use WOActiveImage (described a bit later) to create a graphical link.

> ### *NOTE*
>
> *WOHyperlink was described as a prototypical dynamic element earlier in this chapter.*

HTML Comparison   The WOHyperlink element corresponds to a source HTML anchor (<A>) element.

Essential Properties   The WOHyperlink element must be able to refer to a destination page. It must contain either an `action` or `directActionName` method that produces a WOElement, a `pageName` that produces a WebObjects page, or an `href` to a URL where the page already exists (that is, is not created dynamically by WebObjects).

   You must also either bind text to the `string` property or enter it within the WOHyperlink element. If no text is entered, nothing will be underlined and the user will have nothing to click.

WOActiveImage

This element is just what its name implies: an image on which you can click. Use it outside forms (inside forms, use WOImageButton). For static images, use WOImage (described next).

HTML Comparison   In static HTML, you create a hyperlink reference (generally as an anchor element); instead of putting text within the anchor element, you use an image element (IMG), specifying the image's location in the SRC attribute:

```
<a href="http://www.philmontmill.com">
<img src="../Images/demo.gif" width="172" height="42" border="0">
</a>
```

NOTE

In HTML 4.x, the OBJECT element is preferred to the IMG element; however, IMG remains widely used.

One of the properties of a WOActiveImage element is `imageMapFile`; if you use it, it must be in the same place as the image itself. The `imageMapFile` property lets you dispatch various actions depending on where within an image the mouse is clicked.

Essential Properties   You must specify what the active image does—the page to which it links—and where the image can be found.

Specify the action with either the `action` or `href` properties: `action` is a WebObjects action that returns a response or page; `href` is the standard HTML hyperlink reference.

Use the `src`, `filename`, `data`, or `value` properties to specify where the image is located:

▶ The `src` property is a URL for the image. It is the same as the HTML SRC attribute.

▶ The `filename` property is a relative filename identifying the file within the WebObjects resources that you have identified for your application. Use the `framework` property if the image and component are in separate locations.

▶ The `value` property is a WOElement object; it, too, can be retrieved or created dynamically.

▶ The `data` property is an image retrieved (or created) dynamically by a program; its type is NSData, and you must specify a MIME type in the `mimeType` property.

WOImage

WOImage is the element you use to display a static image—that is, one that does nothing except appear on the page. (See the "WOActiveImage" section earlier for support for images on which you can click.)

HTML Comparison   WOImage corresponds to the HTML IMG element with its `src` attribute.

Essential Properties   You need to specify where WebObjects can find the image when it creates the HTML for the response. Use `src`, `filename`, `data`, or `value` to specify where the image is located:

▶ The `src` property is a URL for the image. It is the same as the HTML `src` attribute.

▶ The `filename` property is a relative filename identifying the file within the WebObjects resources that you have identified for your application. Use the `framework` property if the image and component are in separate locations.

▶ The `value` property is a WOElement object; it, too, can be retrieved or created dynamically.

▶ The `data` property is an image retrieved (or created) dynamically by a program; its type is NSData, and you must specify a MIME type in the `mimeType` property.

WOQuickTime

QuickTime lets you play movies, synthesize music, view virtual reality, display animations, and handle other multimedia features in Windows, Macintosh, and Java. WOQuickTime lets you easily embed QuickTime into WebObjects applications.

NOTE

The properties of WOQuickTime are extensive; they allow you to create interactive interfaces very easily. Consult the WebObjects documentation and examples for more information. This is an important area to Apple, and WebObjects showcases its significant achievements in this area— including the use of streaming video.

HTML Comparison   The HTML OBJECT element is used to place QuickTime movies into HTML pages; the deprecated EMBED element is also used.

NOTE

Although recognized by most browsers, EMBED is not standard HTML. It is not part of the current (4.01) specification.

Essential Properties   QuickTime movies are played within an area on the HTML page. You must specify the `height` and `width` properties of the WOQuickTime element for the playing area: it is unavoidable if you are drawing the page with WebObjects Builder.

In addition, you must specify the location of the QuickTime file. You can do so in either of two ways:

▶ You can specify the `filename` property to identify the file on the HTTP server.

▶ You can specify a URL in `src`.

WOEmbeddedObject

You use WOEmbeddedObject to dynamically create an EMBED element. This allows you to embed objects that will be played by QuickTime (see "WOQuickTime") or that will be manipulated by other plug-ins.

> **NOTE**
>
> *Although recognized by most browsers, EMBED is not standard HTML. It is not part of the current (4.01) specification.*

HTML Comparison   The nonstandard EMBED element should be replaced by the standard OBJECT element. Either provides the functionality of WOEmbeddedObject.

Essential Properties   You must specify the data to be embedded. You have four choices:

▶ The `src` property is a URL for the data. It is the same as the HTML SRC attribute.

▶ The `filename` property is a relative filename identifying the file within the WebObjects resources that you have identified for your application. Use the `framework` property if the data and component are in separate locations.

▶ The `data` property is an image retrieved (or created) dynamically by a program; its type is NSData, and you must specify a MIME type in the `mimeType` property.

▶ The `value` property is a WOElement object that contains the data for the embedded object.

WOFrame

The HTML FRAME element lets you combine several Web pages in a single display. There are ardent proponents and opponents of frames. Frames are particularly valuable in constructing a composite Web page that pulls together information from several servers. For example, you might have a navigation frame at the top or left of a page; the main part of the page could be generated by a WebObjects application in some cases and by other applications in other cases.

Within WebObjects, you can use the WOFrame element to specify a frame to display. Use the WOFrame element within the standard HTML FRAMESET element.

HTML Comparison   WOFrame corresponds to the FRAME element and is used within a FRAMESET element.

Essential Properties   You must specify the page to be displayed in the frame. Therefore, you must provide either a URL (in the `src` property), a WebObjects component name in `pageName`, or a method name in `directActionName` or in `value`. If you provide a component or method name, it must produce a page to be displayed.

WOComponentContent

These elements let you incorporate entire components that you create in your application: typically, they are headers, footers, banners, or other such components. They may contain a common toolbar or set of navigation links that you want at the top (or bottom) of all of your pages.

HTML Comparison   There is no comparison.

Essential Properties   You name the WOComponentContent as you see fit; in your .wod file, you specify its type, with the type being the name of the component to use. For example, if you have named your WOComponentContent as myBanner, your .wod file would contain the line that follows if you wanted the SiteDemoComponent from your WebObjects application to appear in the place of the WOComponentContent element.

```
myBanner:SiteDemoBanner {}
```

WOGenericElement

You can create your own reusable elements that are based on standard (or nonstandard) HTML elements by using certain attributes set within WOGenericElement. A WOGenericElement WebObjects element creates an HTML element with only a starting tag (like the IMG element).

HTML Comparison   There is no comparison.

Essential Properties   You must provide an `elementName`: the name for the HTML element that is generated.

WOGenericContainer

WOGenericContainer is similar to WOGenericElement, but it represents an element with both a starting and ending tag.

HTML Comparison   There is no comparison.

Essential Properties   You must provide an elementName: the name for the HTML element that is generated.

FORM Elements

HTML forms let you display data for the user, but more importantly, the user can enter data and transmit it back to the HTTP server for further processing. Forms, therefore, are primarily data entry and interface elements.

WOForm

A form encloses a variety of INPUT elements—text boxes, radio buttons, and the like. It includes a Submit button, which causes all data to be transmitted to the HTTP server; it normally contains a Reset button, which restores all INPUT elements to their initial values.

HTML FORM elements must have an action attribute and a method attribute; the method can be get or post, and it determines how the data is transmitted. Briefly, get transmits the form's data as pairs of identifiers (the form element names) and their values in the searchpart of a URL—the action attribute of the form. This makes the data visible if the HTTP request is intercepted; it also limits data to text. The put method transmits the data as part of a MIME-encoded message. It is more secure and is appropriate for larger amounts of data.

HTML Comparison   WOForm produces an HTML FORM element.

Essential Properties   You must specify the action to be taken when the form is submitted. To do so, use either the href property or the action property. WebObjects also allows you to specify the action to be taken in the Submit button's properties (this is what allows you to have multiple Submit buttons in WebObjects forms).

WOTextField

Use a WOTextField element within a form to provide a data entry area. Compare it to WOText—a multi-line input area—as well as to WOPasswordField, in which the keystrokes are hidden with a symbol, such as a bullet •.

HTML Comparison   WOTextFeld corresponds to an HTML INPUT element with type = text.

Essential Properties   You must bind the `value` property. Normally, it is bound to a variable that contains the field's data—that is, both the initial value and (later on) the data that the user has entered.

WOText

WOText is a multi-line field for text display and entry. It can have a scrollbar so that it can contain much more data than its dimensions suggest.

TIP

Use `wrap=virtual` to have users' data entry wrap each line to the width of the text field. If you do not, lines will be very long and usually unreadable.

Compare WOText to the single-line WOTextField element.

HTML Comparison   WOText is the WebObjects version of the HTML TEXTAREA element.

The TEXTAREA element in HTML contains its data between start and ending tags; other form data fields are different versions of the INPUT elements, and their text is set using the VALUE attribute of INPUT.

Essential Properties   You must bind the `value` property. Normally, it is bound to a variable that contains the field's data—that is, both the initial value and (later on) the data that the user has entered.

WOPasswordField

An HTML *password field* is a text field that the browser displays by using a special symbol (such as•) for all characters. When transmitted as part of a form, its contents (the `value` attribute) are transmitted without encryption. Therefore, its security consists only of obscuring what has been typed from curious eyes looking at the monitor. This security, however, is sufficient for many user IDs and passwords.

HTML Comparison   This is comparable to the INPUT element with `type = password`.

Essential Properties   You must specify the `value` property so that WebObjects has a place to store what is entered into the WOPasswordField element.

NOTE

You use the `value` *property to set the WOPasswordField element, even though it cannot be read. Therefore, you may want to make sure that* `value` *is set to blank before using it.*

WOBrowser

Use WOBrowser to present a scrolling list of selections for the user. One or more selections can be made. (You set that option.) Furthermore, you can set a default selection to appear at the beginning.

You can use HTML formatting elements to format the elements in the scrolling list. (The escapeHTML property lets you do this.)

WOBrowser is similar to WOPopUpButton in that it allows users to make choices from a list. There are two significant differences, however:

▶   If users are to be allowed to make multiple selections, WOBrowser must be used instead of WOPopUpButton.

▶   From an interface point of view, the scrolling list of WOBrowser makes it clearer that choices are available—and it can be made big enough so that all (or most) of the choices are in plain view. A drop-down menu shows only one choice at a time.

Constructing a selection list dynamically can be very useful. Consider an e-commerce site that lets users choose various shipping procedures. Next-day delivery may seem pretty straightforward, but, in fact, it usually is not. In the fine print—or on another page of fine print—the curious user may discover that orders placed before 2:00 P.M. or some other cutoff time will be shipped that day for next day delivery—if it is available on the following day. Typically, an order placed after 2:00 P.M. on a Friday will be shipped the following Monday for next day (Tuesday) delivery. Many a customer service representative has had to explain why "next day" means "four days later," in this case.

You could construct a WOBrowser element that takes such details into account. Instead of listing next-day delivery, it could list delivery on Tuesday, or whatever the next day would be at the time of purchase. To do this, you would populate WOBrowser with the appropriate texts during the construction of the component in which it appears.

Another powerful example of the use of WOBrowser is when the contents of a database record's fields are displayed in the WOBrowser element and the current record's value is selected.

HTML Comparison WOBrowser produces a SELECT element with SIZE greater than 1. (A SELECT element with SIZE of 1 or with the `size` attribute omitted is normally displayed as a drop-down menu.)

TIP

The actual interface elements used to implement the HTML SELECT element are up to the individual browser. The HTML standard does not require list boxes, pop-up buttons, or drop-down menus to be used.

Essential Properties You must specify `list`—an array of objects that provides the values for WOBrowser. In the WebObjects ElementTour example that follows, you can see how to create such an array. First, you declare it in the declarations for your component:

```
protected NSArray objectList;
```

Then, within the constructor of the component, create a Java array and use it to create an NSArray, which will be used by the WOBrowser. Bind the `objectList` variable (created here in the component's constructor) to the `list` property by using WebObjects Builder, and your WOBrowser is complete:

```
Object temp[] ={ "one", "two", "three"};
objectList = new NSArray (temp);
```

TIP

Instead of creating an NSArray variable, you can create a method that returns an NSArray variable on demand. Note that if the variables within the array will change, you must either create a method or you must create an NSMutableArray whose data elements can be modified as necessary.

You can also create and populate an array in the `selectedValues` property. In this way, WOBrowser will start off with one or more objects already selected.

While this particular example provides you with no more functionality than the SELECT element in static HTML, the principles apply equally well to an array that is constructed dynamically using database accesses or global variables and information—such as the day of week and time that would be needed for the next-day shipping case.

WOPopUpButton

Pop-up buttons (pop-up menus, drop-down menus—they all mean the same thing) provide a single interface element with a range of choices. Unlike WOBrowser elements, they cannot have multiple selections. Only the current selection is visible, and users are sometimes unaware that they can choose from other values.

Despite their widespread use, pop-up buttons are inappropriate for long lists. A pop-up button listing the countries of the world or the 50 states of the United States is simply too large to function easily. As you try to scroll to your desired selection, you often go past it and have trouble getting back. A pop-up button with the ten provinces of Canada is perfect as far as the number of its choices. (A range of 7–14 is ideal. Fewer than seven are handled well with radio buttons; more than 14 are handled best with a scrolling list in a SELECT element or WOBrowser.)

HTML Comparison   WOPopUpButton generates an HTML SELECT element with SIZE = 1.

Essential Properties   Just as with a WOBrowser element, you must specify list—an array of objects that provides the values for WOPopUpButton. In the WebObjects ElementTour example, you can see how to create such an array. First, declare it in the declarations for your component:

```
protected NSArray objectList;
```

Then, within the constructor of the component, create a Java array and use it to create NSMutableArray (a subclass of NSArray), which WOPopUpButton will use. Bind the objectList variable (created here in the component's constructor) to the list property by using WebObjects Builder, and your WOPopUpButton element is complete.

```
Object temp[] ={ "one", "two", "three"};
objectList = new NSMutableArray (temp);
```

WORadioButton

Radio buttons are similar to checkboxes, but they differ in that only one of a group of radio buttons can be on at a time. (The name is derived from preset station buttons on radios—particularly car radios.)

The group of radio buttons is determined by the buttons' name: within a form, all buttons with the same name attribute are treated as a group. They need not be adjacent to one another, but it is normally a poor interface design choice if they are not.

HTML Comparison   The WORadioButton elements correspond to HTML INPUT elements with type = radio.

Essential Properties   As with HTML radio buttons, you can specify whether an individual button is on by using the `checked` attribute (in HTML) or the `checked` property (in WebObjects).

You can also set a `value` property for each radio button. If a radio button is checked, its value is transmitted as part of its form's data. Thus, if you have two radio buttons with values of AM and PM, if the AM button is checked, the value AM is transmitted along with the name that the two buttons share.

You must specify either `value` or `checked`.

WORadioButtonList

It is often easier to create a WORadioButtonList element rather than individual WORadioButton elements because you are dealing with a single object—the list—rather than a variety of separate buttons. WORadioButtonList wraps an array of objects that contain the radio button values.

The `suffix` property is a string (often a single character or an HTML element) that is inserted after each item in the list. If you use the BREAK (<BR>) element, each radio button will be placed on a single line. You can also insert several nonbreaking spaces or other characters. Note that the same suffix is applied to each item in the WORadioButtonList element. This is not nearly as confining as it may seem at first: a good user interface does not scatter radio buttons around. However, if you wish to place them in a small area—perhaps two rows of two—you must create them using WORadioButton rather than WORadioButtonList.

HTML Comparison   WORadioButtonList becomes a set of HTML radio buttons—that is, INPUT elements with `type = radio` and with a common NAME attribute (which you specify in the WORadioButtonList `name` property).

Essential Properties   The only essential property is a list of objects containing the titles of the radio buttons. You create it just as you do a list for WOBrowser or WOPopUpButton.

In your component's declaration, declare the list:

```
protected NSArray objectList;
```

Then, within the constructor of the component, create a Java array and use it to create NSMutableArray (a subclass of NSArray), which will be used by WORadioButtonList. Bind the `objectList` variable (created here in the component's constructor) to the `list` property by using WebObjects Builder, and your WORadioButtonList element is complete.

```
Object temp[] ={ "one", "two", "three"};
objectList = new NSMutableArray (temp);
```

WOCheckBox

Checkboxes allow users to answer yes or no to various choices. When checkboxes appear singly, users can answer questions such as "Are you over 21 years of age?"

HTML Comparison A WOCheckBox element creates an HTML INPUT element with TYPE = checkbox.

Essential Properties You need to provide the initial state of the checkbox in the checked property. Create a variable in your component and bind it to the checked property.

Declare a variable such as this in your component's declaration:

```
protected int wantsKibble;
```

In the constructor, initialize it appropriately:

```
wantsKibble = 1;
```

NOTE

A slightly more complex way of handling WOCheckBox involves the interplay of two other properties—value and selection. If they are equal when the form is submitted, WOCheckBox is returned with checked true. Setting value by itself will usually not give the results you want: stick to checked if you want to be safe.

WOCheckBoxList

Use a WOCheckBoxList element to create a group of checkboxes. You normally use WOCheckBoxList only when the checkboxes are logically related. For example, in specifying query results, a user might check boxes for Verbose Data Display, Complete Header Information, and Date Of Article. Each checkbox can have its own title (such as Verbose Data Display), and each can be checked or not. They are grouped with a common name attribute that WebObjects assigns or that you can assign to WOCheckBoxList (and that WebObjects will then assign to each checkbox within it).

HTML Comparison The WOCheckBoxList element will be expanded into a set of checkboxes with the same name attribute. When Submit is clicked, all checkboxes that are selected will be transmitted as part of the form. (This is standard HTML procedure for checkboxes in a form that share the same name.)

Essential Properties   The only essential property is a list of objects containing the titles of the checkboxes. You create it just as you do a list for WOBrowser or WOPopUpButton.

Declare the list in your component's declaration:

```
protected NSArray objectList;
```

Then, within the constructor of the component, create a Java array and use it to create NSMutableArray (a subclass of NSArray), which will be used by WOCheckListBox. Bind the `objectList` variable (created here in the component's constructor) to the `list` property by using WebObjects Builder, and your WOCheckListBox element is complete.

```
Object temp[] ={ "one", "two", "three"};
objectList = new NSMutableArray (temp);
```

WOHiddenField

Forms use hidden fields extensively. When a page is dynamically created, information is placed in hidden fields that are then transmitted back to the server (or onto another one) when Submit is clicked.

With WebObjects, you can often manage this functionality by storing data in variables in a component (or the session object). This strategy reduces the amount of traffic to and from the user; in addition, it eliminates the problems sometimes associated with users viewing the source code of their Web pages and seeing the hidden fields. (When the fields contain personal information such as credit card numbers, their visibility in the HTML source can cause problems.)

HTML Comparison   WOHiddenField corresponds to the HTML INPUT element with TYPE = `hidden`.

Essential Properties   WOHiddenField should have a variable bound to its `value` property. If its value is not set, nothing will be returned when the user clicks the Submit button, and there will have been no point to the process.

NOTE

An exception to this occurs when a JavaScript or other script fills the hidden field as a result of user action in other visible fields.

In addition, you should set the `name` attribute of the hidden field so that you can access it and its data. Again, if you cannot access it, there is no point to having it.

WOImageButton

You use WOImageButton within a form as a graphical Submit button. It is similar to a WOActiveImage element in that it generates an action; however, you use WOActiveImage outside forms and WOImageButton within forms (in most cases).

HTML Comparison   This is comparable to the HTML INPUT element with the `type` attribute set to `image`.

Essential Properties   Specify the action with the `action` property—a WebObjects action that returns a response or page. Use the `src`, `filename`, `data`, or `value` properties to specify where the image is located:

▶   The `src` property is a URL for the image. It is the same as the HTML SRC attribute.

▶   The `filename` property is a relative filename identifying the file within the WebObjects resources that you have identified for your application. Use the `framework` property if the image and component are in separate locations.

▶   The `value` property is a WOElement object; it, too, can be retrieved or created dynamically.

▶   The `data` property is an image retrieved (or created) dynamically by a program; its type is NSData, and you must specify a MIME type in the `mimeType` property.

WOSubmitButton

Users click a Submit button to transfer a form and all of its data to the HTTP server, where it is passed on for processing as appropriate.

NOTE

You can use an image rather than a button to submit a form. In WebObjects, the WOImageButton element does this; in HTML, an INPUT element with TYPE = IMAGE does it.

HTML Comparison   A WOSubmit button is the same as an HTML INPUT element with TYPE = `submit`.

Essential Properties   You must specify the `action` property—the method to be invoked when the button is clicked.

NOTE

In HTML, ACTION is an attribute of a form; in WebObjects, `action` is a property of a form, too. However, you can specify an action for a Submit button so that an individual form can have multiple actions, depending on which of several Submit buttons a user clicks. If you do so, you must set the WOForm element's `multipleSubmit` property.

WOResetButton

A Reset button restores all INPUT elements in a form to their initial values.

HTML Comparison   This is the same as an HTML INPUT element with TYPE = RESET.

Essential Properties   There are none.

Programming Elements

The programming elements support traditional procedural programming (repetitions and conditions, for example); they also provide interfaces to Java applets, JavaScript, and VBScript. They are described in this section.

TIP

The first three elements—WORepetition, WOConditional, and WOSwitchComponent—are not just easier ways of generating your HTML pages. Using such programming structures (loops, if statements, and case/switch statements) makes your code easier to read and maintain. Rather than trying to figure out how similar-looking code differs, these structures make it clear what is going on. They are worth using in every programming environment.

WORepetition

The WORepetition element repeats its code to generate similar (or identical) HTML. You can specify that it will iterate a certain number of times, or you can give it a list of objects that it will process one at a time.

HTML Comparison   There is no comparison.

Essential Properties   You must either provide count—the number of times the code should be executed—or list, an array of objects (such as names) that WORepetition will process.

WOSwitchComponent

The WOSwitchComponent element displays a component that is chosen at run time. You bind its WOComponentName property to a string or (more commonly) a method that returns a string; the string contains the name of a component and—optionally—its attributes. Thus, in a form you could dynamically choose to display WOTextField (which is modifiable) or WOString (which is not modifiable).

> **NOTE**
>
> *You can accomplish a similar effect by using the READONLY attribute of the HTML INPUT element. However, using WOString generally causes browsers to display text in such a way that it appears as if it could not be modified under any circumstances. Furthermore, some browsers do not support the READONLY attribute.*

HTML Comparison   There is no comparison.

Essential Properties   You must bind a string or method that returns a string to WOComponentName. You can bind the following method to WOComponentName; it causes either WOString or WOTextField to be generated. In the case of a string, a value is displayed.

A string is declared in the components declarations:

```
protected String fieldValue;
```

Then this method is defined:

```
public String whichComponent ()
  {
  if (  )
    {
    fieldValue = "Some text.";
    return "WOString";
    }
    else
    {
    fieldValue = "";
    return "WOTextField";
    }
  }
```

For this code to work properly, you must declare a binding for `value` (a property of both WOString and WOTextField) in the WOSwitchComponent element that you use in WebObjects Builder and bind `fieldValue` to it using WebObjects Builder as shown in Chapter 14.

NOTE

When you use WOSwitchComponent, any properties that you will be binding in this way must be common to them. In practice, this is not such a big deal: you typically switch between strings and text fields; you rarely switch between text fields and horizontal rules. Furthermore, the `value` *property is probably the one you are most likely to set—and it applies to most WebObjects form elements.*

WOConditional

This element lets you wrap HTML code in WebObjects Builder so that it is (or is not) generated as part of the response to the user.

TIP

WOConditional is a simple if statement: there is no else. You write a method inside your component's Java code (or elsewhere in your WebObjects application) that returns a value of true/false or yes/no. Rather than having to write almost-similar methods to provide the reverse result (that is, to handle the else case of an if), you can use the `negate` *property of WOConditional. If* `negate` *is true (or yes), then the results of your method are reversed. Thus, to create an if/else pair of WOConditional elements, create two identical WOConditional elements with the second one using* `negate`*. (Of course, the HTML code within the WOConditional elements should vary.)*

HTML Comparison   There is no comparison.

Essential Properties   You must bind a method to the `condition` property. That method should return true/false, yes/no, or 1/0.

Here is a sample method you can use as a template:

```
public boolean testForResult ()
  {
  if (a > b)
    return true;
  else
  return false;
  }
```

Replace the underlined section with the test you want to perform. Because this is Java code, you can do anything you want—including querying a database or a legacy system.

WONestedList

This element displays and controls a nested hierarchical list of hyperlinks.

HTML Comparison   There is none.

Essential Properties   You must provide the list array as well as a sublist function which returns the sublist (if any) for the currently selected element of the list array.

WOFileUpload

You frequently want to let users browse their disks to select a file that will be uploaded to the HTTP server. WOFileUpload lets you do so. This is how users can send you images, documents, or attachments to Web-based e-mail and discussions.

NOTE

If you use a WOFileUpload element within a form, you must set **enctype** *for the form to* **multipart/form data**. *A WOFileUpload object on the WOB palette (described further in Chapter 24) includes the form and the right settings to make the process more convenient. See Chapter 23 for more on palettes and other reusable components.*

HTML Comparison   There is no comparison.

Essential Properties   You must bind a string to filePath, which is returned as the full path to the file that is uploaded. data is a property containing an NSData object, which is the file.

WOApplet

Java applets let you write code that is executed on the client machine (where the user's browser runs). See WOParam (described next) for a means of passing parameters to applets. This element and the ones that follow in this chapter are primarily devoted to scripting support for Java, JavaScript, and Visual Basic. You normally do not need to use them with WebObjects unless you are converting legacy code.

NOTE

Java applets are downloaded as byte code and are executed on the user's computer in a virtual machine. JavaScript is an interpreted scripting language that is executed by the user's browser.

HTML Comparison   WOApplet corresponds to the HTML OBJECT element where the included object is an applet. (The HTML APPLET element has been deprecated; the OBJECT element should be used instead.)

Essential Properties   You must bind the `code` property to identify the Java class. You must also specify the `height` and `width` of the applet's area on the page; if you use WebObjects Builder, you cannot avoid specifying `height` and `width` because you draw the object.

WOParam

Use WOParam to set the values of parameters for WOApplet elements.

HTML Comparison   WOParam corresponds to the HTML PARAM element.

Essential Properties   You must provide the name of the parameter and its value—or a means of obtaining its value when the page is created. Thus, you must bind `name` and either `value` or `action`—a method that provides the value.

WOJavaScript

You can insert JavaScript into your generated HTML using the WOJavaScript element.

NOTE

JavaScript—like VBScript—is interpreted and executed by the user's Web browser. Java applets are compiled into byte code, downloaded, and executed by the Java Virtual Machine on the user's computer.

HTML Comparison   WOJavaScript is comparable to an HTML SCRIPT element with `type = text/javascript`. (Formerly, the `language` attribute was used to specify a script's language; that syntax has now been deprecated in favor of the more general `type` attribute.)

Essential Properties   You must provide a JavaScript for the WOJavaScript element. You can do so in one of three ways:

▶ Use `scriptString` to identify an NSString object (or a method that returns an NSString object) that contains the JavaScript.

▶ Use `scriptFile` to identify an NSString object (or a method that returns an NSString object) that contains the name of the file containing the script.

▶ Use `scriptSource` to provide a URL for the script.

You must provide one (and only one) of these.

WOActionURL

The WOActionURL lets you dynamically create URLs to launch JavaScripts.

HTML Comparison   Compare WOActionURL to an HREF attribute of the anchor element that starts with JAVASCRIPT.

Essential Properties   You must provide either an `action` or `directActionName` method that produces a WOElement, or a `pageName` that produces a WebObjects page.

WOResourceURL

This element converts filenames to URLs for use in JavaScript.

HTML Comparison   There is none.

Essential Properties   Use `filename` or `data` to specify the resources.

▶ The `filename` property is a relative filename identifying the file within the WebObjects resources that you have identified for your application. Use the `framework` property if the image and component are in separate locations.

▶ The `data` property is an image retrieved (or created) dynamically by a program; its type is NSData, and you must specify a MIME type in the `mimeType` property.

WOVBScript

You can insert VBScript into your generated HTML by using the WOVBScript element.

NOTE

VBScript—like JavaScript—is interpreted and executed by the user's Web browser. Java applets are compiled into byte code, downloaded, and executed by the Java Virtual Machine on the user's computer.

HTML Comparison   WOVBScript is comparable to an HTML SCRIPT element with `type = text/vbscript`. (Formerly, the `language` attribute was used to specify a script's language; that syntax has now been deprecated in favor of the more general `type` attribute.)

Essential Properties   You must provide a VBScript for the WOVBScript element. You can do so in one of three ways:

▶ You can use `scriptString` to identify an NSString object (or a method that returns an NSString object) that contains the script.

▶ You can use `scriptFile` to identify an NSString object (or a method that returns an NSString object) that contains the name of the file containing the script.

▶ You can use `scriptSource` to provide a URL for the script.

You must provide one (and only one) of these.

Implementing the Request-Response Loop

IN THIS CHAPTER:

Classes that Implement the Request-Reponse Loop

The Request-Response Cycle in Action

In Chapter 16, you saw how dynamic elements do the nuts-and-bolts work of WebObjects, implementing interface elements and providing basic programmatic controls. This chapter focuses on the basic implementation of the request-response loop in WebObjects. It consists of two sections:

1. In the first, the major classes involved with the request-response loop are described. These include WOElement, WOMessage, WOContext, WORequest, and WOResponse.

2. In the second section, the methods that actually implement the request-response loop are presented: `takeValuesFromRequest`, `invokeActionForRequest`, and `appendToResponse`.

Classes that Implement the Request-Reponse Loop

The WOElements class is the abstract superclass of all the elements described in the previous chapter. It is described in the following sections, along with its related objects—WOContext, WOMessage, WORequest, and WOResponse. These classes perform much of the work of WebObjects, particularly the implementation of the request-response loop. You use them (or their descendants), but you will rarely need to directly instantiate or override them because the lower-level classes in WebObjects do that for you. However, you do need to know how these classes work.

> **NOTE**
>
> See the WebObjects Framework reference (downloadable from the WebObjects site) for full descriptions of all classes and their methods in WebObjects. Not all of the methods of the classes described in this chapter are listed here.

WOElement

The abstract superclass of all user interface elements on a Web page, WOElement encapsulates the data and functionality common to them all. You never directly create a WOElement object; however, you manipulate its methods and the data with which it works through the descendants that you do work with.

In addition to a constructor, WOElement has three methods:

▶ **`takeValuesFromRequest`** This method extracts data from the incoming HTTP request.

▶ `invokeActionForRequest`   After extracting data from the request, an action may be invoked by the WOElement.

▶ `appendToResponse`   This method adds some HTML to the response being prepared to be returned to the user in response to the request.

The default methods do nothing (`takeValuesFromRequest` and `appendToResponse`) or return null (`invokeActionForRequest`).

Each of these methods takes two parameters:

▶ `WOMessage`   The first parameter is a descendant of WOMessage: either aWORequest (`takeValuesFromRequest` and `invokeActionForRequest`) or aWOResponse (`appendToResponse`).

▶ `WOContext`   The second parameter collects all of the contextual information that applies to the WOElement object—references to the session, the WebObjects application object, the HTTP request, and so forth.

Each of these classes is described in the sections that follow.

WOMessage

Like WOElement, WOMessage is an abstract superclass. Its two descendants handle requests and responses in the request-response loop. Its methods are available to both of those descendants, and they fall into two broad categories: the HTTP message (either the request or the response message) and user info—an important WebObjects means of passing data around within the processing of the request-response loop. (A constructor method also exists.)

Before looking at the HTTP message and user info categories, the framework concepts of dictionaries and data objects are explored because they are used in both of those categories.

Dictionaries

The programming framework on which WebObjects is built (which is also the basis for Cocoa on Mac OS X) includes a dictionary class—NSDictionary. When instantiated, NSDictionary objects contain pairs of items, with each pair representing a dictionary entry. One item is a key (usually a string), and the other is a value (an object of class NSObject or java.lang.Object). Storage and lookup of dictionary entries is fast and highly optimized. Such pairs are common throughout the world of computer programming. For example, the key "name" may match the value Voltaire; the key "city" may match Lisbon; and so forth. An NSDictionary object can be used to store (and then to retrieve) whatever data needs to be stored.

NOTE

Keys for entries are unique; therefore, a single dictionary can contain only one "name" and only one "city." Multiple dictionaries can be in use, and they can have identical keys with different values.

Natural language dictionaries are very large; however, NSDictionary objects are frequently small, with only a handful of entries. Utility methods let you retrieve an array consisting of all keys—or of all values. By doing so, you can quickly search to see if a specific key or value exists in the dictionary. Thus, an NSDictionary object lets you access its data in any way that you want to.

NOTE

Dictionaries are a way of organizing memory. Instead of relying on positional identification of data ("the first 20 characters are the name, the next 10 are the city..."), data can be identified based on its meaning and without regard to characteristics that might change. This type of design is characteristic of modern programming—XML provides identification of the data contained in documents. Until powerful computers were available, fixed formats had to be used to identify data: there simply was not enough processing power to quickly decode "name" and to look up its corresponding value. Decades of programmers (and users) had to count character positions and rely on documentation to tell them which information was where in files and in memory.

When you use an NSDictionary object in WebObjects methods, you need only know the basics described in this section. Often, WebObjects methods themselves wrap around basic NSDictionary methods to allow you to look up and—where appropriate—add entries to a dictionary. The underlying methods used most often are `objectForKey` and `setObjectforKey`.

The first method returns an object (or `null`) for a key value; the second adds an entry consisting of the key and value that are passed to the method. (Only NSMutableDictionary objects can have new entries added to them in this way.) Additionally, if a key already exists, `setObjectForKey` will replace the object with a new value. No duplicate entries exist in a dictionary.

HTTP Message Manipulation

Incoming requests and outgoing responses are just HTTP messages for most WebObjects applications (except for Java clients). WOMessage provides methods to manipulate the data in the HTTP message; those methods are available in both WORequest and WOResponse, although some of them make more sense in one object than in the other.

Header Manipulation   HTTP headers provide the control information about the content of the message that follows. Headers contain both required and optional information. Although in most cases it is sufficient to think of a single HTTP request followed by a single HTTP response, in fact, the initial request can be a whole sequence of negotiations between the HTTP client and the HTTP server. Such negotiations can involve back-and-forth messages to determine if a user's cached page is still valid, for example.

The WebObjects WOMessage header methods let you inspect and set whatever headers you want. Within WebObjects, message headers are stored in a dictionary, and the basic dictionary manipulation routines—retrieving by key, retrieving all keys, retrieving all entries, and so forth—are all available. In addition, dedicated methods let you inspect and set the HTTP version of the message (`httpVersion` and `setHTTPVersion`).

NOTE

Cookies—which often contain information that behaves like message content—are implemented in HTTP as part of the message headers. Because they can be used to store and retrieve content, they are discussed in the next section.

Content Manipulation   Following the HTTP headers, many HTTP messages contain a body consisting of a document's content; that document can be XML or HTML (the original form of message content). Other content-manipulation routines let you handle cookies and let you control the text encoding of the message data.

Most content is either XML or HTML. Basic routines allow you to perform three operations in either format:

▶ You can *set* the message's content. You prepare the content for the message, and in setting it, you replace any content that may already have been there.

▶ You can *append* some data to the existing content (if any) in the message.

▶ You can *get* the message's existing content.

When you are working with XML, everything is a document (or document fragment). Thus, the `set` and `get` methods work with XML document objects. In HTML, you set and get a sequence of bytes.

With XML, you can append only an XML document fragment (because everything is a document or document fragment). With HTML, you append a character string.

NOTE

As is the case with many of the methods in this section, these methods are called by descendants of WOMessage; you do not normally invoke them yourself.

Cookies are used to store data on the user's computer. WebObjects provides a class—WOCookie—that helps you use them. WOMessage has methods (addCookie, removeCookie, and cookies) that let you manipulate WOCookie objects. Before launching into cookie-land, remember that WebObjects Session objects can manage state for you, and frequently cookie information (particularly session-based cookie information) should be managed within the Session object.

Finally, methods let you retrieve and set the text encoding for a WOMessage object. The default encoding in WebObjects is ISO Latin1, which is appropriate for English, Spanish, Portuguese, and many other European languages. Some computer systems display other text formats—Unicode, Japanese, ASCII, and the like. Some character sets (Unicode, for example) have more characters than ISO Latin 1; others (ASCII, for example) have fewer.

TIP

If you are using English, leave the message encoding alone.

User Info

Each WOMessage object can have an NSDictionary object associated with it. You can place any entries you want in this dictionary, and it can be used by the WOMessage object (or its descendants).

WOContext

Each method of WOElement takes a WOContext object as a parameter, in addition to a WOMessage object. A WOContext object contains references to the WOApplication, the session (WOSession), the current page (WOComponent), and the current WOElement (using an element ID). It also refers to both the request and the response objects.

NOTE

Some of these objects may not exist—ever, or at a specific time. A WOResponse object does not exist until after the WORequest object has been processed; a direct action may never have a WOSession object. In every case, though, if an object exists, it is unique. A WOSession object may have a number of requests and responses, but each one belongs to only one WOSession object.

WORequest

WORequest, a descendant of WOMessage, is a WebObjects class that encapsulates HTTP requests. Usually these come from user actions—either from typing in a URL for a direct action or by clicking on an interface element on a page. WORequest objects can also be created automatically by adaptors such as those supplied with WebObjects that allow databases to interact with the WebObjects application itself.

Most of the WORequest methods are accessors that let you retrieve data from forms and their elements, from cookies, and from the HTTP header values.

WOResponse

Like WORequest objects, WOResponse objects are HTTP messages—and they are descendants of WOMessage. Its methods let you access both the HTTP headers and the HTML content of the response to the user.

The Request-Response Cycle in Action

These objects—WOElement (generally an interface element), response and requests flavors of WOMessage, and WOContext—work together with WebObjects to implement the request-response cycle.

You do not often need to create these objects or to override their methods. WebObjects does this for you in most cases. Here's how it works.

Users normally initiate a request-response cycle by submitting input to WebObjects. The input is transmitted to an HTTP server (such as Apache), and from there, it is sent to a WebObjects adaptor. That adaptor receives the HTTP request from the HTTP server; it creates a WORequest object from the HTTP request and sends it to your WebObjects application.

If your application does not yet exist, WebObjects creates it by using the `constructor` method. If it does exist, WebObjects calls the `awake` method. (The details of these methods do not matter; suffice it to say that they prepare your application to continue or start its work.)

If a session is needed to process the user's request, this task is handled in the same way: if the request exists, its `awake` method is called, and if it does not, its `init` method is called. The same steps are repeated with the request page object. As this process continues, the WOContext object is updated with references to the application, session, request page, and other necessary data.

NOTE

The URL of the request contains identifiers for the application, page, session, and element.

takeValuesFromRequest

When all necessary objects have been created or awakened, WebObjects next calls each object's takeValuesFromRequest method. This method is implemented in WOApplication, WOSession, WOComponent, and WOElement. For interface elements, the bindings that you created with WebObjects Builder let WebObjects move data from the WORequest object and place it in appropriate variables in your application. Thus, WebObjects Builder and its bindings provide enough information to WebObjects so that you do not have to write any unloading code: takeValuesFromRequest does it all.

If you want to manipulate data entered by users in standard interface elements, you can create overrides of those standard interface elements and implement takeValuesFromRequest for them. Such an override can reformat the data; it can also handle the case in which a single input needs to be placed into two or more application variables. (You can bind only one to an interface element using WebObjects Builder.)

CAUTION

Remember that you are preprocessing input at this point. Do not get carried away and start computing results or otherwise carrying out a user request. Furthermore, note that the **takeValuesFromRequest** *processing occurs only if data from an HTML form has been transmitted in the request. If no data is sent (merely a request for a new page), this processing is skipped, which makes perfect sense. However, if you have decided to hide some special processing in a* **takeValuesFromRequest** *method, assuming that it will be called in response to a user request, you will be disappointed.*

If you override takeValuesFromRequest, here is what it should look like:

```
public void takeValuesFromRequest  (WORequest request, WOContext context)  {
   super.takeValuesFromRequest (request, context);
   //your additional code here
}
```

You must call takeValuesFromRequest in the superclass before you call your own code: calling the superclass's method allows the propagation of takeValuesFromRequest through all of the appropriate objects that are interested.

TIP

If you add a single line of code and break your WebObjects application, look for a missing call to a superclass (such as the line starting with **super** *in the sample here).*

invokeActionForRequest

The `invokeActionForRequest` methods of WOApplication, WOSession, your various WOComponent objects, and their assorted WOElement items are called in the same way as `takeValuesFromRequest` until one of them handles the request. Note that while `takeValuesFromRequest` is propagated to all interested objects, `invokeActionForRequest` is propagated only until one of them handles the request.

NOTE

The **`invokeActionForRequest`** *methods are bypassed when a user directly requests a WebObjects page by typing in (or using a bookmarked) URL that includes the WebObjects application name and the name of the component that generates the requested page. WebObjects URLs are discussed further in the next chapter.*

Whereas it is common to override `takeValuesFromRequest` to preprocess input, overriding `invokeActionforRequest` is less common. The only general reason to do so is if you want to dynamically change the action that is carried out in response to a user request. For example, this can occur if a user has requested an action that is inappropriate and cannot be carried out: you can either produce an error message or you can substitute the correct action.

One example of this type of substitution is when a user attempts to complete an online purchase before having submitted delivery or credit-card information: in this case, the credit card or delivery page must be presented rather than the final checkout page (which the user may have requested). Another example of page substitution is when a blank search request is submitted. Note that in both of these cases—and many others in which you might be inclined to override `invokeActionForRequest`— you can prevent the need to switch response pages by improving the interface.

Good interface design prevents errors from occurring and prevents illogical and out-of-sequence actions. In the online purchase situation, clearly numbering the steps of the process helps users to understand that a sequence is involved, and you can disable buttons in the numbered sequence until the proper moment. In the case of the blank search request, you can catch the blank input before the page is submitted by using JavaScript or other WebObjects features.

appendToResponse

As a result of either `invokeActionFromRequest` or of a direct request to a component, a WebObjects component begins to generate a response. Like `takeValuesFromRequest`, the `appendToResponse` method is implemented in WOApplication, WOSession, WOComponent, and WOElement. It is propagated among all of the relevant objects by calls to each object's superclass object.

As with `takeValuesFromRequest`, you may override `appendToResponse` for post-processing of results. These overrides may include reformatting output (as is the case with `takeValuesFromRequest`), and they may include a variety of additional post-processing tasks.

The `appendToResponse` method will always be called (unless, for some reason, there is no response to a request); however, consider whether post-processing is truly post-processing or should be made part of an action itself.

Separating your functionality into pre- and post-processing simplifies ongoing support and maintenance. If you discover that you need an initialized variable as you are writing an `appendToResponse` method, go back to a constructor or to `takeValuesFromRequest` and perform that initialization there. It may seem like extra effort, but it will pay off in the long run. A typical override of `appendToResponse` looks like this:

```
public void appendToResponse
  (WOResponse response, WOContext context)
  {
    super.appendToResponse (response, context);
    //your additional code here
  }
```

Make certain that the `super.appendToResponse` call is not omitted (and that it occurs before your own code). This call is the mechanism by which all interested objects construct the response in the proper sequence.

Using Direct and Component Actions

I n Chapter 16, you saw how dynamic elements implement HTML functionality and the additions to it that are part of WebObjects. In Chapter 17, you saw how the request-response loop is implemented so that interactions between users and WebObjects proceed properly. Now it is time to look at what dynamic elements and the request-response loop accomplish, how the request-response loop is initiated, and how actions are carried out. This is the level with which users interact.

Here are the major sections of this chapter:

▶ **WebObjects URLs**   This is a basic WebObjects URL: typing it in or clicking it launches a WebObjects application within WebObjects itself.

▶ **WOApplication**   The overall WebObjects application object keeps track of everything going on in the application's environment—sessions, state, and the like. You must override WOApplication for each WebObjects application that you write. Note that WOApplication is the first class described in this book that you *must* override. Typically, the override of WOApplication is called Application.

▶ **WOAdaptor**   WebObjects adaptors interact with the non-WebObjects world of HTTP servers and databases. These objects can be customized as needed so that the WebObjects code remains platform- and environment-neutral.

▶ **WORequestHandler**   Request handlers actually run the request-response loop that was described in Chapter 17.

▶ **WOComponent and component actions**   Components are basically Web pages; they can be associated with actions that are fired by WebObjects as necessary. You override WOComponent for your Web pages; however, if you use WebObjects Builder, the code will be generated for you to handle the most basic operations, and you may never have to know that you are overriding WOComponent.

▶ **WODirectAction and direct actions**   Direct actions are actions that can be addressed without a Web page.

TIP

Most programming for basic WebObjects applications involves creating new components and direct actions. In addition, you need to override WOApplication for your own WebObjects application; however, the extent to which you need to customize your override varies from none at all to a lot.

WebObjects URLs

Uniform Resource Locators (a subset of Uniform Resource Identifiers) are specified in Internet standards and protocols. They consist of a scheme (http) for the Web, followed by the identification of a resource on the Web. (A URI identifies a resource without necessarily providing its access method—the scheme. Thus, www.philmontmill.com is a URI.

The resource identification can consist of a domain name preceded by the name of a computer resource; it can also consist of only a domain name. The domain name can be an IP address (a quartet of digits such as 192.168.1.25), or it can consist of a name that can be resolved into such an IP address by using a domain name server. Following the resource identification, a port may be specified; in the case of http, if it is not specified, 80 is assumed.

The resource identification and optional port can be followed by a slash; in turn, the slash can be followed by directory names—separated by slashes—culminating in a filename. That file is normally the identifier of a page to be returned to the user. This URL identifies part of the WebObjects documentation on Apple's site:

```
http://developer.apple.com/techpubs/webobjects/pdf/pdf.html
```

This identification—what follows the http:// and ends with the next slash (or the end of the URL)—identifies the http server to which the request is sent. In the case of the Apple WebObjects documentation, the http server is running on port 80 of the computer named developer located in the apple.com domain. (The domain name server for apple.com is responsible for routing messages to the developer computer appropriately.) Here, a file pdf.html is located within the pdf directory, which, in turn, is located within the webobjects and techpubs directories on developer.

NOTE

In the section that follows, the word "application" is used in several different ways; unfortunately, this reflects the varying terminology of the different technologies involved. From the point of view of your http/Web server, one or two applications (the http server and the WebObjects adaptor) are running. From your point of view, your WebObjects application runs in conjunction with the WebObjects adaptor (the application visible on the server.)

Using WebObjects in a cgi-bin or Server Directory

If the http server is to send the request to a dynamic application server (such as WebObjects) running as a separate process, the name of the server's cgi-bin directory follows the resource identifier. That directory is often named cgi-bin. Then, the name of the script or application appears in the URL. Each time the http server receives a request, it creates a process by running the script or application indicated in the URL. When the request has been fulfilled, the process is killed.

For WebObjects, the name of the program running in the cgi-bin directory is WebObjects. This is, in fact, the WebObjects adaptor—the program that mediates between WebObjects applications and the http server. (See the "WOAdaptor" section later in this chapter.) The WebObjects adaptor is specific to the http adaptor; it can serve a number of WebObjects applications. Following a slash, you enter the name of the WebObjects application you want to use.

The host name need not be a registered domain name; it can be the name or IP address of a host on your local area network. For example, you can launch WOInfoCenter by using the following URL (provided that you have installed WebObjects on a local computer with the address 192.168.1.9):

```
http://192.168.1.9/cgi-bin/WebObjects/WOInfoCenter
```

Inside the cgi-bin directory, the WebObjects program—the WebObjects adaptor—will run the WOInfoCenter WebObjects application.

The WebObjects application is located in the DocumentRoot directory of your http server. It may be located within another folder, as in this case:

```
http://192.168.1.9/cgi-bin/WebObjects/Tests/Movies
```

You can pass parameters to the resource that the URL specified by adding a query or searchpart (the names are equivalent). The searchpart is preceded by a question mark, and it consists of one or more pairs of data elements—names, followed by values. For example, here is a WebObjects URL for OpenBase Limited; a single parameter (page) is passed in with the value home.

```
http://store.openbase.com/cgi-bin/WebObjects/OpenBaseStore?page=home
```

You can rename the directory in which the executable code runs. Apple does this with the Apple Store. Here is the URL for the Apple Store:

```
http://store.apple.com/1-800-MY-APPLE/WebObjects/AppleStore
```

You parse this URL just as you would any other one in this section. The scheme is http; the domain name is apple.com. The specific computer resource is store. The cgi-bin directory has been renamed cleverly: its name is 1-800-MY-APPLE (the telephone number for the store). The WebObjects adaptor (still named WebObjects) runs the application called AppleStore.

TIP

This method of renaming the cgi-bin directory and/or the WebObjects adaptor can be very useful in converting the lengthy string of a URL into an advertising message. It can also be helpful in not publicizing your directory structure or the way your site is structured and supported. Apple wants to publicize its use of WebObjects (and rightly so). Your objectives may be different.

WebObjects URLs can contain even more components than those listed here. As people navigate through your site, their session information and other data can be passed in the URLs that WebObjects generates automatically. (For more information, see the sections "WOComponent and Component Actions" and "WODirectAction and Direct Actions" later in this chapter.)

Using WebObjects in API Mode

Instead of running a process in the cgi-bin directory, you can link the process code to the http server. In general, the application you want to run is compiled into a dynamic-link library (DLL) or object code that is specific to the API of the http server.

Why This Matters

Once an interactive user is working with WebObjects, URLs are of little import. They are significant in two cases, however:

▶   URLs can provide an entry point to your application. The user types in a URL that you provide—or that URL is a link attached to a button or other interface element in a non-WebObjects environment.

▶   Users can bookmark URLs to easily return to them later.

You can control the first case to some extent; the second (bookmarking) is not under your control to the same degree. Users can bookmark a page whether you want them to or not. Providing appropriate entry points to your application can ensure that users get where they want to go with as little difficulty as possible. You will see how direct actions can help you achieve this when they are discussed at the end of this chapter in the section called "WODirectAction and Direct Actions."

WOApplication

Your WebObjects application starts with a descendant of WOApplication. You override WOApplication and put any customized code that you need into your overridden class.

If you are using Project Builder and WebObjects Builder, the code for this override will be created for you:

```
import com.webobjects.appserver.*;
import com.webobjects.eocontrol.*;
import com.webobjects.eoaccess.*;
import com.webobjects.foundation.*;
import java.io.*;
import java.util.*;

public class Application extends WOApplication (){
  public Application () {
    super();
    system.out.println ("Welcome to " + this.name() " "!");
    /* ** put your initialization code here ** * /
  }
}
```

This is the constructor for your Application class; it must call its superclass's constructor. (That is how all of the basic WOApplication construction takes place.) The comment shows you where to put your specific initialization code— but hold off before coding away. WOApplication objects themselves have a lot of environmental data stored in them, and you may not need to do much of the initialization that you will need to access. Furthermore, your Application object as a descendant of WOApplication has references to its various sessions and other environmental references. In many cases, your initialization code will be able to be placed in another, more specific object.

Your override of WOApplication is normally called Application. You can name it something else if you want; to do so, you must place code in your application's main function to instantiate your override of WOApplication with its other class name.

The simplest strategy is to use the standard class name Application for your override of WOApplication.

NOTE

The name of your WebObjects application itself should reflect what the application does—CompPlan, for example, implements a Comprehensive Plan application. Within your named WebObjects application, using standard file structures and names makes it easier to maintain the application in the future. Remember that your subclass of WOApplication (Application) is the central object in your WebObjects application. (The use of the word "application" in several different senses has already been discussed.)

Using Multiple WOApplication Instances

WebObjects applications tend to run as multiple instances on a server. If you are accustomed to using a personal computer with personal productivity tools such as a word processor, you may not be accustomed to the idea that several copies of a program can run at the same time. Modern operating systems such as Mac OS X, Windows NT/2000, and UNIX (with its cousins such as Linux) incorporate advanced process management controls to allow multiple tasks to run at almost the same time. The computer's resources are shared sequentially among the various tasks as the tasks need the resource; each task is given a small slice of time to use, and then the operating system allocates the computer's resources to the next process that is ready to operate.

With WebObjects, the instances of your WOApplication can run on one computer or on several computers that are coordinated by WebObjects. Obviously, instances of WOApplication that are located on separate computers can process data simultaneously: they have no resources in common to contend over (except possibly a database). Even on a single computer, different WOApplication processes can ensure that throughput is faster than with a single process.

The Role of WOApplication

Your descendant of WOApplication (typically called your Application object) is responsible for communicating with one or more adaptors. It receives an http request and then coordinates whatever is necessary to return the response to the adaptor. A primary part of this work is creating and managing sessions for individual users. Sessions implement the statefulness that is absent from http and that is required for sequences of transactions that add up to e-commerce and other Web-based activities. Session management includes not only the creation of sessions, but also their destruction—either in response to an explicit command or as a result of a time out.

In addition to managing sessions and state, your Application object is a good place to store information that may be needed by component objects or other parts of your WebObjects application. Through the WOContext object, any request or response—or object handling a request or response—can gain access to the Application object and thus, to its methods to retrieve data.

An Application object is not a substitute for a database and is a poor place to store transient and changing data; however, it is an excellent place to store commonly used strings that will be needed on many pages and that change relatively infrequently.

NOTE

The date or time is not such a string; copyright information may be an appropriate string to store in the Application object. In the case of copyright information, you can load it into a variable in the Application object and then place it in the appropriate places on various pages by using an accessor method in Application. That way, if it changes, you can propagate the change throughout your WebObjects application.

Like other objects discussed in the previous chapter, WOApplication implements `takeValuesFromRequest`, `invokeActionForRequest`, and `appendToResponse` to carry out its role in the request-response loop.

WOAdaptor

A WebObjects adaptor handles communication between an http server and WebObjects. It may be a freestanding process, or it may be compiled or linked into the http server (using the API interfaces described previously in the section "Using WebObjects in API Mode"). The adaptor is critical because it means that the WebObjects environment can function independently of a particular server (and vice versa).

Adaptors are specific to http servers; for instance, the Apache adaptor is not the same as the Netscape (NSAPI) adaptor or Microsoft Internet Information Server (ISAPI) adaptor.

NOTE

For further information on adaptors, see the WebObjects documentation on installation and deployment. See in particular Deploying WebObjects Applications. (Visit http://developer.apple.com/techpubs.)

The WOAdaptor abstract class provides the framework for interacting with the actual adaptor. The adaptor itself may be written using object-oriented techniques or one of the WebObjects frameworks: this object provides an interface to that adaptor.

In general, only the WOApplication class communicates with WOAdaptor. Your override of WOApplication normally communicates with WOAdaptor only through the superclass's calls to WOAdaptor. In other words, WOAdaptor is important to know about, but do not touch it unless you are writing your own adaptor.

WORequestHandler

Another abstract class, WORequestHandler, has three concrete subclasses, which handle requests for components, direct actions, and resources. WOApplication returns the appropriate request handler by calling its own `requestHandler ForKey` method indicating whether a component, direct action, or resource request handler is desired.

The key used in `requestHandlerForKey` is wo for components and wa for direct actions. You can see these keys in URLs for component actions; they follow the application name, as in the following URL:

```
http://store.apple.com/1-800-MY-APPLE/WebObjects/
  AppleStore.woa/82/wo/ZAnAM0E1AifBL6pe2X/
  0.3.0.3.28.23.0.3.1.3.1.1.0?69,107
```

This lengthy URL is an actual URL generated during a visit to the Apple Store. The request handler key (wo) is underlined. Other parts of the URL are identified in Table 18-1.

URL Syntax	Meaning
store.apple.com	Computer name and domain name
1-800-MY-APPLE	Cgi-bin directory
WebObjects	Adaptor
AppleStore.woa	WebObjects application name
82	Application instance number (used when multiple copies of the application are running)
wo	Request handler key
ZAnAM0E1AifBL6pe2X	Session identifier
0.3.0.3.28.23.0.3.1.3.1.1.0	Component identifier
69,107	Data

Table 18-1 *URL Syntax Demystified*

You do not need to worry about creating these monstrous URLs because WebObjects does it for you. However, during deployment and debugging, you may need to look at them. In particular, the session identifier may be helpful in determining if a trafficking problem has occurred.

The default request handler is normally a component request handler; you may want to make the direct action request handler the default. You must do so if your first action is a direct action rather than a component action. (That is because the initial URL—of the form http://store.openbase.com/cgi-bin/WebObjects/ OpenBaseStore?page=home—does not contain a key for a request handler and the default will be used.)

You change the default request handler to a direct action request handler by overriding the WOApplication `defaultRequestHandlerClassName` method in your Application object. The override should return `WODirectActionRequestHandler` rather than the standard `WOComponentRequestHandler`. Here is the code:

```
public string defaultRequestHandlerClassName () {
    return "WODirectActionRequestHandler";
}
```

NOTE

*If you want to use your own request handler as the default (rather than one of the standard request handlers), you can override **SetDefaultRequestHandler** and pass in your WORequestHandler object.*

Having determined which request handler to use, the WOApplication object (or Application object that overrides it) calls that request handler's `handleRequest` method.

WOComponent and Component Actions

A component action is handled by a WOComponent object or a descendant thereof that you create. As always, it is initiated by a request from a user in the form of a URL, such as the lengthy one described in the previous section.

NOTE

Remember that WebObjects creates the URL: it is not typed in. In fact, it cannot be typed in because WebObjects creates the session ID and component identifier on the fly so that they are unique.

The WORequest object has been passed into the request handler by WOApplication in conjunction with the adaptor that passed the http server's request into the world of WebObjects; the other two objects that will be needed to implement the request-response loop (WOResponse and WOContext) are created by the `handleRequest` method; it returns the WOResponse object as its result.

The request handler for a component action initiates a sequence of events that results in the appropriate component carrying out the requested action. First, the session (which is in the URL) is accessed (or created, if necessary). That session is then asked to locate the component with the appropriate name. Within a given session, only one instance of each component exists with a unique identifier; multiple instances of a given component (page) may exist, but their identifiers will be different. Having the session object control the component allows the same page template to contain different data within the session.

Once the appropriate component has been located or created, the request-response loop is activated. The `takeValuesFromRequest` methods of the application and session objects are called; the method of the component is then called and it calls that method for all of its template's objects. In this way, every object involved with the request has a chance to remove the data which is relevant to it.

Similarly, the `invokeActionForRequest` methods of the application and session objects, component, and its template's elements are called. And finally, the `appendToResponse` methods of those objects are called.

Two other methods exist in all of these objects and are called in the same way. At the beginning of the cycle, the `awake` methods of the application, session, component, and component's template elements are called; on completion of the cycle, the `sleep` methods of those objects are called. You can override any of these methods in any of these objects to do pre- or post-processing before the request or after the response has been dealt with. (If you need to do pre- or post-processing involving the request or the response, you override `takeValuesFromRequest` or `appendToResponse`.)

TIP

As always in object-oriented programming, make your overrides as surgically precise as possible: override the smallest and most proximate object that you can. The major WebObjects classes are described in this chapter so that you understand where to put your code; do not expect to override those major classes (except WOApplication).

WODirectAction and Direct Actions

A component action is initiated through the process described in the previous section; note that the session involved—which changes from one person's visit to another—finds or creates the component. To initiate an action directly from a URL that a user can type in (or that can be bookmarked), you need a method of dispatching that does not involve a session. That is where direct actions come in.

For example, you can get to Apple's knowledge base using the following URL:

```
http://kbase.info.apple.com/cgi-bin/WebObjects/kbase.woa/26/wa/expert
```

A descendant of WODirectAction (an abstract class) named expert is invoked with this URL. The request handler for direct actions (identified by the key wa underlined in this URL) creates the instance of expert, which is the name of the DirectAction class that subclasses WODirectAction. The request handler does not create an instance of expert. This is significantly different from component actions, where the session creates the instance of the object (a descendant of WOComponent) that will do the work.

```
The direct action object then goes about its work.
```

This URL invokes an action or method called `logoutClicked` in the direct action object named ISWODirectAction. (In standard usage, the action is named `logoutClickedAction`—"Action" is appended to the name of the action.) A WODirectAction method called `performActionNamed` handles the dispatching. That method appends "Action" to the string that is passed in, and that, in turn, calls the method that is so named (or does whatever is necessary). This method (or the default method if no name such as `logoutClicked` was given) is responsible for unloading data from WORequest and for returning WOResponse or WOComponent. WOResponse is returned to the adaptor—either directly or by calling the `generateResponse` method of WOComponent if that is what was returned.

State and Session Management

IN THIS CHAPTER:

Identity, State, Persistence, and Transactions:
An Introduction

Where State Happens

Designing for State

Using Sessions Effectively

This chapter addresses the issues involved in *state management*—the range of concerns that come into play when you need to store data from one Web page to another as a user traverses your Web site. These issues are inherent in interactive systems, and they predate the Web (and even the Internet). In this chapter, you will study the issues and principles involved in managing state and learn how to apply them in a WebObjects application.

You can implement state in a variety of ways and in many places, ranging from cookies stored on a user's computer to a database that interacts with your WebObjects application. This chapter describes each type of state storage, when you would use it, and how it works.

The design of your site and your application influences how its state requirements will be organized and how they can be met. You will find information on how to design your site and application effectively; you also will find tips for using session objects to manage state.

Identity, State, Persistence, and Transactions: An Introduction

The basic communications protocol of the Web (HTTP) is stateless. To a large extent, each Web page that you request is independent of the others. There is a reason for this independence: it makes the HTTP specification much less complicated than if state were accounted for.

Unfortunately, this architecture means that every application that wants to implement *state*—that is, some form of persistent data such as a shopping cart, the contents of which are retained as the user goes from page to page—must do so in its own way. WebObjects provides a variety of tools for implementing such functionality. In this chapter, you will not only see how WebObjects handles the issues, but how you can use other tools and techniques to manage (or avoid managing) state.

Handling state immediately uncorks a genie's bottle of issues that are technical, legal, and even moral. Fortunately, these issues have been explored in depth over the decades in which interactive computer systems have been used. This section provides you with a background of those issues. But before exploring the issues, some examples of state are provided to help you understand why they are important.

CAUTION

If you feel that this background material doesn't apply to you and you just want to get on with your WebObjects application, hold your horses. You will not only save time by not having to reinvent the work that has gone before, but as a responsible designer, you also have an obligation (perhaps even a legal one—check your contract!) to be aware of the best practices in this area and to implement them accordingly. There are unpleasant consequences to mishandling data that you use in managing state. The material covered in this chapter is very serious business indeed!

Examples of State

A common example of state is a shopping cart on an e-commerce site: you click from page to page, sometimes adding items to the shopping cart. When you are done, you click Check Out, supply billing and shipping information, and your shopping cart is converted into an actual order. Its persistence while you are clicking from page to page is a commonly cited example of state.

Another equally common example has nothing to do with e-commerce: when you use a searching tool on the Internet, you may be given an option to refine your search when results are returned. Particularly if no results—or millions of results—are returned, broadening or tightening your search net can be helpful. Sometimes, you modify your search by simply typing it in again; in other cases, you can simply add the modification to the previous search. In other words, you type in "and not by Rodgers" and click Search Again to narrow the results of a search of Broadway musical scores. For this to work (that is, for you not to have to type in the entire query again), the initial query must be stored. That query is a state.

Counter-examples of state also abound on the Web. Think about those relentlessly annoying situations in which you must continually provide information that the computer (or the Web site) could store for you. One major financial services company (which shall remain nameless for obvious reasons) has a Web site that brings together its various operations such as banking, investments, insurance, mortgages, and the like. Consistent graphics provide a unified look and feel. Unfortunately, each area of the site requires its own password. Furthermore, the rules for the passwords vary from area to area: in one, the password must be 8–14 characters long and include at least one number and one letter; in another, the password must be no more than eight characters long. It is easy to construct a password in one area that is invalid in another. As a result, clients must keep track of a multitude of passwords on this one Web site.

In a similar vein, a major library online circulation system requires patrons to enter their library card number no fewer than three times to reserve a book. The examples are endless.

You can avoid handling state. In the shopping cart case, for example, you can require that users make all of their choices at once from a long list of items. They may need to use a pencil and paper to jot down inventory numbers as they go, but the responsibility for maintaining state is pushed onto them. But handling state in your application makes it easier for people to use that application; that can translate directly into increased sales and other easily measured benefits. Handling state (that is, recognizing a user and remembering that user's history) is in fact one of the hallmarks of good customer service. When the waiter in a restaurant remembers that you prefer milk (not cream) with your tea (not coffee) in the morning, you are inclined to return; likewise, the bookseller who remembers that you like English murder mysteries or the assistant who remembers that you do not want to take calls before noon will earn high marks from you at least in the "life's petty problems" category.

Although this chapter deals with state from a technical point of view, never forget that from a user's point of view, state is convenience and efficiency. It can also be friendliness, even when generated by a computer. After all, when you return to a Web site and are greeted with a personalized message such as "Welcome back, Jenn," you are likely to react positively. Your name in this case is an example of stateful data: somehow or other, the Web page had to find a way to insert it onto the page.

You need to confront four specific issues in this general area of managing state:

▶ **Identity**   The process of preserving data and restoring it appropriately. If your name is not Jenn, "Welcome back, Jenn" is not going to seem so pleasant. This issue involves identifying the data that you store and the user who is at the other end of the HTTP request.

▶ **State**   The collection of data that is stored—the contents of a shopping cart, your credit card, or your name.

▶ **Persistence**   The mechanism used for storing and retrieving the state.

▶ **Transactions**   A series of separate events that must be taken as a whole. The simplest transaction involves two events: delivery of goods and payment for them. Both must be completed for a transaction (in this case, a sale) to be completed. Transactions are a special case of state.

Identity

Identity is one of the biggest problems you must address when managing state. The technical issues are trivial, but the practical and interface issues are monumental. It is easy to collect data (such as the contents of a shopping cart) and store it off somewhere. The problem comes when you need to retrieve it. How do you know which shopping cart's data to retrieve?

Somehow, you must identify the user before you store the data; then you must reidentify the user when you need to retrieve the data. The simplest case is when someone sits down at a computer, accesses your site, and clicks from page to page. The headers of an HTTP request contain a variety of information that can be used to identify the user, including the IP address from which the request comes. You can use that information to identify the user without asking for any additional data.

You can also explicitly identify the user by asking for a name or a password. In either case, you have something to identify the data that you will store and then retrieve.

Or will you? Errors can occur in both directions: you can identify someone incorrectly and you can fail to identify someone. In the case of using implicit information such as the data in the HTTP header, you will not be able to tell if one person uses two computers or two browsers. The situation may be as simple as one computer crashing and the user logging on with another IP address (assigned automatically when reconnecting to the Internet in some cases). The identification in the new HTTP headers will not match that in the old headers. The reverse can happen when one person gets up from a computer and another person sits down—and inherits a partially filled shopping cart.

If you ask for explicit identification, you run the risk of creating separate individuals based on minimal typing variations in names; asking for an e-mail address may seem like a way to uniquely identify an individual, but many people have multiple e-mail addresses (home, work, private matters, and so on).

In other words, identifying who is using a computer at any moment is a complicated task. It is not a technical challenge, but your job in developing a WebObjects application may well include addressing this nontechnical issue.

Privacy

When you can identify the state data to an individual, you encounter another issue: *privacy*. There is increasing awareness of the need to respect individuals' privacy on the Internet. Laws in many countries limit the reuse of information that you collect. The collection of data—even if your Web-site visitors request it—may be governed by law. All Web sites should have a privacy statement that is prominently posted.

Errors in releasing identifiable data can have serious consequences. Before greeting a returning shopper with a partially filled shopping cart, you need to make certain that you have the right match between shopper and cart. In short, you must do the impossible: unambiguously identify your user. Because this is impossible to do in all cases, your system design should take into account how you wish to err—on the side of accidentally giving the wrong person some information about someone else, or on the side of forcing someone to reenter data.

 ### TIP

In practice, this turns out to be a relatively easy choice. If you are implementing an online loan application system, for instance, you should not be releasing previously entered information to someone unless you are certain that you have the right person. However, if the information is not personal or sensitive, and if it is not identifiable, the risks are much lower. Thus, in a community bulletin board system, showing the previous page incorrectly (showing someone else's previous page) is unlikely to have serious repercussions because all data is public and you would be unable to tell whose previous page you saw.

Collateral Information

It is common to collect collateral information to verify identity. A mother's maiden name, the last digits of a social security number, and any number of other common items of information are collected in this way.

Unfortunately, once you have this information, it can be more dangerous than you suspect. For example, if you allow people to pick a password to allow them to log on to your application, many people will pick a password that they use in other situations. They may pick a password that is the same as their bank account password. This is such a common and reasonable thing to do that your database—which contains the most innocuous of data—suddenly becomes a prime target for hackers and thieves who can collect unencrypted passwords, social security numbers, mothers' maiden names, and the like.

Automated Data Collection

In addition to the information that your users will expect you to store, there is more information that you may choose to store. Users may not be aware of this; they may even specifically not expect you to collect information such as the following:

▶ The URL of the page from which the e-commerce site was entered

▶ Any record of browsing or shopping that has not resulted in a purchase

Privacy laws (and your site's stated privacy policy) may govern this type of data collection and storage. In general, the collection and use of data that cannot be identified as belonging to an individual is not a problem. Thus, collecting the click trail of a user who visits your site is fine: no one knows who that person is. The click trail can then be used to help market your goods and services. At the moment that you associate that click trail with an individual (when, for example, a purchase is made), the data becomes identifiable and must be safeguarded.

TIP

A computer's IP address is not a good identifier for data. However, under some circumstances (such as always-on Internet connections like DSL and cable), it is sufficient to identify data—at least in the short term—because IP addresses tend to remain the same over a period of hours or even days. Therefore, even though IP addresses are not reliable in all cases, they are usable in enough cases so that you should treat incoming IP addresses as identification for the sake of privacy concerns.

State

State is the collection of data that you store and retrieve as needed. It is easy to think of state as a shopping cart or as the last query that has been executed against a database or in a search engine. However, while each of these is an example of state, from a user's point of view, state is the entire environment associated with your Web application. Users expect that entire environment, data and all, either to be maintained (by you) or to change in predictable or explainable ways.

Thus, for a user, your e-commerce application may be expected to store the following items:

► Contents of a shopping cart

► Previous purchases

► Credit-card information

► Shipping information

► Previous page viewed (the Back button in a browser)

► Size preferences

► Shopping preferences (list items by price, availability, or other criteria)

These are all types of state data; their storage and retrieval will involve a variety of mechanisms by a variety of players. (The previous page, for example, is maintained by a user's browser.)

Persistence

State is what is stored and retrieved; *persistence* is the mechanism that is used. State is like any other data: it can be stored in memory or on disk or other mass storage devices. There is nothing special about state in this sense.

WebObjects implements session objects largely to manage state. You can store data in a session object with the expectation that it will be available to that session: that is, to an individual visitor to your application who remains reasonably active. (Sessions expire after a period of inactivity.)

WebObjects also provides a number of ways in which you can explicitly store data in databases and other such data stores. The decision of which type of persistence to employ depends on the type of state data you are storing.

For example, if you are implementing an e-commerce Web site, do you want to allow unchecked-out shopping carts to be preserved? If so, for how long? Some e-commerce sites allow shopping carts to remain unchecked out for as long as six weeks. No WebObjects session object will be around for that long; you must store such data in a database. On the other hand, a customer's current bank balance can reasonably be stored in a session object. The balance for most bank accounts is calculated once a day during end-of-day processing; as a result, today's balance that is stored in a session object will be useless or even misleading tomorrow.

Thus, in deciding on your strategy for implementing state, decide not only what you want to store (state), but also how long you want to store it for (persistence).

TIP

Once again, choose the level of risk you want to take. Is it worse not to have data you could have stored or to have data that may be outdated? This is the time version of the dilemma you have with the identification of data.

Transactions

Transactions are a special case of state. They consist of a set of events (often involving an exchange of value) that must be treated as a single unit, such as a purchase that involves the transfer of goods or services as well as the transfer of money. Because a transaction involves a set of events, some relation among those events must be created; often it is done by preserving the state of the transaction as events are added to it.

NOTE

Transactions need not involve state. Each event in the transaction can contain all of the identifying information, and the final transaction processing can tie together all of the events. However, transactions frequently do involve state.

Transactions can involve far more than just a pair of events. When purchasing an item, for instance, not only does money need to be transferred, but the item needs to be shipped—and it needs to be removed from inventory.

TIP

The Transaction Processing Performance Council (TPC) is a nonprofit corporation that defines transaction processing, establishes benchmarks, and distributes performance data to the industry. You can find out more at their Web site: http://www.tpc.org.

Transaction processing can be implemented in databases or in HTTP servers. Because a transaction is an all-or-nothing operation, a variety of databases updates may need to be performed (or undone) to complete the transaction. Transaction processing is most effectively done by that entity that has the most visible control over the items being updated.

Your WebObjects application may hand over the data for a transaction to a database or another application for processing.

NOTE

Transactions can occur within a WebObjects session. A session can be the same as a transaction, but normally it is not: it is a much larger entity and it is much less formal. A session is the sequence of interactions between a given user and your WebObjects application; in almost all cases, this sequence is driven by the user's choices. A transaction is a carefully defined and structured entity; it can be initiated by a user, but it is controlled by the transaction's logic. You do not have to create a WebObjects session for each transaction.

Where State Happens

You have seen that state is not a single item of information or even one type of information. Each collection of state data can be maintained in different ways and in different places. The following sections describe where state happens.

URL and Form-Based State

State data can be passed back and forth in HTTP messages. No part of the processing stores state; the information is part of whatever HTTP message is being sent or received. For example, here is the URL of a WebObjects direct action used on Apple's iCards site:

```
http://icards.mac.com/WebObjects/iCards.woa/55/wa/category
  ?name=birthday&wosid=5D7000qp600c1600c4
```

Here, the WebObjects adaptor (called WebObjects) is asked to query the iCards WebObjects application (the 55th instance of it, in fact) by using the standard wa direct action request handler for the specific direction action named `categoryAction`. (WebObjects appends the string Action to the name of the action to construct a method name.) A searchpart (underlined) appears at the end of the URL. (It is shown on a separate line only for reasons of space: the URL is only one line long.) Searchparts are always introduced by a question mark, and they consist of pairs of items: names and values. Here, the name of a type of card (`birthday`) is passed in, as is the ID of a WebObjects session to be used in processing the request.

You can also transmit the data from an HTML form as part of an HTTP message. You do so by using the POST method. (This was described in Chapter 2.)

NOTE

When using the POST method of form processing, you frequently send and receive hidden fields in forms. With WebObjects, you can forget about using hidden fields. Instead, you can use variables within your WebObjects application's session or components to store that data between accesses to pages.

In either of these cases (searchparts and POST methods), all of the state data is transmitted back and forth in the HTTP messages; no separate data store is necessary. This strategy is impractical for large amounts of data; however, it can be very useful in transferring data between different types of environments—from WebObjects, for instance, to ColdFusion, and vice versa.

DESIGN TIP

Use URL and form-based state data for small amounts of data as well as for data that needs to move between WebObjects and other environments.

Browser State

Browsers can store state. They normally store one or more lists of pages you have visited. (This is how the Back button works.) They also allow you to bookmark pages: that, too, is a form of state storage.

Storing URLs stores state not just in the page addresses, but also in data that may be placed in searchparts, as discussed in the previous section. Such URLs (along with session-based WebObjects URLs and other dynamically created URLs) may become invalid over time as the data in them expires. Worse, they may point to other data—someone else's most intimate data, if you are really unlucky as a developer (and lucky as a voyeur).

In addition to lists of URLs, browsers typically have caches in which they store pages. This speeds up performance because the cached pages can be loaded quickly. Caching in a browser is a joint effort of the client (the browser and the user) and the server (the HTTP server and the site manager). Caching information at the client side is controlled, usually by a choice of three options:

▶ Never cache pages.

▶ Cache pages for a single session (execution) of the browser.

▶ Cache pages forever.

The cache is limited in size (sometimes settable by the user), so the second and third options may not actually be carried through if there is not enough space for the cache.

The HTTP message can contain information that can be used for caching. It contains an `expires` header that specifies when the attached page is no longer valid; it also contains a `last-modified` header that tells when the page was last modified. Starting in HTTP 1.1, the message can also contain a `cache-control` header that contains explicit caching instructions (such as `no-cache`). Because these headers are visible to all participants in routing a message (that is, routers, Internet service providers, firewalls, and the like), any of them can act on the caching instructions. However, these headers are optional: not every message has them.

There is an ongoing tension when it comes to caching: users, browser developers, and network providers want as much caching as possible because it speeds things up; Web-site developers want as little caching as possible so that their latest data is always available.

NOTE

Some network administrators believe that the single biggest speed boost to the Internet would be widespread use of caching. A remarkably small number of HTTP messages use caching headers.

Like it or not, unless clearly identified as noncacheable, your site's pages will be cached in various places all over the Internet. And, if so marked, your site will be less responsive and require more telecommunications resources because every page has to be sent every time to every user.

Caches are specific to individual computers and to browsers. Thus, someone who uses two computers (or two browsers on one computer) will have two (or more) separate caches. You have little control over this. However, two WebObjects methods do provide you with some tools. They are described later in this chapter in the section, "Using Sessions Effectively."

DESIGN TIP

Store state data using browsers only if you have another plan available. You can prevent browsers from storing data, but you cannot force them to do so.

Client State

You can cause data to be stored on a user's computer by using cookies. Like caches, you have limited control over cookies. Users can choose to accept or reject cookies either unconditionally or conditionally. Furthermore, like with caches, cookies are stored separately on each computer and in each browser's environment.

Cookies are frequently used to store passwords and names so that "Welcome back" messages can be displayed appropriately. Cookies work extremely well when one person uses one computer. In the case of public-access computers in a public library, however, cookies are an unwelcome disaster in most cases—too many people use the computers. Even in shared computers in a small office or a household, cookies can interfere with one another.

Despite the uncertainty attached to cookies (they are specific to computers, not to people, and they can be turned off), they can be helpful for saving small pieces of state. They can also be helpful in developing a sophisticated identification mechanism that relies both on a cookie and on other pieces of saved data that you compare within your WebObjects application.

DESIGN TIP

If you control cookies on the user's browsers (as, for example, in a corporate LAN), you can rely on them. Otherwise, remember that they may not always be turned on. Note, too, that storing information on clients makes that information specific to the client—the specific browser and computer. If your users need to access your application both from home and from work, you need to store the data more globally.

WebObjects State

WebObjects can save state, too, in two ways:

▶ Its *variables* contain data (frequently because you have bound them to dynamic elements on Web pages). Those variables and their data can also be manipulated and stored (as in a database).

▶ It maintains a *cache of pages* that it has served up; those pages may contain data in addition to their HTML elements.

In both cases, the session object comes into play: data is normally stored at the session level, separately for each user, and pages are cached for each session. (You can store data at the WebObjects application level so that it is available to all users and all sessions, but that type of data storage is normally reserved for relatively unchanging data.) As you will see later in this chapter, WebObjects automatically creates and maintains sessions for you: all you have to do is declare variables and bind your interface elements to them.

DESIGN TIP

Relying on WebObjects to store state data is the easiest choice when that data needs to be preserved during a single user's interaction with your application. For more persistent data, read on.

Database State

A database (or even a flat file) can also store state. In a very real sense, a customer's data is a form of state; certainly an unchecked-out shopping cart is state, just like a partially completed mortgage application form is state. You might choose to store these incomplete operations in a database devoted just to them so that your primary database has only complete transactions. However, the boundary between incomplete and complete operations is often not nearly as clean as you might suspect. (A complete mortgage application may be sent back for revision, and that revision can be in a state of limbo as the applicant searches for information that may be several years old.)

Maintaining state in a database has its pros and cons. Increasing the number of database accesses can slow down a system; however, the database is accessible from a variety of computers, browsers, and applications (not just from WebObjects). Accordingly, your incomplete operations can be picked up in many places and at many times.

DESIGN TIP

Use databases to store state data if you need it to be available over relatively long periods of time (hours or days rather than minutes) and from different computers.

Server State

An HTTP server can store state. Typically, it caches some pages. Unlike a client or browser cache, you may be able to control what the HTTP server caches. You may be able to place certain pages in certain locations to improve the speed with which they are served. This is helpful particularly for static pages.

Your main interaction with the HTTP server and state data may be to set the `expires`, `cache-control`, and `last-modified` headers for files coming from specific directories on the server. This is not a WebObjects concern per se.

DESIGN TIP

If possible, perk up your Web site by making all cacheable pages cached by using appropriate headers.

Intermediate State

Finally, you can find information cached in data stores all over the Internet. Routers can read the HTTP headers, and if there is caching information, they may optimize their network's performance by caching them and retrieving them as appropriate.

In addition, companies such as Akamai and Exodus are providing Internet-wide caching and mirroring so that an individual Web site is actually served from a variety of locations on the Internet.

DESIGN TIP

If your Web site is mirrored or cached, be sure you know how to use that service as well as how to turn it off—either in general or to prepare for an update (such as a changed corporate logo).

Designing for State

At the start of developing a WebObjects application, you must consider how you will handle the issues of state. Needing to deal with data that is preserved from page to page as a user navigates through your site makes your task much more complicated than dealing with a site that does not preserve data. However, maintaining state almost always makes your site easier to use, and sometimes it is an absolute requirement for your application.

Identifying Your Needs

State is one of those features (like security) that is far easier to plan for at the beginning of a project than attempting to retrofit it later. One way of designing for state is to make a list of each item on each page that needs to come from somewhere else. "Thank you, Anni" on a response page requires that the user's name come from somewhere—where? Make a three-column list to keep track of these elements:

▶ What page (or WebObjects component or other object) requires the data?

▶ What is the data?

▶ Where does it come from?

The third element (where the data comes from) is what you need to determine as you design for state. You can leave it blank to start, or you can make a guess; most application-design processes iterate through several strategies as the application takes shape.

One answer to the third question is prohibited: one page cannot take data from another page. Thus, the source of data cannot be a Web page. It can be the WebObjects component that creates the Web page, but it cannot be the page itself. In identifying where the data comes from, make sure you can get to it. When you use WebObjects Builder to lay out a page and to bind dynamic elements to variables in your WebObjects application, you can bind them to variables in your component, in the WebObjects session, and in the WebObjects application. To bind them to variables in some other entity (or to programmatically connect them using Java), there must be a path to the other entity. If you cannot find a path to the other entity, chances are you are trying to do something you shouldn't.

For example, you might think that one user's WebObjects session should be able to access data in another user's WebObjects session. This is very hard to do. If there is shared data, share it in an entity that is visible to all sessions—quite likely a database. (The WebObjects application itself is sharable, but remember that you can have multiple WebObjects applications deployed and that the data in one instance is not available to other instances.)

Once you have determined which data you need and where it comes from, you will have the beginnings of a strategy for managing state. If all of the shared data is shared among different users, your state management strategy is likely to be based on a database. If the data is shared within the pages of a single user's session, it is likely to be based on WebObjects sessions. (In systems of any complexity, both strategies are likely to be used.)

Improving Your Design

Before leaving your state management design, review it, looking for efficiency improvements as well as for usability enhancements. On the efficiency front, remember that the page with the message, "Thank you, Anni" is going to cost more than a comparable page with the message, "Thank you." The customized page cannot be cached in a user's browser or in intermediate nodes on the Internet. A page that says "Thank you" and that repeats information (such as an invoice or order confirmation) is likely to be an essential part of your application, but a page that has only a single item of variable data may not be essential.

DESIGN TIP

One way to provide customization with noncustomized pages is to use frames. A relatively unchanging frame can contain a text string such as "Logged On as Anni" or "Welcome, Anni!" When a static page appears in another frame saying, "Thank you," the entire frameset does have the user's name in it.

Consider state management from the other side, too. When you determine what data you need to store, see how else you can use it. If you are producing an order confirmation, you will need to be presenting all of the data from some kind of data store; adding the customer's name (or birthday or any other information) imposes almost no burden because the page's requirements already dictate managing state.

Using Sessions Effectively

The most common type of state management for WebObjects applications is the short-term storage of information from one page to use on another during the same session. The WOSession object lets you handle this almost effortlessly.

WebObjects creates and maintains a session for each user when component actions are used. Direct actions may involve the use of sessions. As anyone who has done so will attest, writing the code to create and maintain sessions is complex and daunting; WebObjects handles that for you. The sessions are there (if you use component actions); all you have to do is access them.

TIP

Session objects are a good place to store information that a number of components will share throughout the session. Information that needs to be passed from one component to another can be passed directly without being stored in the session object. This can make your session objects smaller (and thus, your application).

Storing and Retrieving Session Data

Project Builder creates default classes for you; one of them is an override of WOSession called Session. (The override of WOApplication is called Application; it has been discussed in Chapter 18.)

If you are going to store data in a session object, all you have to do is declare variables for the data you will store. In the Session.java file, you will find a shell for the Session object. For each variable you will need, add a line such as the underlined code in the following example. (The rest of the code is generated by WebObjects ProjectBuilder.)

```
import com.webobjects.foundation.*;
import com.webobjects.appserver.*;
import com.webobjects.eocontrol.*;

String userName
public class Session extends WOSession {

  public Session() {
    super();

    /* ** Put your per-session initialization code here ** */
  }

}
```

Follow the normal procedures for good coding: make the name meaningful. If there is any ambiguity, add a comment. For example, in the case of a user name, you might want to indicate whether this is the name that is stored in a database—a key of retrieval—or a user-chosen nickname. Is the name formatted in a certain manner (last name first), and does it contain honorifics or titles? It is good programming practice to initialize all variables. In Java, variables are initialized to 0 (false for Booleans), and strings are null. If you want another value, initialize the variable in the declaration or in the class's constructor.

Here is an initialization in a declaration:

```
String userName = "Customer";
```

Here is initialization in a constructor:

```
public Session (){
  super ();
  userName = "Customer";
}
```

If you initialize a variable in a constructor, remember that you must call the superclass's constructor first; also remember that you must have previously declared the variable.

TIP

Initializing variables in constructors rather than in declarations is necessary if the initialized value comes from a file or database that needs to be read or otherwise processed to get the data needed for initialization. If it is a constant, it can be initialized in the declaration.

Once you have declared the variables that will store the session's state, you access them by binding them to interface elements. You can do this by using the graphical user interface of WebObjects Builder, or you can write code in the .wod file for the component you are dealing with. (This code is generated by the WebObjects Builder graphical user interface.) Here is the code to bind a dynamic element (a text field named `NameEntryField`) to the `userName` variable declared in the session object:

```
NameEntryField: WOTextField {
  value = Session.userName;
}
```

If you are using the default session object, all you need to do is make sure that the variable's name (underlined) matches the name of the variable you have declared.

To store state variables in a WebObjects application object, follow these instructions exactly, but substitute the Application class for the Session class. (ProjectBuilder automatically creates both for you.)

NOTE

You can store variables in components; however, components come and go. There is a permanent page cache to which you can add specific components. (See "Controlling the WebObjects (Server) Cache" later in this chapter.) In general, though, data in a component that needs to persist is moved to a more permanent location.

For most basic WebObjects applications, this is all there is to state management.

Setting Timeouts

WebObjects automatically creates sessions, and they are maintained as long as there is activity. Sessions automatically time out after an hour. This value (an hour) is a default for WebObjects, and you can change it. Two methods in WOApplication access the value: `setSessionTimeOut` and `sessionTimeOut`. The first method takes one parameter (a number of seconds); the second returns the current value. All sessions created by WOApplication will have this default timeout value.

Timeout values are normally determined by the type of application you are developing. Timing out after a brief period of inactivity is the norm when the application allows the user to update or view sensitive data: for example, what if someone has left a computer to get a cup of coffee, and in the meantime, a passersby manipulates the database? When data is not sensitive, or when your users are in controlled environments, longer timeouts are appropriate.

You can set timeouts for individual sessions. The accessors in the WOSession object are `setTimeOut` and `timeOut`. They function in the same manner as the WOApplication default timeout accessors, but they control only the session in which they are set.

Controlling the WebObjects (Server) Cache

WebObjects stores pages that have been generated for each session. By default, up to 30 pages are stored. All of the variables in the component that produces each page are stored in this way, and you can access them. When a component is needed for a session, the WebObjects cache for that session is checked: if the component is found, it is reused. If it is not found, it is created afresh.

You can control the size of the cache by using the WOApplication object's `setPageCacheSize` and `pageCacheSize` accessors. The parameter to the first is an integer that is the number of pages for the cache; the second accessor is a function that returns an integer value.

CAUTION

You can set the size of the cache to 0 and thereby turn off page caching. If you make this choice, make sure you know why you are doing so. In general, it is not a good idea to turn off page cache. It will cause WebObjects to always create a new page when one is requested, and any data that you store in the component will be lost unless you explicitly handle it.

Unlike client-side caches, you can force a specific page to be cached. A separate cache is available for these manually cached pages. The accessors `setPermanentPageCacheSize` and `permanentPageCacheSize` work exactly like the general page cache accessors described in the previous paragraph. They, too, are methods of WOApplication.

TIP

The permanent cache is a good place for important pages that could otherwise be flushed from the cache by a flurry of unimportant pages. Navigation pages used in frames fall into this category, as do boilerplate thank you or error pages.

To use the permanent page cache, you use the WOSession object's `savePageInPermanentCache` method. It takes one parameter: a WOComponent object (or a descendant thereof—typically your page).

NOTE

The `savePageInPermanentCache` *method is a method of WOSession; each cache (both permanent and temporary) is specific to a session. You set the sizes of the caches with methods of WOApplication, and you save components with WOSession. There is a comparable* `savePage` *method in WOSession that stores pages in the temporary cache; WebObjects automatically calls it for you.*

Controlling the Browser (Client) Cache

Although your control over a browser cache is limited, you can prevent pages from being cached. (You cannot force them to be cached.) Two methods help you do this. You can do it either for all messages or for an individual message.

The `setPageRefreshOnBacktrackEnabled` method in WOApplication adds an `expires` header to each outgoing HTTP message. It is set to the date and time of page creation; in other words, the page as sent has expired. According to the HTTP protocol, it can be displayed, and it can even be cached—but it cannot be displayed from the cache if requested again.

If you use it, you call `setPageRefreshOnBacktrackEnabled` to turn this feature on and off for a series of messages—possibly for your entire application. For that reason, it may be called when you initialize the WOApplication object.

The `disableClientCaching` method of WOResponse affects only that one message. You call it if you want to leave client-side/browser/user caching in place (a good thing) and turn it off only in special cases.

NOTE

You cannot turn caching on for a user or a browser. Whether it is on or off is the user's choice (or the network administrator's choice). Your only option is to prevent caching if it happens to be on. You also cannot find out if it is on. These rules are part of the HTTP protocol specification.

Storing State Explicitly

The basic WebObjects architecture for managing state works for a wide variety of applications. In some cases, you need to store state yourself. You can do so by storing data in databases or flat files; you can also do so by modifying the WOSessionStore objects in which WebObjects actually stores state.

If you are storing state, you need to determine if you are augmenting or replacing the WebObjects mechanisms. For example, if you store intermediate results of a multipage data-entry operation, those results might be stored in a database as well as in the session object. In that case, you must account for the possibility of inconsistencies.

Awake/Sleep Opportunities

The `awake` and `sleep` methods of component, session, and application objects are called at the beginning and end of each request/response cycle. Neither method takes any parameters. You can override these methods to do processing to prepare for or recover from a request/response cycle.

Session Stores

A descendant of the WOSessionStore object handles the actual storage of information for sessions. The standard implementation stores that information in the application's memory. You can create your own WOSessionStore object to save data elsewhere (on disk, for example). If you do, you need to implement two methods in your override of WOSessionStore.

The `saveSessionForContext` method is called as needed to store the data. It takes one parameter—a WOContext object. The context provides pointers to all of the necessary objects that must be stored.

The `restoreSessionWithID` method does the reverse. It takes two parameters: a session identifier and a WORequest object. The session identifier is created (if necessary) when the session is saved; it is stored in the WOContext object.

TIP

If you want to manage your own state storage, you can do so with a database or flat file; you do not need to override WOSessionStore. Much of the data in WOSessionStore is private to WebObjects; much of what you probably want to maintain is your application data. For example, you might want to maintain private WebObjects session information if you implement your own session store that is independent of WebObjects. This would allow a WebObjects application instance to crash and allow its session data to be recovered.

CHAPTER

20

XML and WebObjects

IN THIS CHAPTER:

XML Basics

Using XML with WebObjects

XML (eXtensible Markup Language) is becoming an increasingly important tool on the Web. A standard promulgated by the World Wide Web Consortium (W3C) (http://www.w3c.org), it is used as the basis for many projects as disparate as Microsoft's .Net initiative, Simple Object Access Protocol (SOAP), and a wide variety of Web pages. (XML is often used in conjunction with cascading style sheets—CSS.) Many people believe that XML will eventually replace HTML.

In many ways, XML is even simpler than HTML: its rules are stricter than those of HTML, yet it has much more flexibility because it is infinitely extensible (hence the name). WebObjects, like all modern Web technologies, deals with XML. This chapter shows you how WebObjects deals with XML and why it matters.

First, you will learn about XML basics. XML itself is simple, although its applications can become complex. WebObjects (like most XML applications) uses only the most basic aspects of XML. Then you will learn about the two basic areas in which XML matters to WebObjects: you can use the Document Object Model (DOM) to move sections of documents into and out of request and response messages, and you can use XML elements to import and export data to and from WebObjects.

NOTE

Many people underestimate the importance of eXtensible Markup Language. XML is a next-generation standard: it does little if anything that other standards do not do. For example, you can use the combination of XML and CSS to create Web pages that you could also create with HTML. You can use XML as a format for data transfer in the same way that you can use proprietary data formats. Because XML does not generally provide new features, people commonly dismiss it. However, its improvements in efficiency and productivity (learned from the experience with earlier-generation tools such as HTML) can move the Web—and all of modern information technology—to a new level.

XML Basics

XML is a standard for structured data. It addresses documents as a whole using its Document Object Model as well as individual data items such as names or addresses. It is one of the languages (like HTML) that is based on the Standard Generalized Markup Language (SGML) specification that dates to the mid-1980s (ISO 8879: *Information processing—Text and office systems—Standard Generalized Markup Language (SGML)*, ([Geneva]: ISO, 1986)).

XML Element Formatting

Like HTML, XML uses *tags*—information delimited by angle brackets (< and >)—
to describe information in *elements*. Each XML element has two tags: a starting tag
and an ending tag. The ending tag is identical to the starting tag, but it starts with a
slash (/). Thus, an element called name could consist of the following:

```
<name>
Sarah Bernhardt
</name>
```

Sometimes, an element contains no information other than that found in its
starting tag; in such a case, the starting tag can end with a slash indicating that it
completes the element. Thus, you can write

```
<property name = "name" xmlTag = "name" />
```

The property element contains two attributes (name and xmlTag), and the
property element is completed by the slash. (Attributes are discussed in the
following section.) You could also write

```
<property name = "name" xmlTag = "name">
</property>
```

Here, the property element has both a starting tag and an ending tag. Note that
in XML, every element must be terminated with a slash or ending tag as in the
previous code.

While line spacing does not matter in XML, it is useful in describing this code.
The first line is the starting tag, the second line is the text of the tag, and the third
line is the ending tag.

XML elements can contain other elements. Thus, a person element might
contain a name element and an address element, as in this example:

```
<person>
  <name>
    Sarah Bernhardt
  </name>

  <address>
    Paris
  </address>
</person>
```

NOTE

Remember that the line spacing in this example is provided only to make it easier to read: the entire person XML element could be placed on a single line.

XML Element Names and Attributes

Unlike in HTML, in XML, the user specifies the names of elements. You can create a `name` element or an `address` element or an `invoice` element or a `J4293` element—all you have to do is match the starting and ending tags for each one.

Within the starting tag, you can insert attributes. XML attributes are like HTML attributes: they consist of an attribute name, a =, and the value of the attribute. Here is a typical XML attribute:

```
objectID="451138"
```

Multiple attributes can be placed in a starting tag, as is the case here:

```
<name type = "java.lang.String" objectID="451138">
```

The `name` tag contains two attributes: `type` and `objectID`. XML defines this structure and format; it does not define individual tags. XML is designed to be written and read by programs. It uses plain text for its formatting and you can read it yourself, but its primary objective is to be handled electronically.

XML vs. HTML

XML differs from HTML in three important formatting ways:

▶ Capitalization matters. Name is not the same as name.

▶ All attribute values must be enclosed in quotes unless they are numeric. In HTML, values that contain spaces must be quoted, but single-word values (such as 451138 in the previous section) need not be.

▶ Ending tags are never optional in XML. In HTML, ending tags are optional for a variety of defined elements (such as <P>) and are even forbidden for others (such as <IMG>).

Overall, XML differs most from HTML in that its rules are stricter (albeit fewer).

The Document Object Model

The Document Object Model (DOM) is one of the technologies that exists around XML. It is an API designed to let programs manipulate documents that are expressed in elements (XML or even HTML). DOM describes the logical relationships of elements (or *nodes*) within the document. Thus, a document model can define a complex document such as an invoice or a highly structured text document such as this chapter (with its paragraphs, various types of headings, and illustrations); this document model can be independent of the actual data that exists in a given invoice or chapter document.

The document model aspect of XML is useful in transporting documents or parts of documents from one environment to another. (Many people ignore this fact and focus only on XML elements.)

Why Use XML?

XML lets you identify text by placing it within an element that you define (or that is defined for you). That element may have attributes that are part of the definition. Everything—the attributes as well as the text—combines to create a unit of information that any XML-savvy application can parse.

XML provides facilities for describing information. Formatting is generally provided by cascading style sheets that are keyed to XML elements; the style sheets are in other files. In this way, the structure of a document and its information (XML) is separate from its presentation. This separation not only allows different groups of people to work on the data and on the formatting, but it also makes it easy to switch style sheets to accommodate the different needs of various users and output devices.

With its simple format of text data and identification, XML has quickly become the lingua franca of modern information technology. Using XML is probably the easiest way to transfer data from one application, operating system, or computing platform to another (particularly if the other is not determined at the time when the data must be prepared for export).

NOTE

The capacity of contemporary computers and telecommunications makes XML possible. Until fairly recently, binary (rather than text) data was used because the cost of transmitting and translating text into binary data was not supportable, given the computing infrastructure a decade or so ago. With today's technology, however, there's no need to worry about the cost of transmitting the 56 bits it takes to transmit the string 493,200, as opposed to the 19 bits—just about one-third—it takes to transmit the binary number 493,200.

Using XML with WebObjects

You can use XML with WebObjects in two ways:

▶ You can use the Document Object Model to move sections of documents into and out of request and response messages. (This is an easy way to format XML responses.)

▶ You can use XML elements to import and export data to and from WebObjects.

These two uses of XML are very different, but both are explored in the following sections.

XML and Messages

The WOMessage class and its two descendants WORequest and WOResponse implement the WebObjects request-response loop. Normally, these messages are HTML messages sent via the HTTP protocol. However, you can use XML instead of HTML in these messages. To do so, you use DOM documents or DOM document fragments. DOM documents and DOM document fragments can be converted to XML strings; you use the documents and document fragments to actually move the chunks of XML into and out of WOMessage objects.

A DOM document provides the structure of an entire document. A DOM document fragment provides the structure of a portion of a document; the fragment can be inserted into a DOM document. It may take many fragments to make up an entire DOM document. (A fragment can be an individual inventory item, shipping instructions, client information, and so forth; it can also be an entire invoice; or it can be a single XML element.) When fragments are inserted into DOM documents, their elements are inserted; the fragment itself (the container of the elements) vanishes.

NOTE

The WebObjects XML support is provided using IBM's alphaWorks technology, which is now part of Apache's XML framework.

Three methods of WOMessage are used to manipulate DOM documents: `setContentDOMDocument`, `appendContentString`, and `contentAsDOMDocument`.

Setting an XML Message

Just as you can set a WOMessage object's contents by using the setContent method of WOMessage, you can set the contents to an XML string by using setContentDOMDocument. The traditional setContent method uses an NSData object that contains HTML; setContentDOMDocument uses a DOM document that contains XML. You are responsible for preparing the XML code in the document that will become the message.

Adding XML to a Message

You use the appendContentDOMDocumentFragment method to add a document fragment to the end of the message contents. It joins other append methods such as appendContentCharacter, appendContentData, and appendContentString, which are used to add individual characters, NSData objects, or strings to the HTML content of WOMessage. In this case, the sole argument to appendContentDOMDocumentFragment is a document fragment that can be converted to an XML string.

NOTE

The setContent methods replace the entire message contents (if any) with the object passed into the method. The appendContent methods add the data passed into the method to the end of the existing message (if any).

Getting XML from a Message

Finally, you can use contentAsDOMDocument to extract the XML from a message. (This is comparable to the content method that returns the HTML in an NSData object.)

XML and Data

In addition to using XML for the request and response messages, you can use XML to encode and decode data. This is particularly useful if you need to import or export data from other environments.

WebObjects uses the terms "encode" and "decode" to describe the process of converting binary, structured data to another format (normally some variation of a flat file). Although this chapter deals only with XML, WebObjects and its classes can encode and decode using a variety of formats. You need to implement the encode and decode methods to provide the custom input and output formatting of your objects.

WebObjects gives you a lot of control over how you use XML. You can handle data in three basic ways:

▶ **Fields**   You can encode or decode individual data elements—single fields or variables.

▶ **Objects**   You can encode or decode objects and the fields or data elements within them. This can involve embedded XML elements.

▶ **Mapping**   You can map specific XML elements to specific WebObjects data structures. This strategy is particularly useful if your data structures do not match those of a system with which you must communicate.

Figure 20-1 shows a WebObjects demonstration application that encodes and decodes data by using each of these three strategies. Each strategy is described in the sections that follow; the complete code is provided at the end of this chapter.

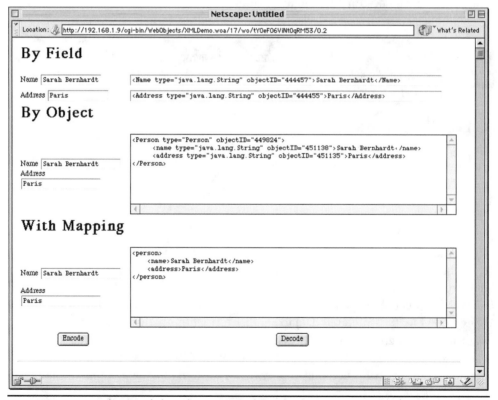

Figure 20-1   *Encoding and decoding XML with WebObjects*

The demonstration application works as follows. You can type anything you want into the fields at the left (names and addresses); when you click the Encode button at the bottom, whatever you have typed is encoded and displayed in the fields at the right. You can type anything you want into the fields at the right (or modify the data that has been encoded). When you click the Decode button, the decoded data will be placed in the name and address fields at the left. In this way, you can experiment to see how the XML or raw data changes.

Encoding and Decoding Fields

If you merely want to encode or decode individual fields, and if those are standard types (such as String objects), you can use the following technique.

In the first pair of data fields, individual variables are encoded. To do this encoding, you need a WOXMLCoder object. You can declare and create one by using the following line of code:

```
WOXMLCoder coder = WOXMLCoder.coder();
```

With the WOXMLCoder object, you can use its `encodeRootObjectForKey` method to construct the XML, as this line of code does:

```
nameXMLstring = coder.encodeRootObjectForKey (personName, "Name");
```

Assuming that the variable `personName` is bound to the `name` field on the Web page, its contents will be encoded using the XML element title `Name`, as shown in the first line at the right in Figure 20-1. The variable `nameXMLstring` is bound to the first field at the right of the figure. The second line of XML is created by using the following line of code:

```
addressXMLstring = coder.encodeRootObjectForKey (personAddress, "Address");
```

In this case, `personAddress` is assumed to be the variable bound to the `address` data entry field. The default encoder generates the relevant attributes for the XML element (its type—a Java string—and its `objectID`—internal to WebObjects).

To decode the XML that is generated, first create a WOXMLDecoder object. As in the previous code you can create and store it in a variable (such as the variable coder t). Or you can create the decoder dynamically as you need it: that method is used here.

TIP

Create and store a coder or decoder in a variable if you will be using it several times; create it inside an expression if you need it for only one use.

Next, create an InputSource object to be passed into the constructor of the WOXMLDecoder object. In turn, the constructor of InputSource requires a StringReader object that wraps around the string variable that is bound to the actual HTML data entry field. Assuming that the XML field at the right in Figure 20-1 is bound to a variable called `nameXMLString`, the following code will decode the XML into the data seen at left when you click the Decode button.

NOTE

StringReader is a Java class; InputSource is part of the SAX package that parses XML. SAX is included with WebObjects and you must import it, like the code at the end of this chapter demonstrates. StringReader and InputSource do just what you would expect them to; you can use them without further investigation just by copying this code.

```
StringReader stringReader = new StringReader (nameXMLstring);
InputSource is = new InputSource (stringReader);
Object anObject = (WOXMLDecoder.decoder().decodeRootObject (is));
personName = ((String)anobject);
```

In reusing this code snippet, simply replace the two underlined words with the name of the variable containing the XML (`nameXMLstring`) and the name of the variable into which you want to place the resulting string. Note that this works for strings; if your variable is of another type, you will need to cast it to that type in the final line of code. Note, too, that `decodeRootObject` creates an object.

Encoding and Decoding Objects

As you can see from the second example in Figure 20-1 (encoding and decoding by fields), you can also encode and decode complex objects. To do so, a Person object is created: it has two fields (name and address). Here is an excerpt of the declaration for Person. (All of the code is provided at the end of the chapter.)

```
public class Person extends NSObject implements WOXMLCoding  {
    String name;
    String address;
```

If you implement the WOXMLCoding interface, you must implement two methods: a constructor that takes a WOXMLDecoder object as a parameter, and an `encodeWithWOXMLCoder` method. If you implement the WOXMLCoding interface, then calling `encodeRootObject` or `decodeRootObject` in the previous example will automatically call your methods.

NOTE

If you want to encode or decode objects other than standard simple objects such as String objects, you must use this technique or the mapping technique that follows.

The following code is a sample constructor that includes a WOXMLDecoder object. As in all constructors, you must set each variable to an appropriate value. In this case, there are two variables (`name` and `address`). Each is decoded from an XML element. (Use `decodeObjectforKey` for String objects; similar methods let you decode Boolean, Double, Float, and Int objects.)

```
public Person(WOXMLDecoder coder) {
    name = (String)(coder.decodeObjectForKey ("name"));
    address = (String)(coder.decodeObjectForKey ("address"));
}
```

In reusing this code, simply replace the underlined text. Note that while the variable name is `name` and its key is also `"name"`, this need not be the case. The XML key must be what is in the XML element. In other words, if you had encoded the `name` variable with the following code

```
nameXMLstring = coder.encodeRootObjectForKey (personName, "customer");
```

you would decode it with

```
name = (String)(coder.decodeObjectForKey ("customer"));
```

You implement encoding the same way. Here is a sample encoding method:

```
public void encodeWithWOXMLCoder(WOXMLCoder coder) {
    coder.encodeObjectForKey(name, "name");
    coder.encodeObjectForKey(address, "address");
}
```

Again, replace the underlined text with your variable name and with its XML element name. To encode the variable `name` as `"customer"` change the first line of code to this:

```
coder.encodeObjectForKey(name, "customer");
```

The advantage of implementing encoding and decoding inside an object is that you never have to worry about it again: calling `encodeRootObjectforKey` or decodeRootObject for the object (as opposed to individual fields in the previous example) will automatically do the work.

DEBUGGING TIP

Remember that your constructor must safely set all object variables. Some may need to be set to predetermined variables rather than to decoded values.

In Figure 20-1, look at the XML that has been generated in the By Object section. Notice that the XML elements for the name and address are the same as those generated in the By Field section at the top. (The type and objectID attributes are automatically inserted.) But you can customize the encoding and decoding by using mapping.

Using Mapping

Finally, you can use mapping to customize the XML that is generated or that is read. To do so, use a mapping file to map XML elements to WebObjects objects and variables.

A mapping file contains a model such as this one:

```
<model>
  <entity name = "Person" xmlTag = "person">
    <property name = "name" xmlTag = "name" />
    <property address = "address" xmlTag = "address" />
  </entity>
</model>
```

Each element has two critical attributes: name and xmlTag. The name attribute refers to the object or variable name in your WebObjects Java code; the xmlTag attribute refers to the identifier of the element in the XML file. In this case, the two are identical, but here is what the model would look like in an alternative implementation. (The personName variable maps to an XML element called ID, and the WebObjects Java class is called Student. It maps to an XML element called WhoItIs.)

```
<model>
  <entity name = "Student" xmlTag = "WhoItIs">
    <property name = "personName" xmlTag = "ID" />
    <property address = "address" xmlTag = "address" />
  </entity>
</model>
```

The XML that corresponds to this might look like this:

```
<whoItIs>
<ID>Samuel Clemens</ID>
<address>Hartford</address>
</whoItIs>
```

The `entity` element is the WebObjects object; the `property` elements are the variables within that object. Note that you can have objects within objects; in such cases, entities are placed within other entities in the model.

When you control both sides of the encoding and decoding, it makes sense to use the same (or similar) names for the XML elements and the WebObjects classes and variables. But, as this example suggests, you may be interacting with systems that are not under your control. Mapping is the technique you use to put data from an external system into your own objects.

Encoding with Mapping   To encode with mapping, you need a mapping file, as described in the previous section, and you need the following code. For encoding, you create a coder just like you did in the previous example, but you use the `coderWithMapping` constructor. It takes the URL of a mapping file. The following code constructs such a coder and encodes an object called myPerson; the XML is placed in a variable called `personmappingXMLstring`. The whole XML is placed in an element whose name is Person, which is defined in the previous mapping file.

```
personmappingXMLstring = WOXMLCoder.coderWithMapping(model).
  encodeRootObjectForKey(myPerson, "Person");
```

Decoding with Mapping   Decoding is just as simple, although it involves a few more steps because you must create an InputSource and a StringReader object (as you did to decode fields). Here is the code:

```
stringReader = new StringReader (personmappingXMLstring);
is = new InputSource (stringReader);
personForXMLmapping =
  (Person)(WOXMLDecoder.decoderWithMapping(model).
    decodeRootObject(is));
```

You can reuse this code by replacing the three underlined words as follows:

▶   Use the name of the String variable that is bound to the text data entry field in place of `personmappingXMLstring`.

▶ Use the variable of the object you are creating instead of
`personForXMLmapping`.

▶ Use the class name of the object you are constructing instead of `Person`.
(This is the same as the `name` attribute of the entity in the XML file.)

Using a Mapping File   In the WebObjects examples that come with WebObjects,
you can find code that lets you identify and use a mapping file. Here is the relevant
section of code that helps you construct a URL for a file that will be stored in a
String object named model. (Note that model is the URL, not the model itself.) The
code works on both Windows and other operating systems. (It adjusts for slash (/)
and backslash (\) file delimiters.) It identifies a resource file with the name that is
stored in the `personMappingFile` static variable, which you place in the
Resources folder of your WebObjects application. See the full code listing in
the next section for more details.

```
if (model == null) {
  String prefix = "file://";
  String path = application().resourceManager().
    pathForResourceNamed(personMappingFile, null, null)
  // adjust prefix for Windows style paths
  if (System.getProperty("os.name").startsWith("Windows"))
    prefix = "file:\\";
  model = prefix + path;
};
```

XML Sample Code

The code that is used for the demonstration application shown in Figure 20-1 is
presented here. Annotations are provided only for those few sections that have not
been commented on previously.

```
import com.webobjects.appserver.*;
import com.webobjects.eocontrol.*;
import com.webobjects.eoaccess.*;
import com.webobjects.foundation.*;
```

Be sure to import the WebObjects XML package, as well as SAX and java.io. All
are provided with WebObjects, but you must include the following three lines of code:

```
import com.apple.webobjects.xml.*;
import org.xml.sax.InputSource;
import java.io.*;

public class Main extends WOComponent {
```

The Person object (defined later in this section) encapsulates name and address data. Three instances are created: one each for the By Field, By Object, and With Mapping sections of the screen shown in Figure 20-1.

```
public Person person, personForXML, personForXMLmapping;
```

The following four variables are bound to the four text fields at the right in Figure 20-1. The first two are the two fields used in the By Field section; there is one variable each for By Object and With Mapping.

```
public String nameXMLstring;
public String addressXMLstring;
public String personXMLstring;
public String personmappingXMLstring;
```

The next variable is the URL of the model file; the one following is the name of the file that you placed in your application's Resources folder.

```
public String model;
protected static String personMappingFile =
  "personmapping.xml";

public Main (){
  super();
```

Create the three Person instances:

```
  person = new Person();
  personForXML = new Person();
  personForXMLmapping = new Person();
}
```

The following method is bound to the Encode button:

```
public WOComponent doEncode() {
```

Create a coder and encode the two fields for the By Field section:

```
WOXMLCoder coder = WOXMLCoder.coder();
nameXMLstring = coder.encodeRootObjectForKey
  (person.getName(), "Name");
addressXMLstring = coder.encodeRootObjectForKey
  (person.getAddress(), "Address");
```

Encode the personForXML object into `personXMLString` (the text field at the right of By Object).

```
personXMLstring = WOXMLCoder.coder().encodeRootObjectForKey
  (personForXML, "Person");
```

If necessary, create the model URL. Then encode `personForXMLmapping` into `personmappingXMLstring` by using the mapping file `model`.

```
if (model == null) {
  String prefix = "file://";
  String path = application().resourceManager().
    pathForResourceNamed(personMappingFile, null, null)
  // adjust prefix for Windows style paths
  if (System.getProperty("os.name").startsWith("Windows"))
    prefix = "file:\\";
  model = prefix + path;
  };
personmappingXMLstring = WOXMLCoder.coderWithMapping(model).
  encodeRootObjectForKey(personForXMLmapping, "Person");

return null;
}
```

This method is bound to the Decode button.

```
public WOComponent doDecode() {
  Object anObject;
  InputSource is;
  StringReader stringReader;
```

Create StringReader and InputSource objects to decode name and address fields. Use the Person accessors to set the variables in the Person object.

```
stringReader = new StringReader (nameXMLstring);
is = new InputSource (stringReader);
Object anObject =
  (WOXMLDecoder.decoder().decodeRootObject (is));
person.setName ((String)anobject);

stringReader = new StringReader (addressXMLstring);
is = new InputSource (stringReader);
person.setAddress ((String)(WOXMLDecoder.decoder().
  decodeRootObject (is)));
```

If any data is in `personXMLstring`, decode the `personForXML` object from it.

```
if (personXMLstring.length() > 0) {
  stringReader = new StringReader (personXMLstring);
is = new InputSource (stringReader);
personForXML = (Person)(WOXMLDecoder.decoder().
  decodeRootObject(is));
}
```

If any data is in `personmappingXMLstring`, decode the `personForXMLmapping` object from it by using the `model` URL.

```
if (personmappingXMLstring.length() > 0) {
  stringReader = new StringReader (personmappingXMLstring);
is = new InputSource (stringReader);
personForXMLmapping =
  (Person)(WOXMLDecoder.decoderWithMapping(model).
  decodeRootObject(is));
}

  return null;
  }
}
```

This is the code for the Person class:

```
import com.webobjects.appserver.*;
import com.webobjects.eocontrol.*;
import com.webobjects.eoaccess.*;
import com.webobjects.foundation.*;
```

Include the WebObjects XML package:

```
import com.apple.webobjects.xml.*;
import java.lang.*;
import java.net.*;
import java.math.*;
```

You must implement the WOXMLCoding interface if you use By Object or With Mapping encoding and decoding.

```
public class Person extends EOGenericRecord  {
   String name;
   String address;
```

This is the constructor with default data:

```
public Person () {
   name = "Sarah Bernhardt";
   address = "Paris";
}
```

These are standard accessors for the class:

```
public String getName () {
   return name;
}

public void setName (String inName) {
   name = inName;
}

public String getAddress () {
   return address;
}

public void setAddress (String inAddress) {
   address = inAddress;
}
```

You must implement a constructor that takes WOXMLDecoder as its parameter. Note that you do not care if this is a mapping decoder or not: your code works the same way. Remember that this is a constructor: you must set all variables (including those that do not come from the XML).

```
public Person(WOXMLDecoder coder) {
  name = (String)(coder.decodeObjectForKey ("name"));
  address = (String)(coder.decodeObjectForKey ("address"));
}
```

To complete your implementation of the WOXMLCoding interface, implement the following method, which encodes each variable in your class that needs to be stored.

```
public void encodeWithWOXMLCoder(WOXMLCoder coder) {
  coder.encodeObjectForKey(name, "name");
  coder.encodeObjectForKey(address, "address");
  }
}
```

CHAPTER 7

Advanced WebObjects Topics

IN THIS CHAPTER:

Debugging Tips and Tools

Database Performance

Handling Errors

T his chapter explores some of the many advanced WebObjects topics. You can find further discussions on Apple's discussion site for WebObjects (reachable at http://www.apple.com/support) as well as in documentation and other resources at http://developer.apple.com.

Many of the most critical issues that affect WebObjects performance turn out to be specific to the application and its installation. Unlike many software products that are installed in many environments (a word processing application, for example, may have millions of individual installations and users), most WebObjects applications have only a single installation. The care and feeding of such an installation is obviously quite different from that of a mass-market product.

However, the unique WebObjects installation may, itself, have hundreds of thousands of users—or more. Thus, you need to be aware of the extraordinary visibility of your application and of its performance.

Debugging Tips and Tools

In order to keep track of what is going on with your WebObjects application, a variety of tools are available. They include:

▶ Logs

▶ Monitor

▶ Warning messages

Each of these can provide you with information about what is happening inside your application as it is running.

Furthermore, there are steps that you can take in advance of problems to attempt to find out what might happen and how to prevent it (or ensure it, depending on the case). These include:

▶ Code reviews

▶ Stress testing

▶ Normal operations

Finally, ad hoc analysis tools for the database (OpenBaseManager, in the case of OpenBase) can help you get to the bottom of apparent anomalies in performance.

All of these issues are discussed in this section.

Logs

Each WOApplication object (the ancestor of your Application object in most cases) maintains a WOStatisticsStore object that stores statistics on the operations of the application. You can gain a reference to that object by using the WOApplication accessor as in this code:

```
myApplication.statisticsStore()
```

At the end of each request-response cycle, the WOSession object's `recordStatisticsForResponse` and `descriptionForResponse` methods are called. The latter ultimately calls a similarly named method of WOComponent that you can override. If you override `descriptionForResponse` in your component object, you must always call the `super` implementation first in order to record basic information. After that, however, you can add your own information.

You can store the information obtained in this manner in a log file. You call the `setLogFile` method of the `statisticsStore` to set the filename and the rotation—the number of days after which it should be overridden. The entries in the log file are in Common Log File Format (CLFF), and you can use standard utilities to read them.

Monitor

As you will see in Chapter 28, the Monitor application is used to manage WebObjects applications and their deployed instances. It collects statistics on the performance of each application instance on each host that supports your application.

Warning Messages

You can generate warning messages from your application (as you do commonly in traditional applications); however, because of the complexity of a WebObjects application with its multitude of instances, they can be less than helpful. Using the log from the statisticsStore object provides additional information.

Code Reviews

In terms of proactive steps, nothing beats careful manual review of critical code. As your application is built and deployed, the critical areas will become clear. Some are obvious from the beginning (the heart of your transactions, for example), while others emerge as problematic only during testing or even deployment.

For critical areas of your operation, review the code to look for the normal Java (and standard programming) pitfalls. Look for variables declared but never used (particularly instantiated but unused objects); look for memory leaks, and look for debugging code that has been left in production versions.

Stress Testing

Stress testing means pushing your application to its limits. It may mean running a load that is double, triple, or even ten times your standard production volume. Depending on the nature of the application, you may need to know what its limits are. At what point do you bring your Web server host to its knees? At what point do you need additional instances?

When the crunch of a major real-life stress incident occurs, you need to know what will alleviate the problem. The three most common solutions are additional memory, more bandwidth, and more processing power (including more computer hosts).

Normal Operation Metrics

Finally, the most important piece of information to have for debugging is information about normal performance, and that often is the hardest to come by. When people are complaining about performance, it is too late to do the baseline measurements so that you can tell if the problem is real or a matter of perception.

It is ludicrous to collect data on the performance of each component in your application. However, for the critical ones, have debugging code available to write to logs of the statisticsStore object so that you can see what is happening.

A side benefit of having normal operation metrics is that in the heat of the moment, you will not have to start from scratch: you will know how to collect the necessary statistics for your application.

Database Performance

Most WebObjects applications rely on databases, and the performance of the database has a great deal to do with the performance of WebObjects itself. There are three techniques you can use inside WebObjects and your Enterprise Objects Framework model to change database performance. In addition, logs both from WebObjects and from your database can help you diagnose problems.

Batch Faulting

As you saw in Chapter 10, you can use batch faulting to retrieve collections of records all at once. You can programmatically determine these records, or you can turn on the Batch Faulting feature in EOModeler and let the model and WebObjects determine the records to be retrieved.

Batch faulting can improve performance in some cases; however, since a multitude of records can be retrieved at a time, more memory is needed for your application, and the retrieval itself may take longer than you expect.

Tuning a database application of any sort requires intimate knowledge of the data and its uses that comes only with careful study of the application. Sometimes, the relatively unsophisticated user (at least on the database side) will be the most knowledgeable about how the data actually is used and how the database should perform.

You set batch faulting in the advanced options pane of the Inspector window for whatever entity you have selected in EOModeler.

Prefetching

Like batch faulting, prefetching was described in Chapter 10. It lets you specify a relationship to be fetched all at once so that when you need the subsidiary records, they are all in memory. The same caveats apply to prefetching as do to batch faulting: increased memory use, possibly lengthy fetch operations, and wasted retrievals if your hypotheses about the behavior of the data and the users are not borne out.

You set prefetching for a selected Fetch Spec in EOModeler.

Caching

Another performance modification you can make is to cache retrieved data in memory. As with all of these options, increased memory use may lead to decreased database accesses. Caching in memory is good for read-only data of limited scope. If it is not read-only data, then the cost of comparing the cached data to database data quickly eliminates any savings. Thus, in setting caching, you usually will consider also setting the data in the selected entity as read only.

You set batch faulting in the advanced options pane of the Inspector window for whatever entity you have selected in OpenBaseManager.

SQL logs

You can have WebObjects write out the SQL that it is executing to a log. You turn this on in one of three ways:

▶ When you build the application in Project Builder, you can add the following line to the build parameters:

```
-EOAdaptorDebugEnabled YES
```

▶ You can enter the following command on the command line in Terminal (insert the name of your application rather than SiteDemo):

```
defaults write SiteDemo EOAdaptorDebugEnabled YES
```

▶ Or, you can execute the following line of code from within your application:

```
EOAdaptorContext.setDebugEnabledDefault(true);
```

Output of the SQL log is directed to standard error, and it can be viewed with the Console application on Mac OS X.

Database Load

Many database managers provide you not only with reports of their performance but also with real-time, graphical displays of what is happening. OpenBaseManager provides this through the Monitor Database Load button in the toolbar. For the selected database, it provides a constantly updated display of the numbers of selects, inserts, updates, deletes, and other database accesses. (The display is updated once each second.)

A log of administrative accesses to the database is also available in OpenBaseManager. You can access it by selecting a database and then choosing Show Log from the Database menu.

Handling Errors

When errors do occur in creating pages to be returned to the user as part of the request-response loop, WebObjects reports them to the user. You can customize these messages either by modifying the default error page or by implementing your own error page.

Customizing the Default Error Page

A single error page is used for all WebObjects applications running on a server. It is located at the following place on Mac OS X:

```
/System/Library/Frameworks/JavaWOExtensions.framework/Resources
```

You can modify this page with WebObjects Builder. Note that your modifications will affect all WebObjects applications running on that server. There are two sets of typical modifications you may consider.

The first set of modifications customizes the page to add information, such as a person to contact for help or to whom to report the problem. This is appropriate for in-house WebObjects applications where you can profit from the feedback or where you need to support online users in your organization.

The second set of modifications involves removing information from the default page. If you are not running an in-house application, but rather it is provided to a variety of people on the Web, perhaps you want a generic Oops page that does not reveal the structure of your application (in page or component names) and does not present what may be gibberish to the user.

Remember that any customization you make to the default page will apply to all of your WebObjects applications.

Implementing Your Own Error Page

If you implement your own error page within your application, you can customize it on a component basis. There are four Java exceptions that are posted and that you can intercept:

1. If WebObjects cannot restore a session (usually as a result of a timeout), it posts an exception and the WOApplication object's `handleSessionRestorationErrorinContext` method is called. You can override it, and if you do, you need to know that it has one parameter— the context. From that, you can obtain any information you need as you process the exception.

2. If it cannot create a session, it winds up calling the WOApplication object's `handleSessionCreationErrorinContext` method with the same context parameter.

3. If it backtracks too far, it calls the WOApplication object's `userhandlePageRestorationErrorinContext` method, also passing in a context.

4. Otherwise, if an exception occurs, it posts a generic exception and the WOApplication method `handleException` is called. This method contains the exception as well as the context. You can use the exception that is passed in to figure out what to do and what error message to display. For example, `handleException` may receive an exception such as `EOValidationException`. This is important to intercept: if you cannot validate user data, you need to explain what and why so that the user is able to correct the problem. You can also create your own named exception that you intercept here.

You can override the handleException method of your override of WOApplication. If you do so, here is the basic code.

```
public WOResponse handleException (
  java.lang.Throwable anException,
  WOContext aContext) {
```

Declare a WOComponent that you will use to return the information to the user. Then, extract the description of the exception from the exception object.

```
WOComponent errorPage;
String exceptionDescription = anException.toString();
```

You need to identify the type of exception that has been posted. Once you do so, you can create the specific type of error page that you want to use (shown in italics). You do so by replacing the boldfaced code in the following lines with the exception you are looking for.

```
if (exceptionDescription.indexOf(anExceptionName) > -1) {
    System.err.println ("anException error");
    errorPage = pageWithName("specificErrorPage",aContext);
} else {
  System.err.println ("error" + exceptionDescription);
  errorPage = pageWithName("ErrorPage",aContext);
}
```

Generate a response from the page you have created, and return it.

```
WOResponse response = errorPage.generateResponse();
return response;
}
```

There are many things you can do to improve WebObjects performance, but, as this chapter should demonstrate, nothing is better than collecting the information that you need in order to find out what really is going on. Not only is it important to log failures (and to properly inform the user of them), but it is also critical to monitor—at least occasionally—the normal operations of your application so that you know what normal performance metrics are.

WebObjects has been used for sites large and small. Its diagnostic and management tools are powerful and useful. Use them.

Not only can WebObjects function as a traditional application server, but it also provides a number of newer technologies focusing on the client side and on totally Web-based components. The next part of the book addresses those issues.

Jump-Starting WebObjects and OpenBase

OBJECTIVES

▶ Create database-driven Web sites automatically with Direct to Web

▶ Create Java clients with Java Client

▶ Reuse your frameworks with WebObjects Builder palettes

▶ Create generalized databases and Enterprise Objects Framework models to speed up project development

T he chapters in this part of the book focus on shortcuts to WebObjects applications and on reusing your code and databases. Each technique helps you get your WebObjects application up and running sooner than you might have believed possible.

NOTE

The Apple document, Developing WebObjects Applications with Direct to Web, *is available in PDF format on the http://developer.apple.com site. It provides substantial additional information and guidance on using Direct to Web, including step-by-step tutorials.*

What Is Direct to Web?

Many people consider WebObjects the first application server, and that may well be the case. (It is hard to actually know, since the term "application server" came into existence long after WebObjects did, and, in fact, the term postdates most of the products that today are called application servers.) Its companion product, Enterprise Objects Framework, was one of the first products to provide an object-oriented bridge to databases. (It, too, may have actually been the first.)

These two products arose out of the world of large-scale enterprises. Often, their databases ran on mainframe computers. WebObjects ran on personal computers (as clients) and on personal computers, workstations, or midrange computers (as servers). The tasks for which WebObjects was used were large and varied; the users tended to be equally so. Dell Computer pioneered online ordering of personal computers with a WebObjects Web site, although when Apple bought the WebObjects technology from NeXt, Dell decided to move its Web site to a non-Apple technology. Many financial services companies used WebObjects, as did major corporations in the automotive and other sectors. New ventures as varied as the Apple Store and FlightArrivals.com (which also uses OpenBase) also used WebObjects.

The fact that WebObjects can handle such large-scale operations is a tribute to its architecture and implementation. However, some people believe that WebObjects is only for large-scale projects. Today, that is not the case. First of all, many of the features of large-scale projects (rich media such as QuickTime and database access) are required on small-scale projects. Second, one of the most important lessons of the rise of the Web and the Internet is that the difference between large- and small-scale enterprises and projects does not matter very much; in fact, to the average Web surfer, that difference may be invisible.

Direct to Web is a technology that helps you create Web sites using a database and WebObjects with minimal—even no—programming. You may not need to use WebObjects Builder at all. And, although you do need to use Project Builder during the creation of your Direct to Web application, all you need to do is to create a Direct to Web project, follow through a half dozen assistant screens, and then click a checkbox to launch the application.

Basic interaction with a database via the Web is remarkably simple: you select a record or records to view, you then view details of those records, and you possibly change them. You may add new records, and you may delete old ones. If your project fits into this pattern, Direct to Web may be for you.

Where Direct to Web does not work easily is if you need custom operations. For example, the SiteDemo project described previously in this book automatically shows all public information items with a visibility value of 0 on its starting page. That is a customization that allows users to see the data without knowing anything about a database, and it is not part of the default Direct to Web implementations.

Direct to Web is a great way to build a front end to a database. Often, you can take a complex project and pull out a number of simple database access sections: these can be implemented with Direct to Web. You can then link these small projects with a larger one or with one another: remember links are the key to the Web. The traditional large system architecture with modules and submodules is frequently not necessary in the world of the Internet today.

Creating a Direct to Web Project

The first step in creating a Direct to Web project is creating an Enterprise Objects Framework model using EOModeler. (This was the topic of Part III of the book.) Everything that Direct to Web does is based on such a model. Once you have done that, continue with this section.

In Project Builder, choose New Project from the File menu. Select a Direct to Web application as shown in Figure 22-1.

The assistant next lets you choose the frameworks to include in your Direct to Web project. You can add your own, if you want, but the most common choice here is just to click Next as shown in Figure 22-2.

Figure 22-1   *Create a Direct to Web application*

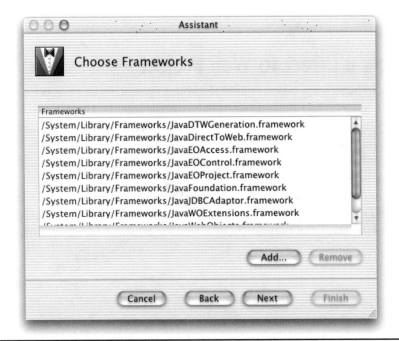

Figure 22-2   *Add frameworks to your project (if necessary)*

Next, select your Enterprise Objects Framework model that you have created as shown in Figure 22-3. It will be copied into your new project's folder, so you can use an EOModel from another project. In this chapter, for example, the EOModel from the SiteDemo project is reused. This is a very common case: you use the same EOModel both for one or more Direct to Web applications and for a larger, custom-written application. In fact, you can use Direct to Web for advanced users' ad hoc queries and procedures while developers work on the main WebObjects application.

WebObjects provides three basic looks for Direct to Web projects: choose the one you want from the panel shown in Figure 22-4. (Each of these is shown in the next section of this chapter.)

Finally, you can choose to build and launch the project as shown in Figure 22-5. If you do, you will see your project in all its glory.

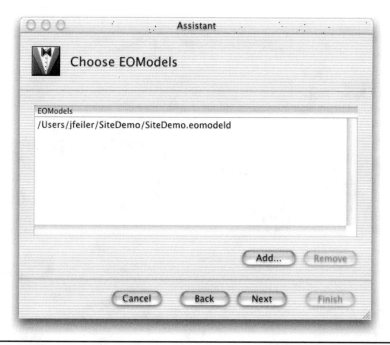

Figure 22-3   *Select an EOModel*

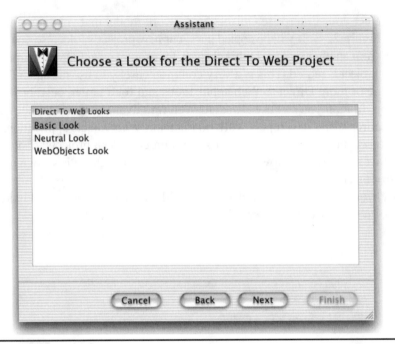

Figure 22-4 Select a look

Figure 22-5 Build and launch the application

Direct to Web Looks

As you are setting up your Direct to Web project, you can choose among three default looks:

▶ Basic

▶ Plain

▶ WebObjects

Basic Look

Figure 22-6 shows the opening page for a Direct to Web application using the Basic look.

Figure 22-6   *Opening window for Basic look*

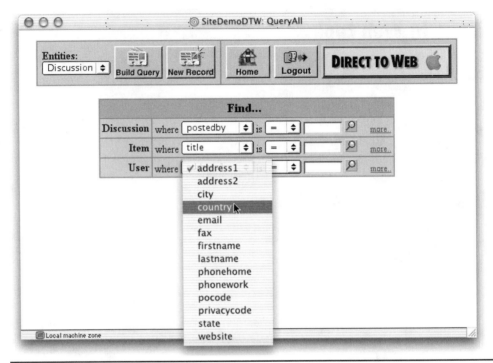

Figure 22-7   *Find page in Basic look*

It allows people to log in with a username and password, but in the default implementation, no processing is done for the username and password. As a result, if you simply click the Login button, you go to the Find page shown in Figure 22-7. (WebObjects refers to this as a *query-all* page.)

The three database tables (Discussion, Item, and User) are picked up from the EOModel. Likewise, the column names (such as those shown in the pop-up button) come from the EOModel. You may want to consider renaming columns from the database in the EOModel so that the names shown here are more meaningful. However, if you are implementing a small application that people will use in conjunction with other applications, beware of renaming fields: users will wonder if Home Phone and phonehome are actually the same field.

Plain Look

The login page for the plain look is shown in Figure 22-8. You will see how you can customize this window, perhaps with a logo or graphic.

The query-all page for the plain look is shown in Figure 22-9.

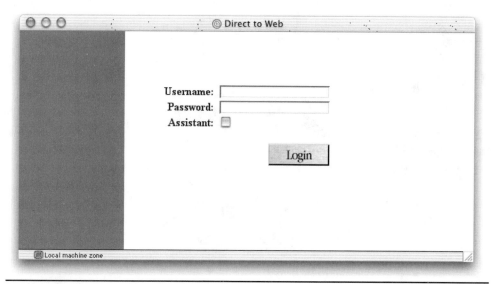

Figure 22-8   *Login window for Plain look*

WebObjects Look

Finally, the WebObjects look login page is shown in Figure 22-10. It includes logos and graphics.

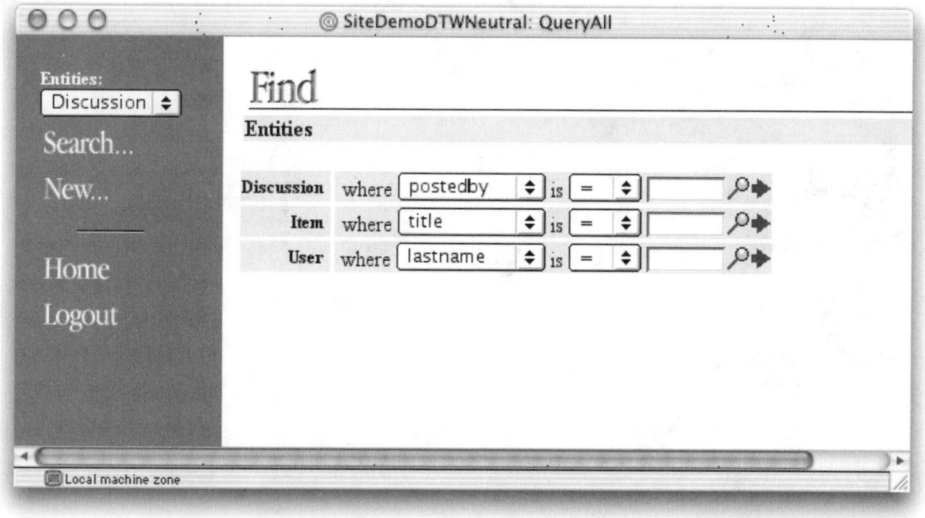

Figure 22-9   *Find page for Plain look*

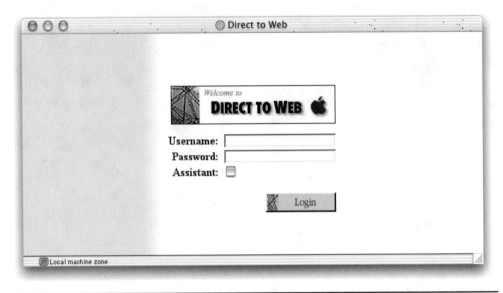

Figure 22-10 *Login page for WebObjects look*

The query-all page for the WebObjects look also contains graphics and the Apple logo, as you can see in Figure 22-11.

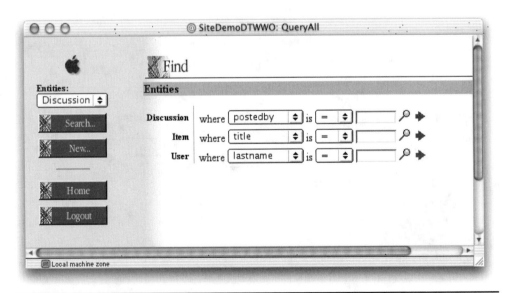

Figure 22-11 *Find page for WebObjects look*

The Build Query button at the top or side of each page lets you open a *query* page in which you can build a more complex query than in the query-all page. The query page is specific to one database table (which you select using the Entities pop-up button). The query page for the Basic look is shown in Figure 22-12.

The New Record button lets you add a record to a database table using an *edit* page. A Basic look edit page is shown in Figure 22-13.

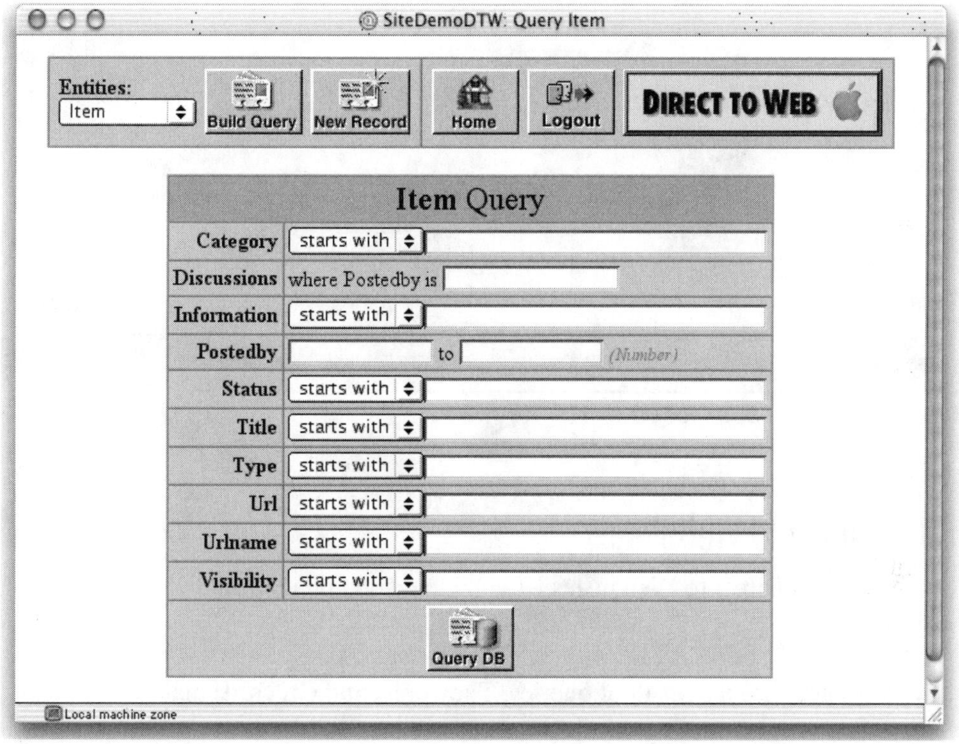

Figure 22-12 *Query page for Basic look*

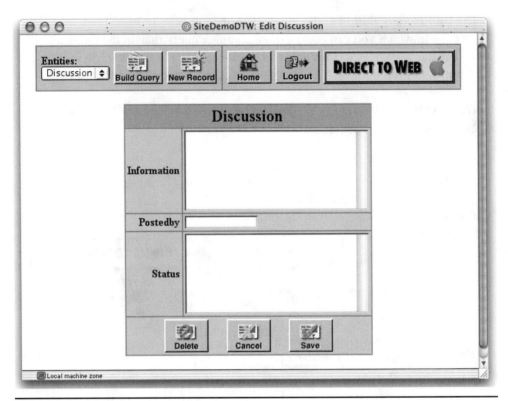

Figure 22-13   *Edit page for Basic look*

Other Direct to Web Pages

Other standard Direct to Web pages let you view and update data, lists of data, and relationships.

▶   *List* pages are the result of queries. They present the records that satisfy the query. They do not have links on them to data records.

▶   A list page that contains hot links to the displayed records is a *select* page.

▶   When you click a link on a record on a select page, you go to an *inspect* page or an *edit* page. An inspect page lets you view (but not change) data; an edit page allows you to modify and save data (as shown in Figure 22-13).

▶ An *edit-relationship* page lets you manage a relationship between two tables. You can add or remove records in accordance with the rules you have set up in EOModeler.

▶ *Confirm* and *error* pages are displayed when appropriate.

Customizing Direct to Web

You can customize your Direct to Web application in two ways:

▶ You can modify the pages using WebObjects Builder and Project Builder. This lets you change their appearance.

▶ You can modify the contents of the pages, adding or deleting columns from database tables, for example.

Using WebObjects Builder and Project Builder

In general, the Direct to Web pages are all built dynamically. As you will see if you look inside the project that is built for you, there are only three components: Main, PageWrapper, and MenuHeader.

Main is the component that presents the login page. If you wish to implement a username/password security system, add it to Main. By the same token, if you wish to remove it, remove those fields from the Main component using WebObjects Builder.

PageWrapper is the basic page into which each of the dynamically built pages is placed at run time. If you wish to change the look of all of the pages (except for the login page), modify PageWrapper. Remember that in modifying it you are modifying the wrapper for all of your Direct to Web pages, so stay out of the center of the page (where the contents will be displayed). If you do modify PageWrapper, remember to test with all of the possible pages that might be generated so that your graphics do not obscure data.

Finally, MenuHeader is the row of buttons at the top or left of each page. You can modify them, too.

Using WebAssistant

Like all of WebObjects, Direct to Web uses Java. You can run WebAssistant on the server to help you customize the content of some of the pages. When you are first creating your project, you build and launch it from Project Builder: your computer is the server as well as the client. You can enable the assistant as shown in Figure 22-14.

As the application is launched, a variety of messages appear in the Project Builder window (you may need to resize it to see them). Figure 22-15 shows a critical message that helps you launch WebAssistant. It begins "DirectToWeb WebAssistant launch line:" and is highlighted in Figure 22-15. (Depending on the width of your window, it may take up more or fewer lines.)

Copy the text between and including "appletviewer" and "openWebAssistant." Paste it into Terminal as shown in Figure 22-16. The contents of this text may vary: most particularly, the port number of localhost (50016 in this example) changes each time you run your project.

Figure 22-14   *Enable WebAssistant to modify pages' contents*

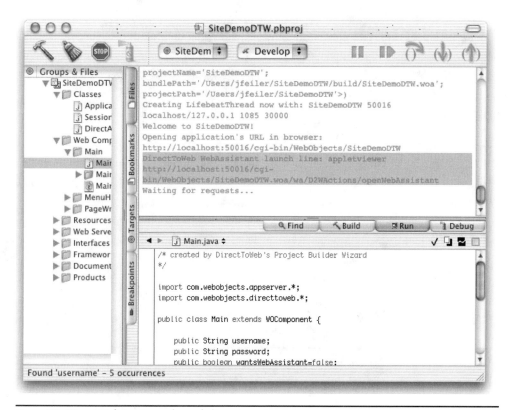

Figure 22-15   *WebAssistant launch line*

Figure 22-16   *Launch WebAssistant*

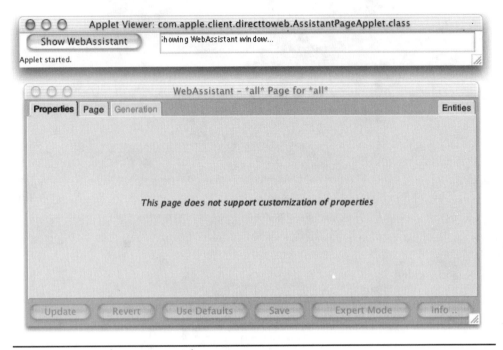

Figure 22-17   *WebAssistant windows*

WebAssistant windows will appear as shown in Figure 22-17. You may find a message such as this one indicating that no customization is possible. Never fear: other pages will let you customize them.

When you navigate to another page, you can either click a Configure button in the MenuHandler section or just bring the WebAssistant window forward: it will be synchronized with the page you are looking at. In Figure 22-18, the WebAssistant window for the default query page in the Discussion table is shown.

The default page allows people to search by any of three columns: information, postedby, and status (shown in the center of the page). Other columns in the EOModel are shown at the left.

If you select one of the columns, you can add it to the displayed set or you can remove it. In Figure 22-19, information was selected and then moved to the nondisplayed set.

At the bottom, buttons let you work with the WebAssistant. Update will update your Web browser's display (although you may have to click the Refresh button or menu command). Save will store your changes permanently for all future users of your application. Expert mode, shown in Figure 22-20, is described at length in the Apple documentation cited at the beginning of this chapter.

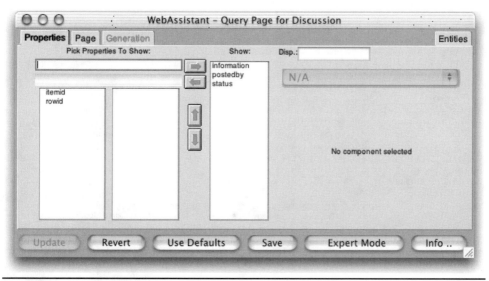

Figure 22-18   *Default query page for Discussion*

Tabs at the upper left of the window let you move through sections of the page. The previous pane controlled the properties. The Page tab lets you adjust the color and set other controls, as you can see in Figure 22-21.

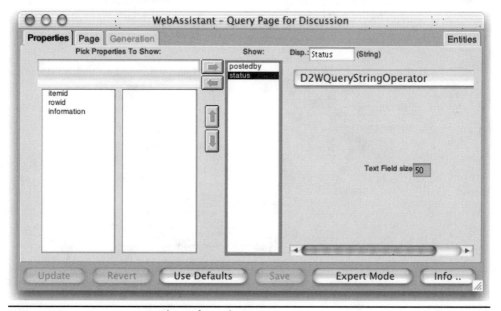

Figure 22-19   *Removing a column from the query*

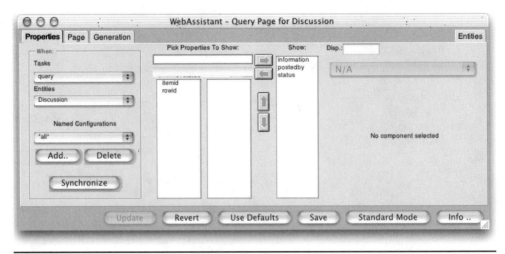

Figure 22-20   *Expert mode for WebAssistant*

The third tab, Generation, is shown in Figure 22-22. It lets you prepare for further customization of your Direct to Web application. The Freeze Component button has the effect of converting your dynamically built page to a WebObjects component, complete with .java file and wrapped .wo file. They are added to your project and you can modify them from there. Generate Template creates a page template (like PageWrapper) that also can be modified. If you have created such a template, you can associate it with an individual page using the pop-up button at the top right of this page.

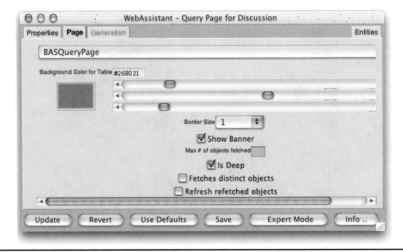

Figure 22-21   *Page settings in WebAssistant*

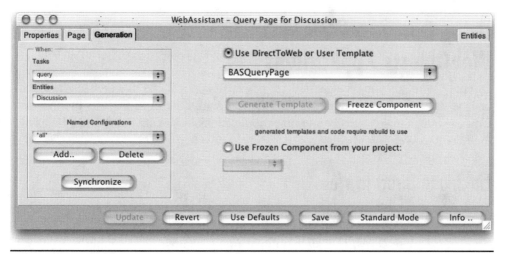

Figure 22-22   *Generations settings in WebAssistant*

By default, the query page with the Basic look uses a template called BASQueryPage. If you created your own query page (using the Generate Template button), you could call it MyQueryPage. It would then be available in the pop-up button.

The settings shown in the previous illustrations are applied in Figure 22-23. Most notably, the background of the data is changed to white, and the information column has been removed from the query.

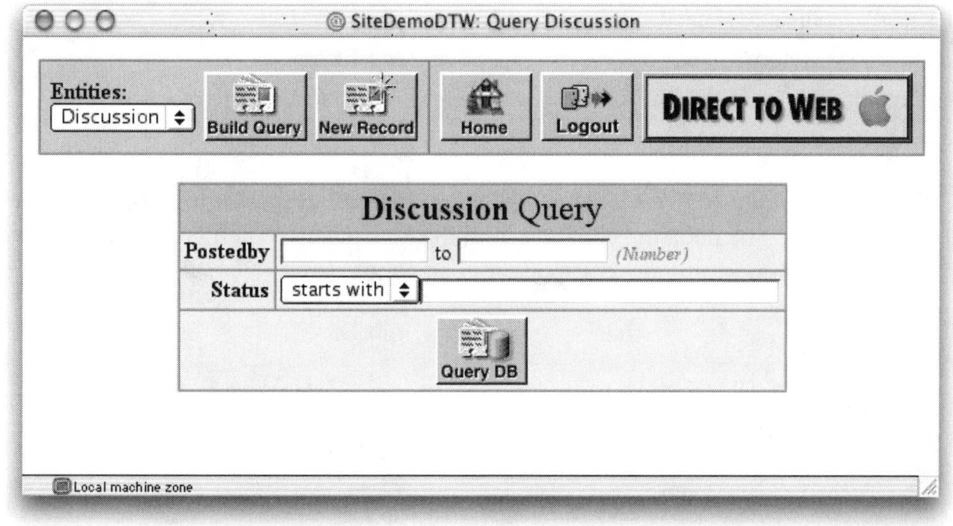

Figure 22-23   *Revised query*

Using Direct to Web in Other WebObjects Applications

Direct to Web lets you create small yet powerful applications that are standard front ends to databases and models you have created with Enterprise Objects Framework. You can integrate them easily into other applications by linking to them and by using the Direct to Web frameworks.

Linking to Direct to Web

In order to create a link to a Direct to Web component, you need to create the component in your standard WebObjects application. Details are provided in *Developing WebObjects Applications with Direct to Web,* but the overall scheme is quite simple.

The action method or other code that generates the component to satisfy the link must create an appropriate interface. These are named to correspond to the names of pages for Direct to Web components described previously. Here are the methods you call and the types of components that they return:

Method	Object Returned
queryPageForEntityNamed	QueryPageInterface
listPageForEntityNamed	ListPageInterface
editPageForEntityNamed	EditPageInterface
inspectPageForEntityNamed	InspectPageInterface
selectPageForEntityNamed	SelectPageInterface
editRelationshipPageForEntityNamed	editRelationshipPageInterface
queryAllPage	QueryAllPageInterface

The methods all take two parameters: the page name and the session. You may need to call additional methods to set data within the new pages. When you are done, you return them as you would any component in an action.

Using the Direct to Web Frameworks

You can also use Direct to Web components inside your standard WebObjects application. You need to add three frameworks to the WebObjects application:

▶ JavaDirectToWeb.framework

▶ JavaDTWGeneration.framework

▶ JavaEOProject.framework

You do this by selecting the Framework group in the Files & Groups pane of Project Builder, and then using Add File from the Project menu. The Add File command will ask you if you want to copy the file into your project and which target you want to add it to—you want to add it to the Application Server target.

Then, use the appropriate Direct to Web components in the WebObjects Builder palette.

CHAPTER
23

Java Client

IN THIS CHAPTER:

What Is a WebObjects Java Client?

Direct to Java Client

Creating a Java Client Project

Writing Java Client Applications

Running a Java Client

Ithe previous chapter, you saw how to use Direct to Web to quickly create front ends for databases using WebObjects and Enterprise Objects Framework. This chapter focuses on an even more exciting aspect of WebObjects: Java Client and Direct to Java Client. With them, you can create Java clients that interact with your WebObjects server application without going through a Web browser. This is a true client/server architecture, and it provides much greater flexibility for you. That flexibility comes about not just in the portability of your Java clients (which can run on any Java-enabled computer) but also in what you can do inside them with your own code.

NOTE

The Apple document Developing WebObjects Applications with Direct to Java Client *is available in PDF format on the http://developer.apple.com site. It provides substantial additional information and guidance on using Direct to Web, including step-by-step tutorials.*

What Is a WebObjects Java Client?

Figure 23-1 shows a Java Client application in action. It uses the same SiteDemo Enterprise Objects Framework model that you have seen elsewhere in this book, and it accesses

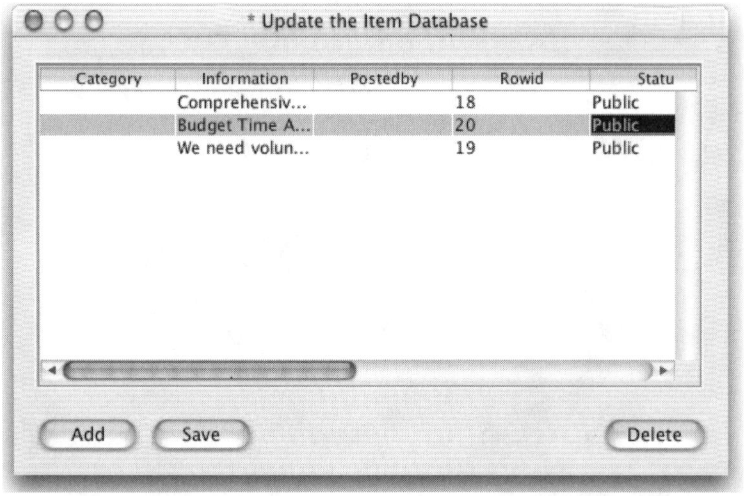

Category	Information	Postedby	Rowid	Statu
	Comprehensiv...		18	Public
	Budget Time A...		20	Public
	We need volun...		19	Public

* Update the Item Database

Add   Save   Delete

Figure 23-1   *Adding a record in Direct to Java Client*

the OpenBase SiteDemo database that is associated with that model. In Figure 23-1, you can see several records in that database. The Add button has been clicked and a new record (number 20) has been added in this figure. It is unsaved (you can tell that because there is an asterisk to the left of the window title indicating unsaved changes).

If you use OpenBaseManager to check the database, you will be able to see that no such record exists. However, clicking the Save button in this window and clicking the Refresh button in the OpenBaseManager window shows you the combination seen in Figure 23-2: the record has been added to the database. Note the Java Client WebObjects window in front of the OpenBaseManager window. Also, the asterisk in the window title is gone, since there are now no unsaved changes.

Similarly, when you delete a record as shown in Figure 23-3, it is deleted from the Java Client view.

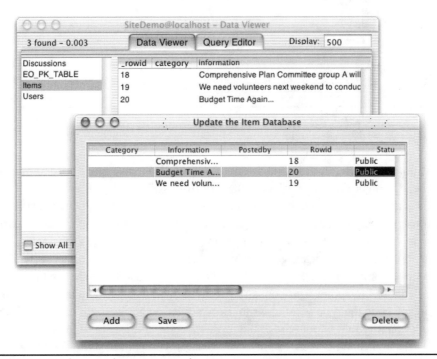

Figure 23-2 *Looking at the new record in OpenBaseManager*

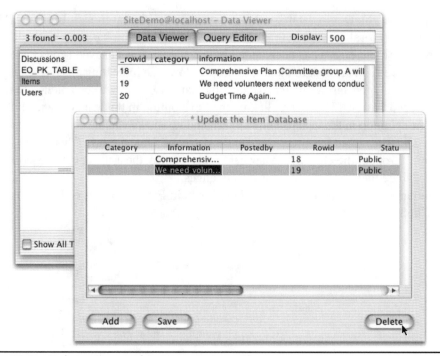

Figure 23-3   *Deleting a record in Direct to Java Client*

It is not deleted from the database until you click Save. Figure 23-4 shows the refreshed OpenBaseManager display that confirms this.

This is all as it should be, but you may not notice the most important part of these four illustrations: you are not looking at a Web browser window. You are looking at a Java applet running on its own inside a Java Virtual Machine (JVM).

The applet is communicating with a WebObjects application on a server (which can be the same computer), but it is not using the protocols shown in the first part of this book. Because the applet is not constrained in the ways that a Web browser is, it can contain any code that you want to write. Browser-based applications can never execute any functionality that is not part of the browser being used. (Plug-in components and other extensions can be used, but in general cases, you cannot write code that will be executed on an ad hoc basis and rely on its being executed by all users and all browsers.)

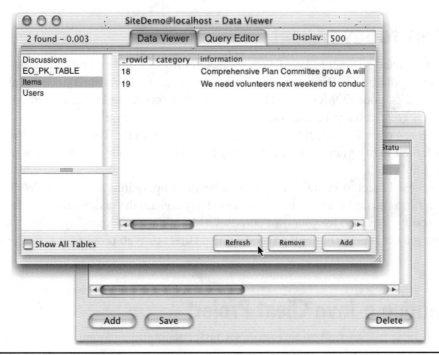

Figure 23-4   *Looking at the OpenBaseManager with deleted record gone*

Java clients, on the other hand, are nothing but Java code, and you can write any code that you want in them. They provide access to any such functionality you want; furthermore, they run on any Java-enabled platform. If you are pushing browsers to their limits or are using features that are not available in all versions of all browsers, using a Java client bypasses all of that confusion: your code is your applet, and that is the end of that.

In addition to providing portability and protecting yourself from getting involved in browser wars, Java applets also provide entry into platform-specific functionality. Although the portability of Java is one of its great features, it is also true that on some platforms (notably Mac OS X), almost the entire range of operating system features and interfaces is available to Java applets. Thus, you can use Java to write Mac OS X–specific code that integrates your database, the Enterprise Objects Framework model, the WebObjects application, and Mac OS X in a very powerful way.

Direct to Java Client

You can create a Direct to Java Client project in Project Builder in much the same way in which you did for Direct to Web: in fact, you answer the same questions about frameworks, your EOModel, and the database that you did in Direct to Web. A Java Client is created for you, and you can use it as is in many cases.

You can open the Direct to Java Client Assistant from the Tools menu in Project Builder to modify your Java Client. It functions similarly to the assistant you used in Direct to Web.

Because Direct to Java Client is so similar in its operations to Direct to Web, this chapter focuses on Java Clients themselves. They contain the underlying code that you can modify or expand for your own purposes. (Modifying and expanding a Direct to Java Client project is much easier than modifying a Direct to Web project for many people.)

Creating a Java Client Project

You start in Project Builder by creating a Java Client project in much the same way in which you create any other project. You name it, select the frameworks to include (the default set is just fine), and select an EOModel on which to base your Direct to Java Client. As with Direct to Web, your EOModel is copied into your new project.

A new question appears as shown in Figure 23-5: you must provide a class and package name for your controller. This is a controller in the sense of model-view-controller architecture (your EOModel is the model, and your window is the view). Your Java Client may ultimately have many classes and packages, but this is the first one, and it is created for you by the assistant. The default name is based on your project name, and it is usually good for most purposes. (The only exception may be when the name is too long.)

You next select a template for your Java Client, as shown in Figure 23-6.

In the most general case, you want the EOF Application Skeleton. For a simple interface to a single database table, select Single Table; and for an interface to a related set of tables, select Master Detail.

The assistant creates the appropriate files in your new project. In addition to files that you have seen before, you will now find your interface controller files in the Interfaces group, as shown in Figure 23-7.

Figure 23-5 *Naming an interface controller class and package*

Figure 23-6 *Selecting a template*

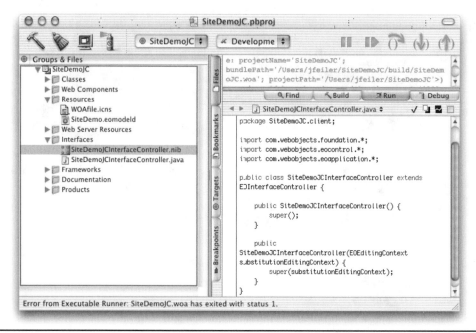

Figure 23-7   *Interface controller files in Java Client*

Writing Java Client Applications

The controller .nib file contains the information that WebObjects uses to create your interface. In it are the bindings between interface elements, the code in your controller .java file, and your EOModel. Double-clicking a .nib file opens Interface Builder, the tool you use to design the interface and create these connections.

If you have used Direct to Java Client, these connections (and the interface) have been created for you. You can examine them in Interface Builder, and you can modify them as well as create new ones.

NOTE

The documentation for Interface Builder, Apple's Creating a Java Client WebObjects Application *(available in PDF from http://developer.apple.com), and Jesse Feiler's book,* Mac OS X Developer's Guide, *all provide extensive help with using Interface Builder. This section summarizes its capabilities for you.*

If you open a .nib file for a Direct to Java Client application, you will see a window with data fields in it. You will also see a window with icons representing the various objects the .nib file deals with. In Figure 23-8, these two windows are at the left, with the data field–populated window at the top.

At the right of the illustration is the Inspector window. You open it from the Interface Builder Tools menu, and it reflects values for whatever object you have selected. In this case, it shows the connections for the highlighted button (Fetch). You will see shortly how to create such connections; for now, it is sufficient to know that you can view them, and that a connection such as this causes a method called `fetch` in a target object to be executed. (If you experiment and do not see this sort of display, note that the two pop-up buttons at the top of the Inspector window must be set to Connections and Outlets.)

Clicking a data field as shown in Figure 23-9 reveals a different type of connection. Here, you can see a visual connection from the text field to the EOModel object

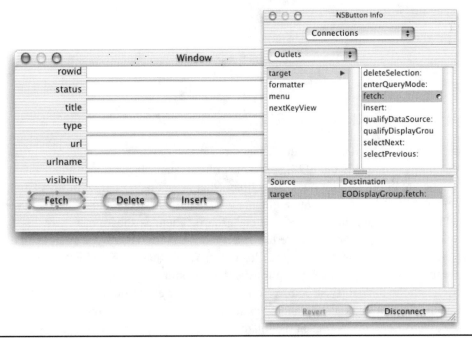

Figure 23-8   *Using Interface Builder*

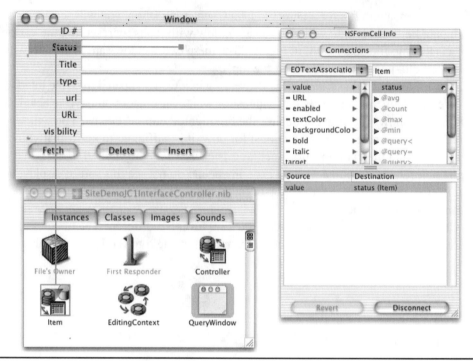

Figure 23-9 *A connection between a data entry field and an EOModel database column*

representing the Item table. In the Inspector window, you can see the nature of this connection: its value is the EOModel table column status.

If you are building your own Java Client (that is, not using Direct to Java Client), you can easily build these input elements yourself. First, open your EOModel (you can double-click the file in the Resources group). Then, as shown in Figure 23-10, drag the element you are interested in to a window. Automatically, a complex data structure will appear as shown in the illustration. (Note that the figure is a composite: you must release the mouse button for the data structure to appear.)

Beneath the data entry structure, you can add a variety of buttons. You do so by dragging them from a palette window as shown in Figure 23-11. You can double-click them to rename them (by default their name is Button). As you move interface elements around, guidelines will appear as you can see here: they help to create well-designed interfaces.

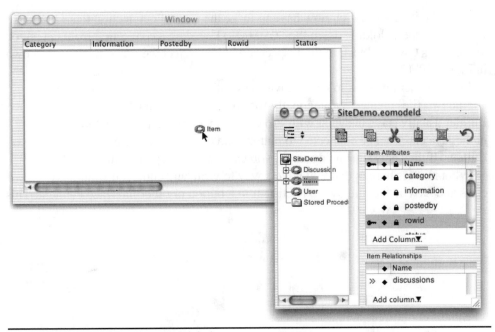

Figure 23-10   *Adding an EOModel element to a view*

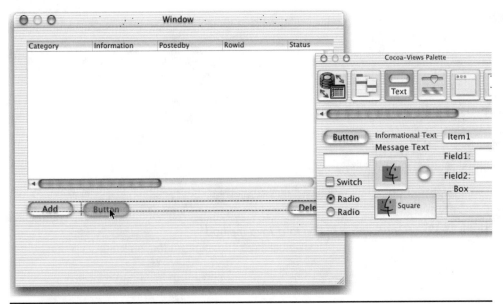

Figure 23-11   *Adding a button to a view*

To make it all work, you now have to forge the kind of connection that Direct to Java Client does. Holding down the COMMAND key, drag a connection from the button to the File's Owner object; in the Inspector window, select the `save` method as shown in Figure 23-12.

File's Owner turns out to be the Java class with the same name as the .nib file: these are the two files created automatically for you in a new Java Client project. Interface Builder usually stays in synch with Project Builder, and so methods that you create in the Java class can be connected to buttons and other interface elements in Interface Builder. If they are not synchronized, you can manually update Interface Builder.

What matters here is that you have a way to write any code you want in your Java class and have it execute by connecting it to a button or other interface element. This

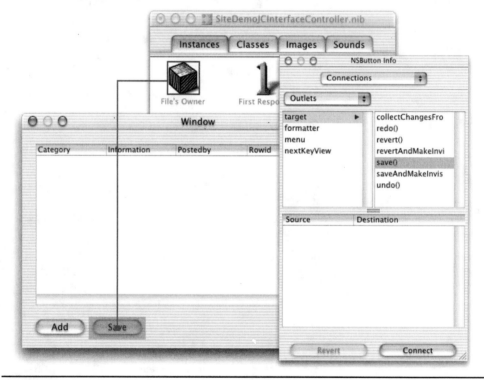

Figure 23-12   *Connecting a button to a Java method*

is the heart of your extensions to the basic Java class. WebObjects, Project Builder, and Interface Builder take care of the database manipulation; you do everything else. This is the hook that you use for the extensions.

While the Save button needs to be connected to the save method in your Java class (actually in an ancestor of it that WebObjects has created), other controls need to be connected directly to the EOModel and its frameworks' functionality. Figure 23-13 shows the connection from the Add button to the Item element of the EOModel: addition and deletion of records is handled there, but saving (that is, committing the change and freezing the edit context) is done by the Java class.

You can use the Inspector window to modify many properties of interface elements: connections are among the most complex. Among the most simple is naming a window: select the window in Interface Builder, and then set its attributes as shown in Figure 23-14.

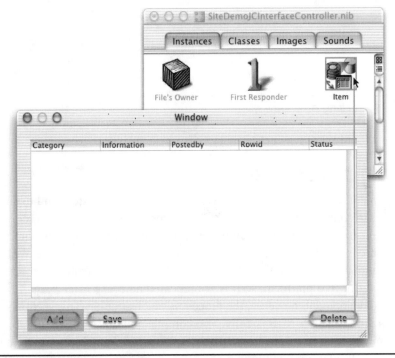

Figure 23-13   *Connecting a button to an EOModel entity*

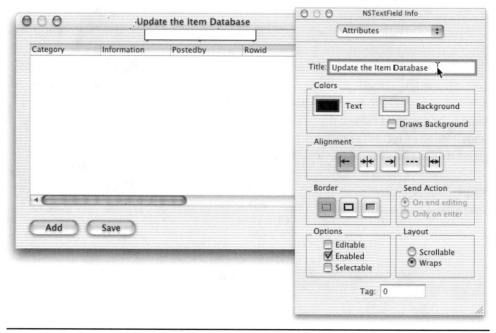

Figure 23-14   *Setting a window title*

Running a Java Client

WebObjects Java Client applications run on personal computers and use Internet connections to communicate with a WebObjects application running on a server (usually a different computer). The WebObjects application in turn accesses databases and other resources. Deploying Java Client applications is covered in the WebObjects documentation that is distributed with the product. It differs from version to version and from platform to platform, so it is not repeated here.

During development, however, the process is much simpler. This section shows you how to do it on Mac OS X. Basically, you compile and build your WebObjects Java Client application as usual in Project Builder. You then launch the server application from Project Builder, and you launch the Java Client application from Terminal.

Do Not Launch a Web Browser

It is important that the Java Client not be launched within a Web browser. In order to prevent this from happening, set the option -WOAutoOpenInBrowser to NO. You do this using the Targets tab in the Project Builder window. Select your target (the larger one at the top that contains the Application Server and Web Server targets). Click the Executables tab and, within that pane, the Arguments tab. Type in the line

```
-WOAutoOpenInBrowser NO
```

Make certain that it is checked to be used at the right. (You can leave such launch arguments in your project and enable and disable them with checkmarks.)

At this point, when you launch your WebObjects application from Project Builder it will be launched, but no Web browser will open. (You can test this to make certain.)

Run the Java Client Application from Terminal

Inside the WebObjects application (inside the .woa wrapped file bundle), you will find the launch script you need. In order to open the .woa package to see its contents, press the CONTROL key to bring up a contextual menu for the package as shown in Figure 23-15.

Show Package Contents opens the window shown in Figure 23-16. Note that you cannot navigate into a package in any other way: the Finder will note open packages. However, once you have opened a package in this manner, its windows behave just like normal Finder windows (which they are).

Figure 23-15   *Opening a package*

Figure 23-16 *Viewing the package contents*

Inside the package, you will find the Java Client application inside one of the appropriate folders—Windows, Unix, or MacOS. It will have your project name followed by _Client.

Launch Terminal, and drag the appropriate client into the command line as shown in Figure 23-17. This figure is a composite: you drag the file into Terminal and release the mouse button; its name and full path then appear as shown in the figure.

If you are a glutton for punishment, you can simply type the entire path and name of the Java Client application. Add a space to the command line, and then add the appropriate URL. It is provided for you when you launch your WebObjects application in Project Builder. (It is highlighted in Figure 23-18.) You will find two URLs in the startup messages: one is for Web server connections, and the other is for direct connections. You want the direct connection URL, which is the second one.

Copy this URL and paste it into the command line following the name and path of your Java Client application (remember to leave a space between the two). Finally, press RETURN to execute the command and launch your Java Client application.

There are a number of other ways of launching your Java Client application; they are described in the WebObjects documentation.

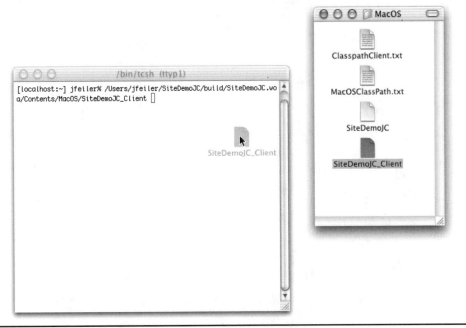

Figure 23-17   *Drag the client name and path to Terminal*

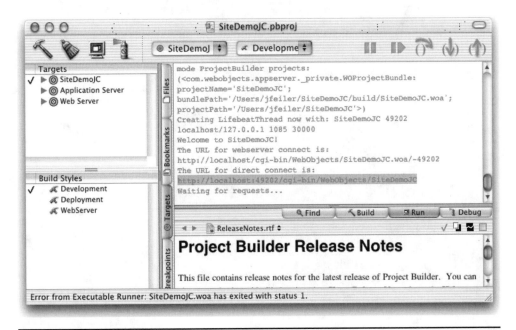

Figure 23-18   *Finding the direct connect URL*

Reusable Components in WebObjects

IN THIS CHAPTER:

One of the primary purposes of using object-oriented programming techniques is to be able to reuse your code. Palettes in WebObjects Builder provide a powerful way for you to reuse code ranging from HTML snippets all the way to full-fledged WebObjects components. This chapter provides an introduction to the palette, how to use it, the default palettes, and how to create your own palette objects. It concludes by showing you how to create reusable WebObjects components.

Using the Palette

To begin, open the Palettes window by choosing Palette from the Windows menu in WebObjects Builder. Across the top of the window is a toolbar showing the palettes that are installed, as you can see in Figure 24-1.

The palettes in your installation may differ from those shown here, but these are the basic WebObjects palettes. Each one is described briefly, giving you a feel not only for what it can do but also for the types of things that you can accomplish in your own palettes.

In order to use a palette item, you drag it into your WebObjects Builder window. Once it is there, you select it, bind to it, and otherwise use it like any other WebObjects entity.

Sometimes, when you drag an object into your window, you will see a message such as the one in Figure 24-2.

Figure 24-1   *The palette*

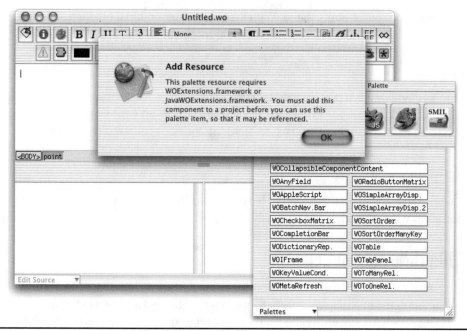

Figure 24-2   *WebObjects Builder complains about a missing framework*

If you get such an error, go back to Project Builder and add the framework using the Add Files command in the Project menu.

WOExtensions Palette

This palette (shown previously in Figure 24-1) lets you insert any of the objects from the WOExtensions framework. These are utility objects that provide you with extraordinarily powerful custom-built objects that handle many routine Web tasks. Most of the commonly used ones are described here.

WOAnyField

This object lets you provide an interface to data retrieved in a display group with almost no effort. In its general form, it consists of the implementation for a user interface to specify the data to be shown. You specify a `keyList`, which is a list of the attributes on which a user can select from the display group, you identify the key group, you provide a binding for `key`, which is the current iteration of the display group, and you provide the source entity name. With these and other optional bindings, WebObjects displays an interface that you can incorporate into a page. Its format is

```
where key is = <value>
```

In this case, `key` is a pop-up menu displaying the items you provide in the `keyList` (name, address, phone, for example), and = is also a pop-up item from the relationships defined by WOAnyField. The `value` field, of course, is entered by the user.

WOAppleScript

As with a Java applet, you specify the height and width of this element and the script that is to be run when it is clicked. Obviously, this is available only on Macintosh platforms.

WOBatchNavigationBar

For example, the WOBatchNavigationBar is an entity that lets users manipulate a list of database items in a display group. It handles navigating from one batch to another; it provides users with the ability to specify the number of items in a batch, and it shows the total number of items in the display group (as a result of a database fetch).

You simply drag WOBatchNavigationBar into your component and connect the necessary bindings. The minimum bindings are the display group itself, but you should add the title of the objects being shown (so that page will display "8 chairs" or "8 tubes" as appropriate). You can also set text styles and colors for that text.

WOCheckboxMatrix, WORadioButtonMatrix, and WOTable

Using WebObjects Builder, you insert HTML code (and often WOString objects) to which you bind properties of the objects in an array that is bound to this component. In this way, you can display each object's data. WOCheckboxMatrix adds a checkbox to each object in addition to the strings or links that you specify; WORadioButtonMatrix adds a radio button.

This is a very convenient way to produce an interface to a variable-length number of objects that is returned from a fetch statement.

WOCollapsibleComponentContent

This component provides the entire interface handling for content that can be displayed in a short summary or in a fuller form. Clicking an interface element that is part of the component (often a disclosure triangle) expands or contracts the data.

WOCompletionBar

Also useful but on a much smaller scale is the WOCompletionBar, which displays a progress or completion bar letting users know how an operation is proceeding. You must set a current value, but you can also (optionally) set colors, formats, a minimum and a maximum, and so forth.

Because the source code to the WOExtensions objects is available as part of WebObjects, these objects are not only a valuable set of tools for quickly building Web pages, but they also represent an excellent WebObjects tutorial. It is definitely worth an hour or two to experiment with each of the items in the WOExtensions palette so that you will get a sense of the types of code you will not have to write.

WODictionaryRepetition

This component loops through each item in a dictionary of key/value pairs and executes the HTML you provide in it. As with the WOCheckboxMatrix element, you can use this to display the data for a variable length dictionary.

Remember that in WebObjects, dictionaries are often used for relatively small amounts of data (including the contents of Java class objects built on your Enterprise Objects Framework model). Thus, you have a very quick way of displaying an object's content.

WOMetaRefresh

After a number of seconds (which you specify) the current page is automatically refreshed with a page that you specify and an action is invoked (also specified). This allows you to implement redirection for pages that have moved on your site; it also allows you to have constantly refreshing pages for news updates and the like.

WOSimpleArrayDisplay and WOSimpleArrayDisplay2

These components display the objects in an array in a single column list. You can specify the number of items to display in the list; if the array is larger than that number, a More link is provided (WOSimpleArrayDisplay) or an image is used to invite the user to look at other items (WOSimpleArrayDisplay2).

In WOSimpleArrayDisplay2, you can specify a link to be applied to each item in the list. The link contains the same action for each item in the list; in your action code, you must look at the item object that is returned to see which one was clicked.

WOSortOrder and WOSortOrderManyKey

Designed for use with a display group, this component provides an image that indicates how the data in the display group is sorted (ascending, descending, or not at all). The image is hot, and clicking it sorts the display group's data.

In the case of WOSortOrderManyKey, a pop-up menu is displayed next to the sort image. It contains the items in the `keyList` binding that you provide; in this way, users can select which of several keys the display group is sorted on.

WOTabPanel

You provide an array of objects to this component, and you specify a field in each object to be used as a tab identifier. When the user clicks a tab, the object corresponding to that element in the array is displayed. Note that this is a convenient way to display a small or variable number of objects; about six should be the maximum.

Premade Elements Palette

Premade elements are mostly HTML elements that you can use in your application. They are shown in Figure 24-3.

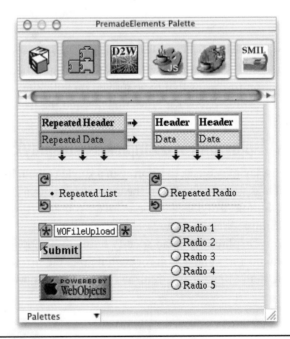

Figure 24-3   *Premade elements provide HTML shortcuts*

They range from the most basic of HTML elements (a "Powered by WebObjects image" that contains a link to WebObjects) to clusters of radio buttons, a set of form elements that let you upload a file, and a repeated list with each item bulleted.

These elements are useful in their own right, but they also demonstrate the sorts of things that you can do with palettes. For example, if you are developing applications for others, you may be able to add your own logo and link to some of the pages. Premade elements of your own making are also useful for standardizing graphical elements such as navigation bars on all the pages of a site.

Direct to Web Palette

The Direct to Web palette is shown next in Figure 24-4.

You will recognize these interface elements from Chapter 22. The default Direct to Web implementation that is built for you by Project Builder uses them in its own pages. As you expand a Direct to Web application to make it more powerful, you may need to add these buttons to the new pages that you create. Note that these elements contain not only the necessary graphics but also the bindings for you to link to your new components. (If you are in doubt about how to connect them, look at the bindings that Project Builder has created in the default component in your project.)

Figure 24-4   *Use the Direct to Web palette to extend Direct to Web applications*

JavaScript Palette

JavaScript snippets are shown in the JavaScript palette, as you can see in Figure 24-5.

JavaScript is very useful in catching data entry errors at the earliest possible moment. Because the JavaScript runs on the user's computer, there is no need to send a message back to WebObjects to perform validation or to notify the user of something that inherently is wrong (too many/few digits in a field, a blank, and the like).

Relying on JavaScript for your editing is not a good idea, though, since users may turn it off in their browsers. It is better to add your JavaScript edits using these palette objects but then to repeat the edits in your WebObjects application. (In fact, sometimes

Figure 24-5   *JavaScript palette provides interaction on the user's computer*

edits are done yet a third time when the database and/or Enterprise Objects Framework model also inspects the data.)

JavaClient Palette

You can add a Java applet to your interface using the JavaClient palette shown in Figure 24-6.

You must specify the applet's width and height on the HTML page as well as the applet class name.

Figure 24-6 *Use the JavaClient palette to add an applet*

WOSMIL Palette

Finally, the WOSMIL palette provides a range of objects to help you manage SMIL as shown in Figure 24-7.

SMIL is an acronym for Synchronized Multimedia Integration Language, a standard of the World Wide Web Consortium. (Full documentation is available at their site, http://www.w3.org/TR/REC-smil.)

Based on XML, SMIL lets you create sequences on a Web page. In a common use, you can specify a region (that is, a height and a width) to use for your media. Using that region, you can then play a sequence such as the following. Before showing the first image, you place an anchor on the region in order to allow users to click it no matter what is playing. The declaration of the region and the anchor are shown here, along with the start of the sequence element:

```
<layout>
  <region id="regiontoplay " width="160" height="120" />
</layout>
<seq>
  <a href="http://www.apple.com" show="new">
```

Next, you can display an image in that region for a duration of five seconds (note the boldfaced code). Here is that code:

```
  <img src="http://animage.jpg" dur="5s" region="regiontoplay "/>
```

Now, you can play a movie from start to finish in the same region.

```
  <video src="rtsp://amovie.mov" region=" regiontoplay " />
```

You can then return to the image and show it without a duration attribute; that is, until the user moves on to another page.

```
  <img src="http://animage.jpg" region="regiontoplay "/>
</seq>
```

As you can see, SMIL is an invaluable tool in presenting rich media, and the WOSMIL palette speeds up development.

Figure 24-7   *The WOSMIL palette*

Creating a New Palette

As you can see, palette objects are very useful not only for speeding up development but also for standardizing interface elements on a given project. You, too, can create palette objects.

You start by creating a new palette from the window at the bottom of the Palettes window. Next, you create the interface elements just as you normally would in WebObjects Builder. When you are satisfied with them, you drag them into the Palette window. You can then rename them and save them as shown in Figure 24-8.

The newly created palette object consists of all of the interface elements that you have selected and dragged into the palette. Thus, if you select a heading, some boilerplate text, and a graphic, all of them can be dragged into a reusable palette object such as Corp Logo shown in this figure.

In many cases, you do not start out to create a palette object. Rather, after having completed a page, you realize that several parts of it might be useful in the future. In that case, you drag them into the palette to create a new object.

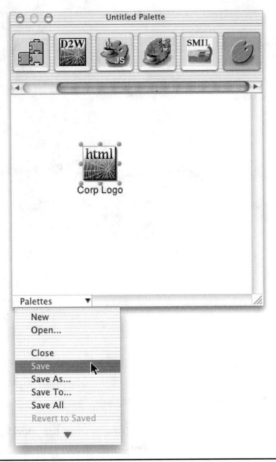

Figure 24-8   *Create new palette objects*

Creating Reusable WebObjects Component Objects

You can also save your entire WebObjects component as a reusable object. Then, it can be included in other components or used on its own elsewhere in your application. (The Toolbar component in the ThinkMovies WebObjects examples demonstrates this.) A reusable component consists of the entire WebObjects component, so your Java code goes along with the interface code. This applies only within the current project; to share objects across projects, you need to use a framework, as described in the next chapter.

Start to create a reusable component object by selecting it (that is, not any of its interface elements such as buttons or WebObjects objects) and opening the Inspector window. Select either Partial document or Full document as shown in Figure 24-9.

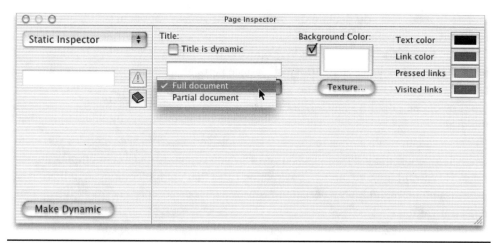

Figure 24-9 *Make your component a partial or full document*

If you will be reusing your component in its entirety and on its own, you should make it a full document. In most cases, however, it will be used like a toolbar or other constituent part of a Web page; those reusable components should be partial documents.

The API button lets you set the interface for your component. It is shown in Figure 24-10.

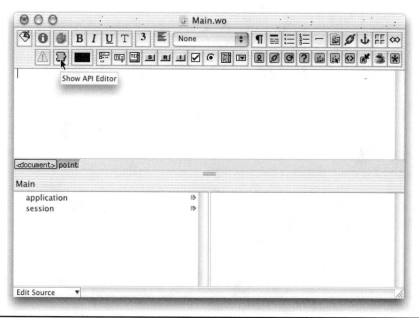

Figure 24-10 *Open the API editor*

The first tab lets you declare the bindings that your component will have when it is reused. It is shown in Figure 24-11.

If you have added keys to it in WebObjects Builder (or if you have declared them in your Java code), you can add them all at once here. You can also create new bindings by using the + and – symbols at the top of the menu bar. As you can see, you can specify the type of each binding and whether it is required as well as whether it can be set by the user.

The Validation tab, shown in Figure 24-12, lets you specify whatever rules you want to implement for the binding. As you can see, you can construct very complex editing rules. Be careful, though, about constructing rules that are too complicated: there is no way around them, and whoever attempts to reuse your component may give up if it does not validate.

Finally, Figure 24-13 shows the Display tab. Here is where you can document your reusable component. You can also provide it with a graphic image that appears as people use it in WebObjects Builder. Obviously, this is preferable to displaying a generic WebObjects image.

The next chapter shows you how to reuse objects with frameworks as well as how to reuse databases and Enterprise Objects Framework models.

Figure 24-11   *Specify bindings*

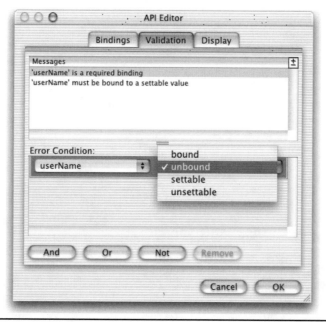

Figure 24-12   *Construct validation rules*

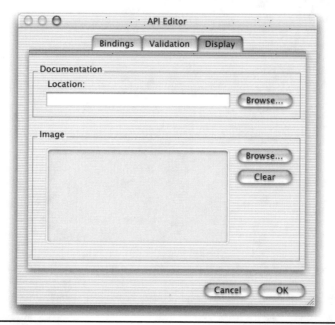

Figure 24-13   *Display rules*

CHAPTER 25

Reusable Databases and Frameworks in OpenBase and WebObjects

IN THIS CHAPTER:

Frameworks in WebObjects

Reusing Databases

Reusing Models

Reuse Considerations

C ode reuse as discussed in the last chapter focused on palette objects and on reusable components within a project. This chapter focuses on larger reusable entities: frameworks that can contain a variety of classes and that can be reused in various projects and databases and data models themselves.

The chapter starts by describing WebObjects frameworks; it then shows you how to implement a framework (that is, how to create one), and then you will see how to use it in your WebObjects applications. Frameworks represent the largest reusable chunks of WebObjects code. You can also reuse your databases and reuse your Enterprise Objects Framework models. There is no reason to start each project from scratch.

Frameworks in WebObjects

WebObjects frameworks contain anything a standard WebObjects application can contain. That means they can contain classes, resources, Web components, and the like. As with reusable palette objects, there are four primary reasons for using frameworks:

▶ You can avoid reinventing the wheel, rewriting common code that you use over and over.

▶ You can enforce standardization for code that is reused, even if it is reused only once or twice.

▶ You can distribute building blocks for applications that do not reveal their source code.

▶ Because frameworks are self-contained, on large projects different developers can work on different frameworks. The integration of frameworks (rather than of individual Web components or classes) may be easier than integrating the smaller units.

A framework can be a collection of unrelated classes and Web components, but frameworks work best when they are clearly targeted and designed for individual purposes. In the real world, frameworks often grow out of applications. As an application is being designed or implemented, sometimes a section of it can take shape as reusable code: other people on the project may need it, or it may become clear that the potential framework has opportunities for reuse in other environments. In other cases, a new project suddenly makes clear that a chunk of a prior project could be turned into a framework and thereby reused.

Implementing a Framework

Frameworks are implemented in Project Builder. From the File menu, choose New Project and then select WebObjects Framework rather than WebObjects Application. The shell of the framework will be created for you, and the correct installation file path will be set.

Creating and Programming a Framework

You program a framework just as you would any other WebObjects application. It does not contain a Main method, but other than that, it can contain components (including WebObjects Builder interface elements), Java classes, resources, and anything else that a WebObjects application can contain. You can create multiple frameworks as you see fit. One approach is to create one set of frameworks that contain only Java classes; such frameworks can be implemented by Java programmers who understand your application's needs; they frequently know very little about WebObjects. Other frameworks can be implemented with WebObjects code and with components built with WebObjects Builder and implemented with custom Java classes.

You do not want to create individual frameworks for individual classes, but it is also the case that creating complex frameworks may make their reuse difficult. Try to strike a balance so that the level of abstraction in the framework makes it easy to reuse.

Note that if you are converting a project or part of a project into a framework, it is generally easiest to create a new project as a WebObjects framework and then to copy the appropriate classes, Web components, resources, and the like from the existing application project into the framework project.

Using Frameworks to Share Database Models

Since a framework can contain resources, it can contain an Enterprise Objects Framework model. You can construct a framework that contains a model as well as the Web components to allow people to enter, browse, search, or delete data from the underlying database. Everything you would put into a stand-alone WebObjects application can be provided, including security. Thus, you can package the entire database part of a project and provide it for reuse by people who are unfamiliar with the database, and with the programming that supports it.

In such a case, the framework is a major constituent of the WebObjects applications that are derived from it. In other cases, the framework is a relatively small reusable piece of utility code.

Frameworks Within Applications

You can use frameworks to share anything from a navigation banner across pages in your WebObjects application to business logic. In fact, these are two of the most common uses of frameworks. By using frameworks for navigational tools, common graphics, and business logic, you can ensure that changes to any of those automatically appear in the next recompilation of code by anyone working on any phase of the project.

Using a Framework

In order to use a framework, you add it to the project using Add Framework from the Project menu. (Do not add the framework using the Add Files command.) You can locate the framework to be added in the dialog that follows.

Frameworks are normally installed in a common directory on your computer. The framework in your project needs to be accessible when your project is built, but it does not have to be distributed separately with your deployed application.

In the examples shipped with WebObjects, you can see frameworks in use. If you look inside the Frameworks folder that is located within the examples folder, you will see frameworks such as JavaBusinessLogic (used in the examples) as well as frameworks that support a number of the palette items. You can open the framework projects to see the underlying WebObjects code.

When you drag a palette item into your application in WebObjects Builder, if it requires a framework, you will be notified of that fact. You must add the framework to your project in order to use the palette item.

Example Frameworks in WebObjects

The WebObjects examples include a folder named Frameworks that contains a variety of frameworks that you can use not only as examples but also in your projects. In addition to the frameworks supporting dynamic elements that were discussed in the preceding chapter, these frameworks are normally installed.

WOComponentElements

This framework implements a variety of interface elements using generic and default routines. You can use the objects in this framework yourself, and you can also refer to the code to see how it is written. The objects in this framework include radio buttons, checkboxes, forms, links, and other basic HTML entities. They also include more complex interface elements that extend HTML, such as nested lists.

WOComponentExamples

This framework contains programming objects for the most part. Implementations of objects to handle switches and case statements are included along with objects to handle lists and nested lists that can be sorted and ordered.

WOSessionStoreExample

This framework implements disk-based persistent storage for WebObjects sessions. It includes garbage collection for sessions that are deemed to have been abandoned. It provides a good reference for how WebObjects session management works.

Reusing Databases

Frameworks let you reuse your work in a very structured, object-oriented manner. You can also reuse your databases, thereby saving yourself work. Reusing databases can be done in a variety of ways, including duplication and partitioning. In addition, there are circumstances in which reusing the data in the database is not only practical but useful.

Duplicating Databases

The very simplest way to duplicate a database is to copy it and use it for another project in which it is relevant. Name and address databases, for example, proliferate in any organization and in any developer's professional life. Creating a new database schema for each project usually guarantees that while the data and structure are the same, field and even table names will vary. These variations can make reuse of derivative works (such as an Enterprise Objects Framework model) problematic.

It can be worth the slight additional analysis effort to look at various needs and construct a generic database or database table to handle certain recurring types of data. The User database table in the SiteDemo example, for instance, contains a variety of columns that are not necessarily needed for SiteDemo, but that can be useful in other environments.

Partitions

You can partition database tables so that the same actual database table is shared among a number of applications. In the case of a name and address table, for instance, a field such as Department or Division can be used to isolate sections of the database table from one another. When retrieving or inserting data, such keys keep otherwise duplicate records from colliding with one another.

If you partition a database table, you obviously enforce the same schema design on all users of that table. This certainly can reduce maintenance efforts; however, it can increase the difficulty of making necessary modifications, since a change to the schema for one partition must be made in all partitions.

Furthermore, by putting apparently disparate data stores together, you can wind up with problems of performance as well as security issues. In a controlled environment (such as in an enterprise), however, such partitioning can be helpful.

Reusing Data

Not only can you actually reuse databases and database tables, but you can also reuse data in them. There are two general cases in which reusing data makes sense:

▶ You can reuse look-up data such as postal codes.

▶ You can reuse test data. This might include test cases that have been specially constructed; it almost might include real-life data that is used to standardize system performance (all of the data from a given year, for example).

In reusing data, make certain that you have the right to do so. Databases can be protected by copyright in some countries. Thus, while the list of postal codes may be in the public domain, a specific database that collects and indexes them may require a license fee.

Of course, you also have to make certain that you do not inadvertently reuse data. If you are duplicating a database or a database table for use in another environment, make certain that all of its data is erased.

Reusing Database Designs and Schemas

Finally, remember that one of the major attractions of relational databases and the Web is that standards exist for the protocols and design technologies such as SQL. As you have seen in the section on OpenBase (Part II) and on Enterprise Objects Framework (Part III), you can generate SQL statements to create and modify databases and their schemas. This SQL is standard SQL, and it can run on other computers and on other databases than those that you are using. For example, you can use Enterprise Objects Framework to create an entity model, and you can generate the SQL to create all the database tables from within EOModeler. You can execute it automatically in OpenBase, but you can also copy that SQL and execute it against another database manager.

Likewise, you can take a database that is implemented in a database manager that you will not be using with WebObjects and use that database to create the SQL statements to recreate its tables and to export its data. You can use those statements and the extracted data to rebuild the same database in OpenBase or another database that you will use with WebObjects.

There are many reasons for this type of operation. One of the most common is the case in which a corporate database provides the source of data that you want to serve up through WebObjects, but where you do not have direct access to that database for WebObjects applications either because of security constraints or because the corporate database is committed to performance issues that do not allow additional online use. Particularly in the case of read-only access by WebObjects applications, you can set up a simple routine to download data from the main database into your own copy of the database. Keeping the database data and schemas synchronized is simple with this type of process.

Data Mining, Warehousing, and Analysis

The final point to consider in reusing databases, schemas, and data is that there are many technologies and methodologies that use duplicated and derivative data for analytical purposes. Data mining, data warehousing, and other phrases describe the use of data that is gathered in the course of processing transactions for analytical purposes.

Much attention is focused on handling transactions, and WebObjects provides advanced technologies for implementing applications of that sort. However, its rapid development and deployment tools makes it highly suited for building analytical tools.

In fact, although WebObjects is not normally marketed as an end-user tool, it is a perfect tool for the creation of ad hoc analytical systems. You can create an Enterprise Objects Framework model that presents selected fields from a database and then let power users develop applications using Direct-to-Web or Direct-to-Java and Java Client technologies.

In addition to the model, you can also provide common graphics and processing routines in frameworks. Armed with these tools, powerful, robust, good looking, and useful applications can be developed as quickly—if not more so—than using traditional end-user tools.

Reusing Models

You can also reuse Enterprise Objects Framework models. They can in turn facilitate the reuse of WebObjects frameworks and components. To return to the example of a name and address database table, you can use a standard model that is attached to a variety of database tables that themselves have various column and table names. In the model itself, those names can be standardized so that WebObjects applications and components can reuse the model although they access different databases or tables.

You can also reuse models in the opposite way. If you have a generic database that handles test or survey data, it might contain fields such as userID, testIdentifier, and date followed by perhaps a dozen fields labeled question1 through question12. (In such a database, testIdentifier is used to partition the database table.)

Rather than use your Enterprise Objects Framework to standardize names in databases that contain various names, you can use your model to differentiate. Thus, in the model for one WebObjects application, the Enterprise Objects Framework model name for an entity named MaritalStatus might map to question1, while in another such model, the name for an entity called Acreage might map to question1.

The actual process in both cases is the same: database table field names are mapped to different names in an Enterprise Objects Framework model. And, in both cases, the objective is to reuse the database or the model to save repeating development, testing, documentation, and maintenance.

Reuse Considerations

As this chapter and the previous one have shown, the structure of WebObjects and its development tools makes it easy to reuse the effort you have put into design, development, documentation, and testing. This is one of the most significant reasons why WebObjects development is so fast and efficient: you start from a very high level, and you can build on the work you have already done.

There is one point that you must remember, however: it is both a caution and an opportunity. In general, the efforts of design, development, documentation, and testing are proprietary. Unauthorized reuse is not a good idea, particularly since it can have the effect of providing information and assistance to competitors. (Even the names of database tables and fields are frequently considered trade secrets by many firms.)

On the other hand, the ease of reuse provides an opportunity for consultants and developers to specialize in the technologies with which they are familiar and to market frameworks and palette items to their clients and to other developers.

Over the years, proprietary code has often been shared among developers and the organizations for which they work. The arguments in favor of doing so include not only the general proposition that sharing can sometimes be a good thing but also the fact that the more a particular section of code is used and reused, the more likely it is to have its bugs discovered and worked out. One of the most powerful arguments in favor of the open source movement is just this: by being able to read and use common code, it can be understood and enhanced for everyone's benefit.

The reuse of design, development, documentation, and testing often changes the role of the developer or consultant. Understanding the data needs of a project and the processing needs of a WebObjects application, developers and consultants become more like business consultants offering an understanding not only of technology but also of how things can be done.

This part of the book has focused on ways to jump-start WebObjects development: using Direct-to-Web, Java Clients, frameworks, palettes with reusable code and components, as well as showing you strategies for reusing database design and implementations. The final part of the book looks at the one remaining issue: deploying databases and WebObjects applications themselves.

Deployment Issues

OBJECTIVES

► Running databases

► Managing security for databases and WebObjects

► Deploying WebObjects Applications

Running a Database on a Network

IN THIS CHAPTER:

Preparing for Deployment

Moving the Database to Production

Location: Where Is the Database?

Time: Keeping It Running

Issues for Small-Scale Networks

This part of the book deals with deployment issues, the sometimes anticlimactic moments after development ceases, as well as the long-term ongoing issues of keeping your databases and WebObjects applications running. This chapter addresses database issues; the last chapter in this part looks at WebObjects. Between them, the chapter on security deals with concerns for both databases and WebObjects.

If there is one overriding message in this part of the book, it is that you should plan for deployment and ongoing operations from the very first day of your project. If you are part of an IT department, you may well be used to such planning. However, if you are one of the new breed of WebObjects users—people more attuned to the Web site world and to small and medium enterprises, these practices may be new to you. It is sad but true that all of your work in developing a WebObjects application can go for naught if you have not properly planned for deployment. At the very least, your project may be seriously delayed.

On the database side of things, this chapter walks you through five basic areas. The first is preparation for deployment: verifying that your database is ready to move. Then, you will see how to move your database into production by updating your Enterprise Objects Framework model. Next, the issues involved in the physical location of your database and its server are discussed; they are followed by the issues involved in keeping things running. Finally, some of the specific concerns of small-scale WebObjects applications and databases are described.

Note that the issues involved in large-scale WebObjects applications and databases are covered by Apple in WebObjects training sessions. In addition, the iServices division of Apple provides training and consulting support: you can find them at http://www.apple.com/iservices. Apple also sponsors the Apple Solutions Experts group of consultants, trainers, and resellers. These independent companies also can assist you with large-scale projects. You can find them through http://experts.apple.com.

Preparing for Deployment

There are two different deployment scenarios. In the first, your deployment will be live as soon as the process of moving files is completed. This is the case in which you are either updating or replacing a system that people use, or in the case where people will begin using a new system right away for production.

The second deployment scenario is the special case in which you will deploy your WebObjects application and its database, but it will not be used for production yet. This may be because users are testing it in the production environment, or it may be because they are loading it with data. In either case, the deployment is real, but you have a period of time before users from outside your organization use the site. (Note that there are many applications that never move beyond this stage. Small-scale applications are written commonly for one or two people—sometimes the application author—to use.)

The final step in your preparation for deployment on the database side should be to synchronize your schema and the model. Open your Enterprise Objects Framework model using EOModeler (you can double-click the model, which is located inside the Resources group of your project), and then choose Synchronize Schema from the Model menu. If any discrepancies appear, they should be fixed at this time. You will rely on the model and database having been synchronized later in this process.

Moving the Database to Production

As part of the deployment of your WebObjects application, you almost always move the database and the application to another computer. Even in the smallest organizations, it is rare for a single computer to be used both for development and for deployment. The exception to this is the case in which the machine is turned into a deployment computer and development no longer takes place on it. It is generally too risky to be creating and testing new code on the same computer as your live data.

The first step in moving a database to production is to physically move it to the new location. You can do this in a number of ways, and one of them is presented here.

First, stop the database if it is running by using OpenBaseManager. Next, duplicate the database.

As a result of your development and testing, you most likely have data in the database. It may be all test data (possibly including corrupted data placed there due to bugs you have fixed). It may be production data that was copied from another database during the project and that is now out of date. Or, it may be live data that you have prepared during your development process. Depending on the circumstances, you may want to delete all of the data in the database, or it might be appropriate to selectively delete data that you have used for testing. Alternatively, you may want to selectively retain some data and delete everything else. Whatever your choice, do it now in the duplicate copy of the database.

Physically move the database to its new location. Usually you use FTP for this transfer. Once it is in its new location, give it the correct name. (You probably could not give it the correct name when you duplicated it because the original database was in the same location and you cannot have two files with the same name.)

To make certain that everything is in order, launch OpenBaseManager on the machine to which you have moved the duplicated database and make certain that you can start the database.

Now make a complete copy of your WebObjects project. Back it up to external media and make certain that the backup copy is readable. This is critical, because you are about to make a change to the project that will break your development environment.

Open your Enterprise Objects Framework model in EOModeler. From the Model menu, choose Set Adaptor Info to open the window shown in Figure 26-1.

Figure 26-1   *Change the database location*

The URL contains the name or address of the computer on which your database is located (localhost in the figure), and the name of the database (SiteDemo). (It is common to see the IP address of your computer instead of localhost: typically, it is 127.0.0.1. In more complex development environments, the name may differ.)

Change the URL to the name or IP address of the computer on which the database is deployed. If the database will have a different name in deployment, change that, too. To confirm that all is well, choose Data Browser from the Tools menu to examine any data in the model and through it in the database. If you prepared for deployment by ensuring that the schema was correctly synchronized, you should have no errors at this time. Because Data Browser accesses the database itself, this process will guarantee that the change to the database name and/or location was done correctly.

In some circumstances, unfortunately, you cannot perform this test. There are cases where the developer does not have access to the production database. If this is the case, you will need your production support team to do this.

This process should result in your database being moved to the production environment and your development environment remaining intact for debugging and maintenance. The copy you made of your WebObjects project is the one you will continue to work on—its version of the Enterprise Objects Framework model still points to the database that you have used during development. The WebObjects project with the model that points to the production database is the one you will move into production (see Chapter 28 for more on that process).

Location: Where Is the Database?

As should be apparent from the steps outlined in the previous section, the database can run on a computer other than the computer on which WebObjects runs. Often they run on the same computer, but there is no need for that to be the case.

Because everything about the WebObjects environment uses standard Internet protocols, you can deploy WebObjects applications on computers that you access only over the Internet. You do not need to physically be able to touch the computer on which your database is running. (It is important to note, however, that *someone* must be able to touch that computer: copies of the database on removable media need to be made on a regular basis.)

Colocation and Data Centers

It is increasingly common to locate Internet, database, and other servers at remote locations. Called *colocation,* this process involves placing your server at a site that has Internet connections (generally very high speed) and sophisticated power management equipment. (Financial institutions, for example, are fond of data centers that are located at the intersection of two different electrical grids and that also have at least a one-day diesel backup generator on site.)

In a colocated environment, your computer is physically transported to the data center and installed by their staff. You may prepare the computer by preloading your databases, WebObjects applications, and the like, or it may be a new computer shipped directly from the hardware vendor. In either case, the first step is for it to be installed at the data center, and for you to confirm that you can gain access to it over the Internet.

Two forms of colocation exist. In the first, your own computer is placed at the data center. In the second, the data center sells or leases the computer to you as part of its support package. The difference between the two is financial, not technical.

Colocation data centers can be enormous sites; the advantages of scale certainly apply to things such as diesel power generators for backup. Colocation data centers can also be very small. In a school, for instance, several servers that are used by teachers and administrators may be located in a central location. There may be no special power backup available, and the network connections may be fairly low speed. But placing the critical computers together provides security benefits. In addition, if one person is responsible for keeping an eye on several servers (scarcely a full-time job), it helps to have them parked together.

If you are placing a server off-site (or even just out of your own office environment), make certain that it is properly managed. Periodically, someone (perhaps you) will log on to check on the status of the WebObjects application and of the databases. Also, someone at the colocation site must routinely perform backups. You may work with these people to set up the backups so that only essential files are backed up. In the case of relatively small databases, you can stop the database and copy it to another location over a network connection, avoiding the necessity of hands-on backup management. However, backing up over a network is often too slow to be practical. The exception to this is databases that do not run 24 hours a day: if you have down time overnight or at any other time during the day, you can run a lengthy backup at that time.

Outsourcing

As you can see, colocated servers require support both at the colocation site and from your own location. One way to eliminate this is to simply outsource the entire running and management of your server. In this way, the backups, checking that databases are running, and the like are done by the data center staff.

In today's environment, you can find both types of services. What is important about colocation is that the data center staff needs to know about Internet connectivity, but that is really all they need to know. (They also need to know how to replace backup tapes as they are filled.) They do not need to know about OpenBase (or whatever database you are using), and they do not need to know about WebObjects. If you outsource your operations, you will need to find a data center that is familiar with the technologies that you use.

In practice, many people are more comfortable using WebObjects-savvy colocation data centers than totally generic ones. That way, if there is a problem, you may get better support.

Hosting

There is a third solution to where to place the databases, and that is Web site hosting. You may contract with a vendor who already runs a WebObjects environment to add your application to that environment. This is similar to outsourcing in that once the database and WebObjects application are transferred you are more or less out of the picture. What is different, though, is that you may need to make your database and WebObjects application conform to the host's standards. These may involve such things as naming conventions; they also may extend to backups that are done at the host site's schedule.

In addition to commercial Web site hosts, you can often find nonprofit organizations and schools that share their hosting facilities with other organizations in the same area of interest.

Environments

The deployment process outlined in this chapter left you with two complete environments: one on the deployment server and one on your development computer. There is no reason to stop at two environments, and there are some reasons to consider several more. Each environment is created just as your deployment environment is. You can then archive an environment to removable media until such time as you need it.

A typical environment is one that is part way between development and deployment. It is an environment in which you can integrate changes from several different developers. On large projects, such a system test environment is common.

Another common environment is one in which a specific set of data is maintained in the database. This may be a controlled set of data against which your application can be run to test that the correct results are obtained. It also can be any of a variety of stress test environments: very large databases, for example, may be needed periodically to assure that your application scales appropriately.

Particularly if your environments rely on databases that are set up in specific ways, it is important to plan for the environments very early on in your development process. It takes time to get all that data into the database!

Time: Keeping It Running

The previous section of this chapter focused on place: where your database is located. This section focuses on the dimension of time: keeping things running.

Maintaining Uptime

It is tempting to think that all WebObjects applications function in a 24 × 7 environment, but this is scarcely the case. It is true that applications running on the Web and that users access at their own convenience normally are available at all times, but many WebObjects applications are used internally. Furthermore, many applications reflect requirements that are time-dependent. Banks in most places do not operate 24 hours a day; their processing is typically done in a more or less draft mode during the day, and the transactions are finalized during end-of-day processing in the middle of the night, which is when funds transfers for electronic banking are sent out.

Know How the Application Should Perform

As part of your project requirements, you should have determined what your application's availability must be. Someone must then make certain that the application meets those standards.

It is surprising to note how frequently performance standards are not specified for a system. The standard may be part of the initial specification; it also may be developed during deployment as you actually measure performance. It is important to know how long it normally takes for specific actions in your application to be carried out. That information can be invaluable when handling irate users. (But beware of explaining to users that the performance they find aggravating is normal. That generally does not work.)

Have Procedures for Problems

In the corporate world, IT staffs spend much of their time developing procedures. As complex technology becomes available to more and more people, some of these procedures need to be copied in small and medium-sized enterprises. Note that not all need to be implemented: the advantages that small to medium-sized enterprises have over the corporate behemoth competitors often derive from their flexibility. On the other hand, you can't wing it in the midst of a problem that is visible on the Web.

Make a list of major problems that can occur, and determine what to do about them. This list can be a single page long: the important point is that you specify before the crisis how you will react to problems.

For example, in the case of a problem that totally breaks your application, you may decide that after half an hour of downtime for testing and troubleshooting, you will reload last night's backup of the database and application. This might result in the loss of data entered since that backup, but it might guarantee that your maximum catastrophic outage is a manageable amount of time (30 minutes plus the time to do the restore and restart the application).

It is human nature to think that each possible solution will do the trick. Before you know it, you can have lost an entire day of processing while you troubleshoot the application.

You need standards for performance, and you also need standards that help you determine if there is a problem. Catastrophic failures are easy to deal with—you know there's a problem. However, if your database manages a library's catalog of books that might contain several hundred thousand records, would you really bring the system down to correct an error in one record, or even in a few hundred records? Again, preparing for the problems helps you manage them. The person who finds the error in the database may care deeply about it and demand that it be fixed right away, but your prepared standard will help you through the problem. (This is similar to the integrated pest management practice adopted by many farmers. They determine the limit of boll weevils or other pests that they are willing to live with in their fields, and they apply sprays and pesticides only when that limit is exceeded. This dramatically reduces the use of chemicals.)

Planning Maintenance

One way to keep your application running smoothly is to plan for maintenance. This may be routine maintenance as it is running (checking the database, checking WebObjects, confirming that performance is within bounds, and the like). This is not just a matter of looking for obvious problems: if your response time is excellent, that may mean that a link to your application is broken and far fewer people than usual are using the application.

In addition to daily maintenance, plan for maintenance during the life of your application. Realistically determine how frequently upgrades to the database or application should be made. If you have planned for an upgrade on a quarterly or semiannual basis, everyone from developers to production staff should know when that will be, and they will know when bugs will be fixed. Having to handle every change to the application on an ad hoc basis will drive everyone nuts.

Planning Backups

The last issue involved in keeping your application running is making certain that backups are done appropriately. The nature of your application should determine how the backups are done. In the case of a bank, for example, backups should be done after end-of-day processing, no matter what time that is. (There have been cases where end-of-day processing runs during business hours of the following day.)

Other backup schedules rigorously adhere to the clock. If your server is colocated or outsourced, you may not have control over when backups are done. If this is the case, at least find out when the backups are performed. This is necessary so that you will know what your exposure to data loss is.

Issues for Small-Scale Networks

Finally, there are special considerations for small-scale networks. As noted at the beginning of this chapter, there are many resources to help you build large-scale applications such as the Apple Store. But now that it is feasible for a school to manage its collection of audio-visual equipment (perhaps 100 items) using WebObjects, small-scale issues emerge.

Perhaps the most important one concerns staffing. WebObjects is not the daunting product that it was a few years ago. This means that developers should not be afraid of it; it also means that some experienced WebObjects developers may be working on projects of a much smaller size than they are used to. Small-scale projects are very efficient, but they often do not have the depth of resources available to a large project team. For all of these reasons, keeping up to date on WebObjects issues is essential. There is a WebObjects discussion list on Apple's support site (http://www.apple.com/support), and you can search its archives as well as follow recent developments.

Coverage is another concern for small-scale networks. If you are doing everything, how will you have a vacation? True, you can take a laptop with you and log in from wherever you are to troubleshoot problems, but that is not a vacation. Whether you are the developer or the manager, you need to confront the fact that there has to be backup support for every application. One way that this can be done is with a buddy system: developers often pair off for this purpose.

CHAPTER

27

Security

IN THIS CHAPTER:

Database Security

Web Security

WebObjects Security

Other Security Concerns

S ecurity is an area of concern in the deployment of databases as well as of the Web and of WebObjects applications. This chapter addresses all three of those issues.

It is worth noting that many people think security is about keeping out intruders and dealing with people who have malevolent intentions. As a result, they commonly think that no one in their organization would harbor such wishes or that their data is so unimportant that no one would want to steal it. Leaving aside the issue that security needs to be in place before there is a problem, consider the fact that security is also a way to prevent errors. It is very easy to accidentally delete files or to find yourself working with the wrong copy of a database (such as a production database instead of a test database). Implementing security is a double-check that helps minimize accidents. Whether you look at it from the standpoint of evil-doers or as a precaution against many mistakes (or both), security should be part of every installation.

Database Security

In common with most database managers, OpenBase lets you implement security for your database. This lets you control who can view and update various records. However, if you refer back to the general architectural diagrams shown in Part I of this book, you will see that database security is not what it appears with an application server such as WebObjects.

WebObjects itself is the database user. If you want to implement a security mechanism in which members of the Finance Department have update access to payroll information while any division chiefs can view that data, you can do so in OpenBase, but it won't make a bit of difference when WebObjects is running.

If users can access a database directly (that is, not through WebObjects applications), you may need to implement your security at the database level for your users, in addition to providing access through WebObjects. You will then need to reimplement security on the WebObjects side. (That is discussed in the following section.)

WebObjects basically needs full access to any of the database tables that it will be using; there are circumstances where a WebObjects application will be doing no updates, and in those cases you can limit its access to reading data.

In view of the fact that WebObjects needs such access to your database, many people believe that there is no reason to implement security at the database level at all. However, it is prudent to password the entire database (thus forcing users who access it through WebObjectsManager to log in) and to create a WebObjects user. You may want to create other users as well.

Host Passwords

You can create a password for your database host server in OpenBase. You do so by selecting a host (not a database) in OpenBaseManager, and choosing Preferences from the application menu. In the center tab of the window, you will find the button that lets you set the password. This window is shown in Figure 27-1.

If you password the host, then people using OpenBaseManager need to log in before they can work with any of the databases on the host. This is a gross but prudent precaution because OpenBaseManager allows people to do really serious things (such as remove database tables). Once the host is passworded, the log-in window shown in Figure 27-2 appears when people try to access a database in OpenBaseManager.

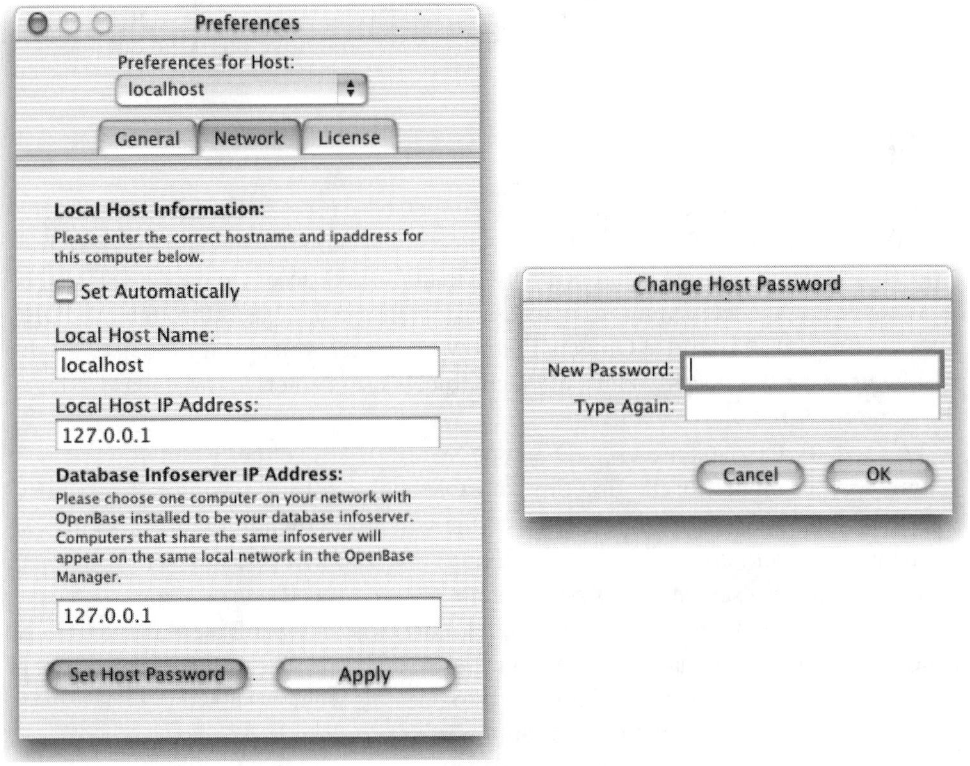

Figure 27-1   *Set the database host server password*

Figure 27-2   *Logging in to an OpenBase database*

This step safeguards the database schemas. Now you move on to the databases themselves.

Setting Up Users

You can establish individual user accounts for database users in OpenBaseManager. This is necessary only if you want to control access to browse data (and queries) in OpenBaseManager. Groups of users are used to implement access to the database itself.

When WebObjects is running, it accesses OpenBase databases through the JDBC interface; in your Enterprise Objects Framework model, you specify the user ID that will be used for this access. Thus, all WebObjects users enter your database using the same ID—that of WebObjects.

You specify the database user ID and password (if any) either when you are setting up your model for the first time in EOModeler or by choosing Set Adaptor Info from the Model menu. In either case, the window shown in Figure 27-3 opens. You enter the username and password (if any) that you will be using for WebObjects access. As you can see here, it is possible not to use a specific user name.

The user that you have set in your model must exist in OpenBaseManager. Here is how to create and manage users and groups for your databases. First, select Users from the OpenBaseManager Database menu to open the window shown in Figure 27-4. You can also click the User Manager button in the toolbar.

The two buttons at the top left of the window let you add and delete users. At the right, you specify user IDs and full names, you select the group to which a user belongs, and you can set a password. The items in the lower part of the right-hand section of the window (email address, for example) are used by RADStudio and are not needed for use with WebObjects.

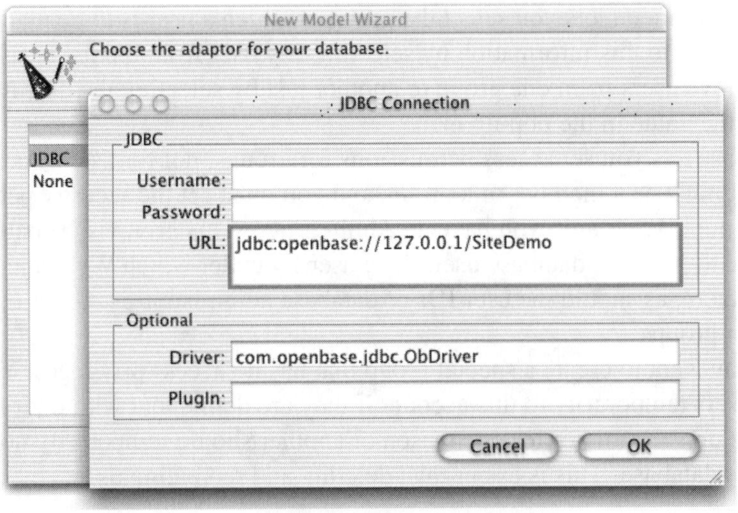

Figure 27-3   *Set the user name and password in EOModeler*

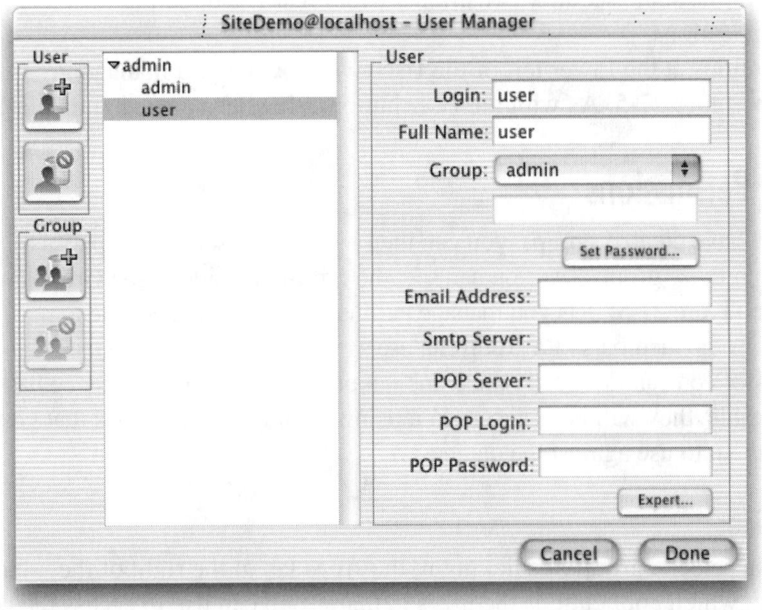

Figure 27-4   *Managing users in OpenBaseManager*

The pop-up menu lets you select the group in which a user is to be placed. You can come back to this information by selecting any user from the list of users. Thus, you can move users from one group to another just by selecting the user name and changing the value in the pop-up menu.

OpenBase lets you set access permissions for groups, not for users. As a result, every user must be a member of a group, and you must set the security permissions for that group. By default, you have an admin group. This group is probably not the right place to put your database users. The user ID under which WebObjects will run might be there, as should the user IDs of database administrators. Other users should be in other groups.

You may want to create a special group that has no access privileges. You can transfer users temporarily to this account if they are delinquent with their library books, are on vacation, or for one reason or another should temporarily not have access to a database. This is easier than deleting and recreating users.

Setting Up Groups

Groups of users are used to control access to databases. All users within a given group have the same security constraints with regard to updating the database and using applications.

The buttons at the lower left of the Users window let you manage groups as shown in Figure 27-5. As with the User buttons, they let you add and delete groups.

Setting Permissions

Once you have created groups, you can then move on to setting the permissions for the users in those groups. As you can see, the right-hand side of the Groups window (shown in Figure 27-5), lets you manage permissions. You will be able to manage what applications the members of a group can use as well as what tables in the database they can access. (You cannot specify the combination of the two, so if someone has access to the Item table, they will have access to it using all of the applications that you have allowed them to use against the database.)

Applications

When you select a group by clicking it, the Apps tab at the right of the window lets you select which applications the users in that group can use to access the database.

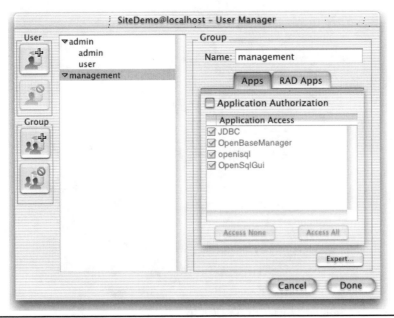

Figure 27-5   *Managing groups in OpenBaseManager*

The admin group always has total access, so you cannot change its applications. Groups that you create, however, can have a variety of application choices.

If you want to implement application-level security, check the Application Authorization box at the right. The list of applications below it contains every application that has been used to access the database you are working with. Select those applications that you want members of this group to be able to use.

Table Security

You can also implement table-level security within a database. Click the Expert button to open the window shown in Figure 27-6.

At the top of the list are OpenBase tables in each database that store items such as relationship. For these as well as for your tables (at the bottom of the scrolling list) you can set security to allow or deny selection (reading), insertion (adding), updating, and deletion.

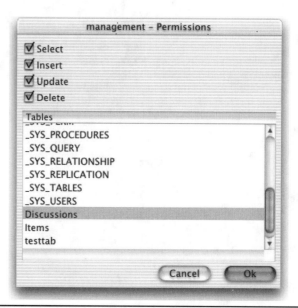

Figure 27-6   *Set table-level security for groups*

Web Security

From the start, the World Wide Web has had a variety of security mechanisms
built into its protocols. In particular, HTTP, the data transport protocol, supports
authentication with user names and passwords; in addition, the Secure Sockets Layer
(SSL) protocol provides a secure way of transferring encrypted and protected data
between a Web browser and a server. Both of those are described here.

Using SSL

SSL requires implementation both in a user's Web browser and at the HTTP server.
Today, most browsers in widespread use support SSL, and most HTTP servers do
so, too. Messages sent using HTTP over SSL are encrypted; in addition, the message
text is protected at both ends using an algorithm that confirms that the message has
not been changed during transmission.

You can identify SSL messages by the schema at the start of a URL—https://
represents HTTP over SSL. Many browsers display an icon (often a padlock) in a
status bar to indicate that a secure connection has been established. Because of the
overhead of SSL when compared to unsecured transmissions, it is frequently used
only for the most secure requests and responses: credit card numbers, for example,
are normally sent in this way.

Authorizing the HTTP Server

There are two aspects to SSL. First, the HTTP server requires a security certificate (SC) signed by a Certificate Authority (CA) indicating that the server is known. There are a number of Certificate Authorities: one of the most widely known is Verisign, located at www.verisign.com.

You need to obtain a security certificate for your HTTP server only once: it will then serve for all of your secure transactions in all of the applications on that server. If you are using a commercial ISP, chances are that it already has such a security certificate in place for at least one of its servers. Frequently, an ISP will offer a variety of e-commerce and secure transaction options, and you can avail yourself of them so that you do not have to worry about them yourself.

There are a number of ISPs that actually will implement the entire financial part of e-commerce; when you get to the part of a transaction that requires a credit card authorization, you can use their facilities, and they will return a code to your application indicating that the credit card has been accepted or declined. Some of these ISPs go so far as to also process the transactions and to arrange for payment of the proceeds to your account.

In addition to services provided by ISPs, you may find financial processing in other places. OpenBase, for example, has stored procedures that can be called from any program or WebObjects application to process credit card payments and perform address verification. All you need to do is send the credit card, expiration, billing street and zip, and a few other pieces of information and it will clear the payment through your account at Verisign.

Redirecting to https://

The standard HTTP header includes an optional field called `location`. If present, it contains the address to which the message is to be sent. You can use the location field to provide an alternate URL that begins with https:// rather than with the standard http://. In that way, WebObjects will pass the message to the HTTP server, and the server will direct it to the user's browser using SSL.

Although WebObjects URL addresses can be quite complex, for the sake of this discussion, they can be considered to have only three parts:

1. They start with a schema—http:// or https://.

2. They continue with a host name, which is the name of the HTTP server or your domain name, which winds up being decomposed to the server.

3. That is followed by the specific set of fields that include application, session, and component identification, such as

   `/cgi-bin/WebObjects/kbase.woa/wo/0.0.6.21.0.7.`

As a response is being prepared by WebObjects, the `appendToResponse` method of the application, session, and component is called. It creates the header for the response using fields that have been set. Normally, this is done internally without your worrying about it; however, to use SSL, you will need to modify that header.

You do this by calling the WOMessage method `setHeader` to set the location field in the header. (You can set any of the header's fields using this technique; the names of the fields are those provided in the HTTP specification, RFC 2616, available at http://www.w3.org/Protocols/.) The `setHeader` method has two arguments: a string and the field name. You compose the string from the three items described previously. This line of code will do it for you. (Note that it is spaced out to show the three entities.)

```
aResponse.setHeader (
  "https://" +
  this.context().request().headerForKey("host") +
  this.context().componentActionURL(),

  "location");
```

Insert this line in an override of `appendToResponse` to change the header. Since `appendToResponse` is called by application, session, and component objects, you can do this at any of those levels. To leave SSL, insert an almost identical line of code, but setting the schema back to http:// from https://.

Using HTTP Authentication

HTTP provides authentication; it is documented in RFC 2617: HTTP Authentication: Basic and Digest Access Authentication, available at http://www.w3.org/Protocols/. Browsers and HTTP servers collaborate on authentication, just as they do on SSL. However, unlike SSL, which uses a trusted third party for authentication, HTTP authentication passes between the browser and the server without a third party. Furthermore, HTTP authentication uses a user name and password, but it does not provide encrypted communication.

In order to provide HTTP authentication, you need to add a `WWW-authenticate` field to the response header. Sample code to do this is provided at http://developer.apple.com/techpubs/webobjects/Topics/ProgrammingTopics.e.html; you also need to consult RFC 2617 if you are not familiar with HTTP authentication.

HTTP authentication is easy to implement on HTTP servers; it is used to keep people out of specific directories to which only privileged users should have access.

You can also use it within a WebObjects application. In practice, however, it often turns out not to be the right tool for security. SSL is the appropriate tool for keeping individual messages secure (credit card numbers, again), and log-on security is appropriate for those cases where you need to retrieve a variety of information about the user who is logging in. That technique is discussed in the following section.

WebObjects Security

In setting up security for your database and its tables, remember that you can implement it not only in OpenBase itself but also in WebObjects. All WebObjects users will appear the same to OpenBase—it is WebObjects itself that is the user in those cases. Practically, it makes sense to allow broad access to WebObjects and to implement security inside your application based on the actual final end user's identity.

Because you implement your own security mechanism inside your WebObjects application, you can implement whatever you want. One common approach is to implement log-on security: on your application's Main page, you request a user name and password. You then validate them against a database to determine if the user should be allowed in.

Some entire sites do require log-on security; others require security or user validation only for certain areas. In designing your application, it is important to consider at what points you will implement security. In general, minimizing the amount of your site that is secured is a good idea. It makes life easier for everyone. Entering a user ID and password deters people from using a site, even valid users. You have probably encountered this yourself as you browse the Web: if you are asked to log on, just to get a weather report or news headline, you may take yourself elsewhere.

Gatekeeper pages can be implemented using the mechanism described here. Main can be the gatekeeper for your entire site, but you may want instead to place a gatekeeper much deeper into your site. You also may want to have several gatekeepers. This can be problematic unless you store information in the session object (user ID and password or else the information that the session user has been validated). If you do this, then when you approach a gatekeeper page, you can check to see if you need to ask for user ID and password.

There is more information on security available from Apple's Web site at http://developer.apple.com/techpubs/webobjects/Topics/ProgrammingTopics.e.html.

Implementing Log-on Security

The shell of this implementation is provided in Direct-to-Web projects that you create in Project Builder. You can do anything you want to validate a user ID. Here is one approach.

In your Enterprise Objects Framework model, create a Fetch Spec that retrieves a record based on a user name. Create a property in Main with that name (perhaps ?userID), Bind the user ID text field to that property, and then execute the Fetch Spec from an editing context. If you have a result and if the password field matches the database-stored password, present the next page; otherwise, present an error.

Here is one way to do that part of the process.

```
EOQualifier qualifier;
EOFetchSpecification loginFetchSpec;
EOEditingContext EC = new EOEditingContext();

loginFetchSpec = new EOFetchSpecification ("loginFetch", null, null);
NSArray results = ec.objectsWithFetchSpecification (loginFetchSpec);
if (results.count() == 1)
  {
    //compare retrieved object's password with input field
    //return positive value;
  }
  // throw  exception or take other action
```

The advantage that this security mechanism has over HTTP authentication is that your fetch statement can return an Enterprise Objects Framework model entity that represents the user in all its glory: the password (encrypted or plain) can be returned, but so can preferences, in-process transactions, and any other information that you want. If you are going to need to retrieve this information for authenticated users, you might as well do it as part of the authentication process.

If you use the Direct to Web project shell, the Login button is a submit button that will cause a new component to be created. It is in that second component's code (perhaps its initialization code) that you can execute this check. Validating a password is a complicated issue, and there are many different approaches. The strictest security encrypts the password; you apply the same encryption to the user-entered password, and test if the stored, encrypted value matches the newly entered and also encrypted value. This prevents the password from being visible in the database.

Direct Actions and Security

One reason for using direct actions is that the pages presented by direct actions are bookmarkable. Standard WebObjects URLs change because the session identifier is part of the URL.

When pages are created dynamically and cannot be bookmarked, you can be reasonably certain that they are only created for a valid user, so long as you have checked the user ID in your log-on security. If someone cannot get past Main without a valid user ID, all is well with standard WebObjects actions.

With direct actions, however, each page can be bookmarked, and you have no guarantee of who is accessing the page. One way around this is not to use direct actions to create pages that you want to be protected.

Be Careful What You Store

If you allow users to select their own passwords, you need to be very careful about how you store them. Most people use the same passwords over and over; you may find yourself with a database that contains passwords for ATM machines or email accounts. If you store user-chosen passwords, look carefully at what other data you are storing. If you store account numbers of credit cards, for example, you are likely to wind up with usable combinations of credit cards and passwords in your database. Not everyone will use their credit card password, but enough will that your database will become much more attractive to thieves and hackers.

Other Security Concerns

In addition to securing your database and implementing security in your WebObjects application, there are several other areas of concern you should think about. This section touches on some of the issues.

Code

Your code itself is one of the biggest security vulnerabilities. With the code, people can see how you validate user IDs. If you develop an e-commerce site, the code may give away information about transactions where credit limits are not checked. Your business logic may in fact be your organization's greatest asset, and all of it is sitting there in your code.

Therefore, consider your code confidential material, and guard it accordingly. It needs to be safeguarded not only from theft but also from damage—inadvertent or malignant. Backup copies of your application and database are invaluable in the case of such damage, but they also pose a security risk. It is amazing how many installations implement fairly good security and then leave backup tapes and CDs in the most exposed areas of the organization.

Servers

Your database and WebObjects server themselves are security risks. If your servers are located off your premises, you need to know that they are protected. Standard colocation contracts provide insurance and spell out the precautions the vendor will take to safeguard your servers. However, if your servers are colocated informally, such precautions may not have been taken.

Your servers are probably worth more to you for the software that is on them than for their hardware value. Unfortunately, for thieves, the reverse is true. Make certain that your insurance covers your servers no matter where they are.

Passwords

Finally, the issue of passwords needs some attention. Whether you allow people to choose their own passwords or create passwords for them, you normally set certain rules. Common rules specify minimum and maximum lengths for a password; other rules require both letters and numbers. Some implementations require passwords to be changed on a regular basis: in extreme cases, after each use.

What has happened is that all of these passwords and the rules for their use have started to lose effectiveness. A few years ago, people were cautioned never to write down their passwords. Today, with the proliferation of passwords, people either write them down or use the same password over and over; both are severe compromises to security.

The rules that you make will help to determine how people manage their passwords; that, in turn, will help make your application more or less secure. On balance, it seems that having fewer rules increases the likelihood of people reusing passwords from other purposes. That may be a good idea, since the passwords that are used frequently are often not written down, and the written copy is the biggest security loophole.

If you do implement rules for passwords, look around your environment. One financial services site was formed from the merger of two other sites developed in two different parts of the company. One site requires passwords of no more than eight characters; the other requires passwords of at least eight characters. With the exception of eight-character passwords, passwords are valid only on one side of the site or the other, and users must use two different passwords to log on. Clearly this is an extreme case, but it is a good example of how the implementation of security can have unforeseen consequences.

Invisible Security

Finally, consider if it is possible to implement security without it interfering with users. Maybe information that is collected as a normal part of using your site can be used to verify a user's identity; furthermore, maybe that is not necessary at all. Remember that users are happiest when they know why something is being done. If you ask them to select a user ID and a password and tell them why, it is easier than just putting up a roadblock. (In some cases, you may make the user ID and password optional: by providing them, users may get improved service or more information, but if they choose not to do so, they still can have access to your application.

Deploying WebObjects Applications

IN THIS CHAPTER:

The WebObjects Deployment Environment

Managing Hosts

Managing Applications

Managing Instances

During your development process, you have been able to run your WebObjects applications from Project Builder. When it comes time to deploy your application on a Web server, you need to follow the steps in this chapter. Note that you may be deploying for production, or you may be deploying on a test machine: in either case, the process is the same.

There are slight variations in deployment techniques on different platforms (directory names are different, for example). Since the underlying WebObjects code is written in Java, the same things happen in the same way, even though files may be located differently. This chapter walks through the architecture on Mac OS X. Its implementation on other platforms may vary slightly. Your primary resources for deployment is the documentation that comes with your version of WebObjects: in addition to platform-related changes, there are some changes from version to version. In particular, WebObjects 5 (which is the first Java release of WebObjects) has changes from previous versions. On Apple's Web site, documentation for older versions of WebObjects may still be available, since people are still using them. If you search the site, make certain that you have current documentation; following the older documentation, particularly in areas of deployment, may not be appropriate.

The ultimate resource is Apple's document, *Deploying WebObjects Applications,* which is part of its Inside WebObjects series. It is available in PDF format for download from the Apple Web site; search for it by title.

The WebObjects Deployment Environment

When you run a WebObjects application from Project Builder, it is accessible only via the port number assigned to it when it launches. This is the port number that shows up in your browser's address field as the application is launched, and it looks something like the following:

```
http://localhost:49752/cgi-bin/WebObjects/SiteDemo
```

In the messages you see in Project Builder as the application starts up, you will see how it is set up:

```
Created adaptor of class WODefaultAdaptor on port 49752 and
address localhost/192.168.0.2 with WOWorkerThread minimum of 16
and maximum of 256
```

The port number (boldfaced in the URL and message) changes each time you execute your application. You can access your application from another computer on the network by using the URL and the changing port number, but that obviously is not appropriate for deployment or anything but the most limited testing.

Furthermore, when you deploy your application, you want to take advantage of the many performance monitoring and tuning tools of WebObjects. This chapter walks you through the process.

NOTE

WebObjects can run very large installations (such as the Apple Store or flightarrivals.com), but it also can run very small ones. The change in Apple's pricing for WebObjects has opened a wide array of smaller opportunities for WebObjects applications. If you are deploying a large-scale application, the resources already described (Apple Solution Experts and Apple iServices) can help you with training and consulting. Long-time WebObjects developers can tell you that deployment is a very complex issue. That is true for the types of applications that traditionally have been deployed. However, if you are deploying a WebObjects application to support booking audio-visual equipment within a school or a WebObjects application that serves up weekly menus and news items for a senior citizens center, the steps in this chapter are probably sufficient. And whether you are deploying a large or small application, the steps are the same (you just do some of them over and over as you install your application on multiple servers).

WebObjects is normally distributed with development and deployment licenses. You may have both, or you may have only one. If you are installing a deployment version of WebObjects, you use the deployment license key you have received. If you have installed a development version of WebObjects and wish to upgrade to a deployment version, you can run the WebObjects License Upgrader and enter the deployment key. A few files are moved around, and the upgrade is complete. Note that you can run both development and deployment on the same computer (although security and performance issues generally argue against doing so in production—for testing, there usually is not an issue).

wotaskd

The WebObjects task dispatcher is a daemon that runs constantly in the background on each WebObjects server. It is installed by default when you install WebObjects with a deployment license, and it runs automatically when the computer starts up. If it stops for any reason, it automatically restarts.

Before beginning installation of your first WebObjects application, check to see that wotaskd is running. Do that by entering the following URL into your browser:

```
http://www.localhost:1085
```

(If your computer is not localhost, enter its name or IP address.)

You should see a display in your browser window like that shown in Figure 28-1.

The contents of the window do not matter at this point: you just want to make certain that you get a response from wotaskd. This daemon will actually dispatch requests to your application as needed. For basic installations, you need do nothing more.

If you do not get a response from wotaskd at this point, consult the documentation and follow the directions provided there. In almost all cases, wotaskd does run after the installation of WebObjects deployment licenses: there is very little that can disturb it. However, if it is not running, nothing will work after this point in the process.

Figure 28-1   *Viewing wotaskd info in a Web browser*

Monitor

You do your day-to-day management of WebObjects applications using the Monitor application, which is itself a WebObjects application. In order to launch Monitor, you need to enter two commands from the command line in Terminal. First, change the directory to the directory in which JavaMonitor.woa is located, using the following command:

```
cd /System/Library/WebObjects/JavaApplications/JavaMonitor.woa
```

On Mac OS X, you can simply type cd (and a space), and then navigate to this directory and drag and drop the JavaMonitor.woa file icon into a Terminal window.

Next, enter the following command. Note that the dot at the beginning of the command is essential.

```
./JavaMonitor
```

This should launch JavaMonitor in your Web browser. (You may need to launch the Web browser first before entering the command.) You will see a window like that shown in Figure 28-2; its actual display will vary depending on your installation and what tab is clicked.

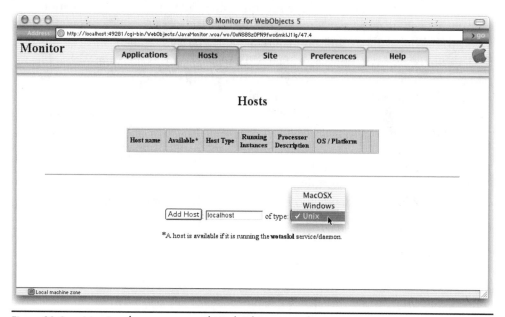

Figure 28-2   *Monitor lets you control WebObjects applications*

Your Application

In order to deploy and manage your application, you need to work with hosts (Web servers), your application, and instances of your application. This section shows you how.

You should know something about how applications run on Web servers. Typically, all of the Web server's pages are located in a directory such as

```
/Library/WebServer/Documents
```

There is a potential security vulnerability if you put applications in that directory, since users of the Web server have access to the directory. As a result, it is best to put only the absolute minimum of files in that directory; typically, these are the resources such as images for your Web pages. When they are downloaded as part of Web pages, they need to be there.

Your WebObjects application itself can be located elsewhere, in a directory accessible to WebObjects itself (actually wotaskd), but not accessible to outside users. On Mac OS X, that directory is

```
/System/Library/WebObjects/JavaApplications/
```

In order for this security measure to work, you need to install the application separately from its resources. Fortunately, Project Builder takes care of this for you when you build an application for deployment. If you look at the Build Settings pane in the Targets display, you will see that SPLIT_INSTALL is YES for WebServer, and NO for development and deployment. By default, a build of the WebServer target of your application does the right thing.

You also need to make certain that your security implementation supports this. The JavaApplications directory needs to be secure; allowing unlimited read and write access defeats the whole purpose. Again, the default implementations and installations do the right thing.

But you do need to do one thing: you must connect your application's executable code to the WebObjects application that will run. That, along with host and instance configuration, is the topic of this section.

Managing Hosts

If this is the first WebObjects application that you are installing, you will need to configure your host. If you have already installed WebObjects applications, your host is configured, and you do not need to worry about it unless you change the configuration or add or delete hosts.

The basic Hosts configuration tab was shown previously in Figure 28-2. To add a host, you type its name and select its operating system as shown there. When you click Add Host, you will see it added to the list of hosts shown in Figure 28-3. It is from this display that you can further configure or delete hosts.

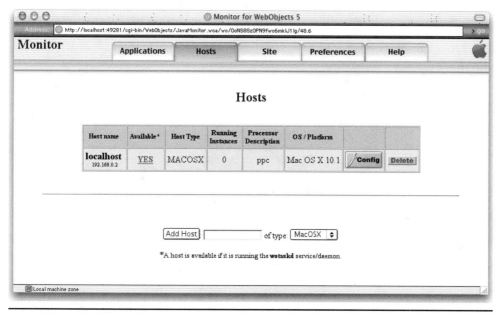

Figure 28-3   *Host list in Monitor*

Managing Applications

When you install a new application (or if you want to reconfigure an existing one), you click the Applications tab to open the display shown in Figure 28-4. This figure illustrates an environment with no applications configured.

As with hosts, you type the name of your application and click Add Application to add a new one. Note that this is the name that people will use to access your application in a URL of the form

```
http://www.yourhostname.com/cgi-bin/WebObjects/applicationname
```

Usually it is the same as the internal name of your application, but it may not be so. Once you have added an application, you can configure it as shown in Figure 28-5.

The most important part of the configuration is the path; this locates the executable code, which is normally located away from your computer's Web server

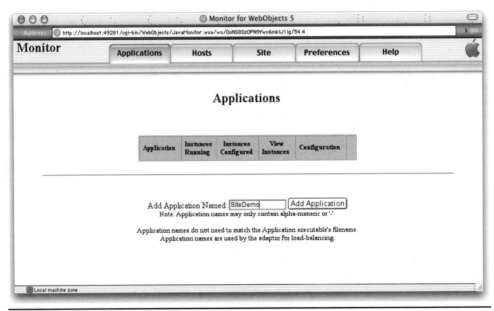

Figure 28-4   *Use the Applications tab to configure your WebObjects applications*

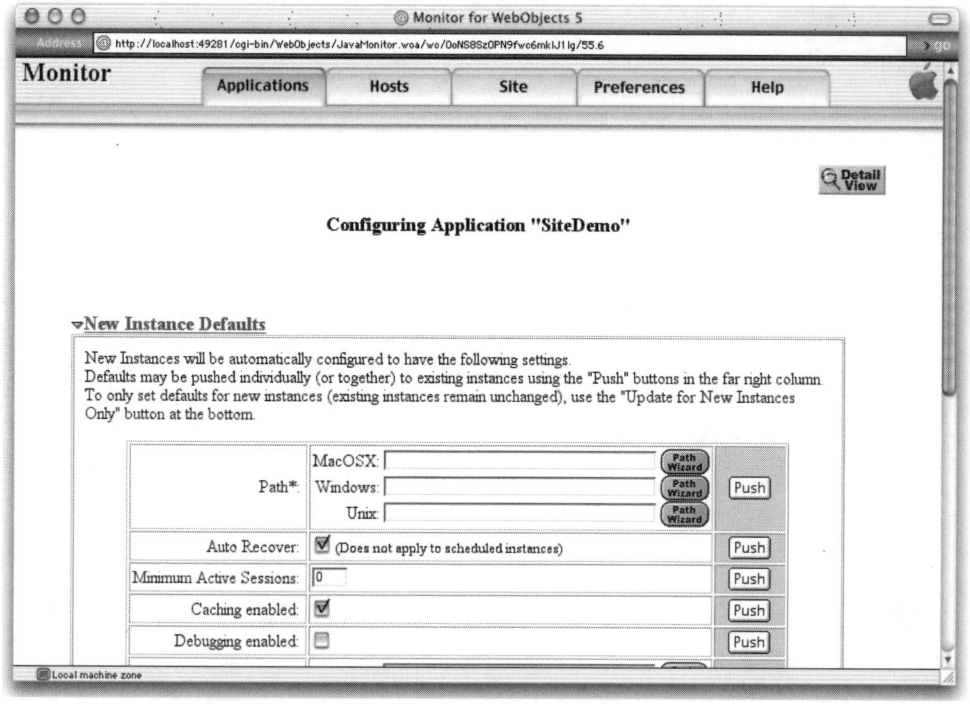

Figure 28-5   *Configure your application*

documents. The Path Wizard button lets you navigate to that file, as shown in Figure 28-6.

The executable file is located within your wrapped file (.woa) directory. Do not select a file such as SiteDemo.woa; go into that directory and select SiteDemo (or whatever your application's name is).

When you click Select, you will be returned to the configuration window as shown in Figure 28-7.

For each of the attributes that you set, you must push the values before they take effect. Each can be pushed separately, or you can push them all using the Push All button at the bottom of the window. Note that the application path is the minimum setting you must make.

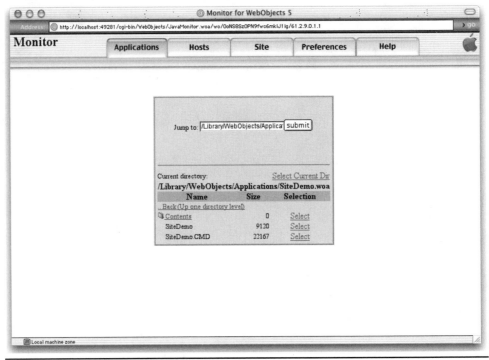

Figure 28-6 *Use Path Wizard to locate your file*

A variety of other settings are available. One of the most useful ones is the e-mail notification setting located further down the page. It is shown in Figure 28-8.

As you can see from the figure, this allows you to specify an e-mail address (or a list of several) to be notified when the application quits unexpectedly. In order to use this feature, you must have configured SMTP values for the host (which you do in the Hosts tab).

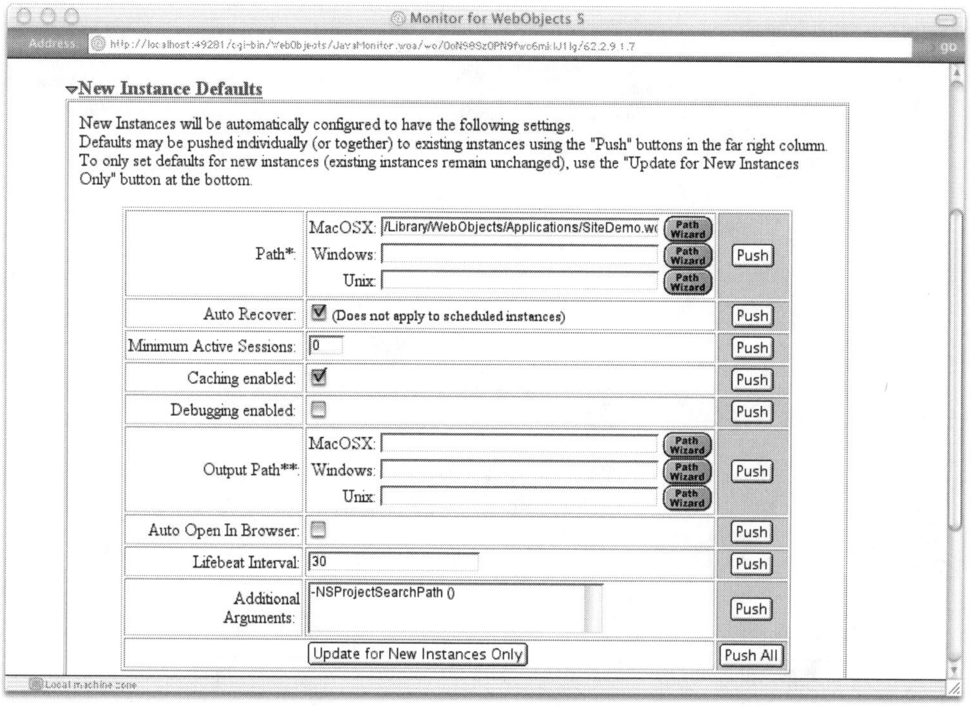

Figure 28-7   *Push attributes*

Once you have added an application, it appears as shown in Figure 28-9.

You can add yet another application, or delete or configure this one. The application's detail view is shown in Figure 28-10. Here is where you do your final work.

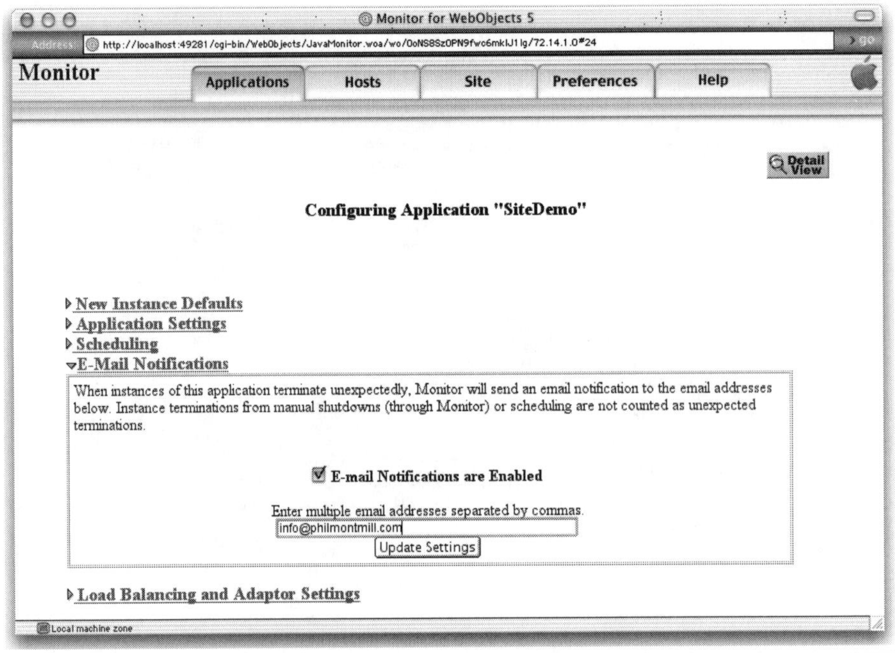

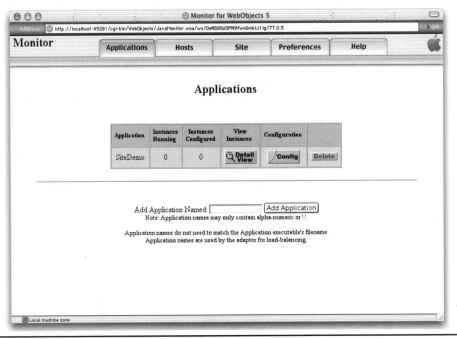

Figure 28-8   *Set e-mail notifications*

Figure 28-9   *Applications view*

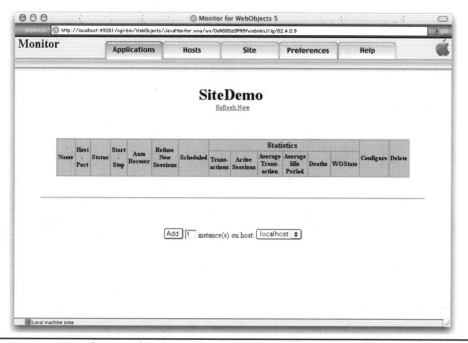

Figure 28-10   *Application detail view*

Managing Instances

The application itself does not run: instances of it run. Each instance handles some of the traffic to the application, as described in the chapters in Part I of this book. Configure the number of instances necessary to manage traffic. The ideal number is determined by the demands of your site as well as by the resources on your servers. You can use Monitor to add and delete instances as necessary. For example, a school's registration system might add instances during the beginning of a term, devoting more resources to registration than to other functions. After the term has started, the number of registration resources might be reduced and the number of event query resources expanded.

You add instances at the bottom of the Application detail view shown in Figure 28-10. When you do so, the instance view shown in Figure 28-11 appears.

You can configure or delete instances, and you can monitor statistics. Note that the instance configuration is the same as the application configuration shown previously; however, it applies only to the specific application.

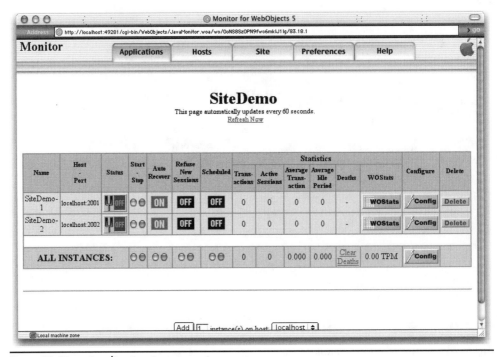

Figure 28-11   *Application instance view*

You can start and stop each application instance or all of them for the application. When you click a Start radio button, you will see the display shown in Figure 28-12.

And, at this point, your users will be able to access your application as shown in Figure 28-13.

There are a number of steps involved in deploying your application, but they really are quite simple. After you have been through the drill a few times, you will be impressed with how routine it becomes.

WebObjects applications let you quickly produce and manage high-quality and powerful Web sites for applications large and small. The WebObjects origins in very large enterprises assure you that it is unlikely your needs will outpace the capabilities of WebObjects. At the same time, the ease of developing and deploying WebObjects applications now makes them feasible for even very small applications.

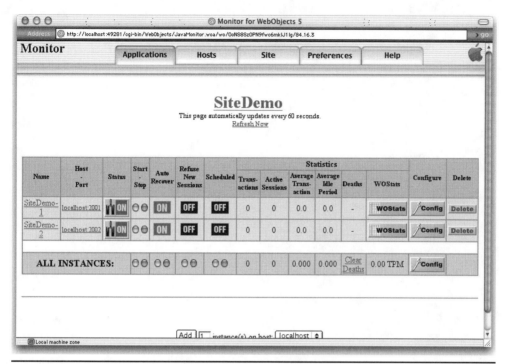

Figure 28-12   *Application instance view with running instances*

Figure 28-13   *WebObjects application is up and running*

Index

INTERNATIONAL CONTACT INFORMATION

AUSTRALIA
McGraw-Hill Book Company Australia Pty. Ltd.
TEL +61-2-9417-9899
FAX +61-2-9417-5687
http://www.mcgraw-hill.com.au
books-it_sydney@mcgraw-hill.com

CANADA
McGraw-Hill Ryerson Ltd.
TEL +905-430-5000
FAX +905-430-5020
http://www.mcgrawhill.ca

**GREECE, MIDDLE EAST,
NORTHERN AFRICA**
McGraw-Hill Hellas
TEL +30-1-656-0990-3-4
FAX +30-1-654-5525

MEXICO (Also serving Latin America)
McGraw-Hill Interamericana Editores S.A. de C.V.
TEL +525-117-1583
FAX +525-117-1589
http://www.mcgraw-hill.com.mx
fernando_castellanos@mcgraw-hill.com

SINGAPORE (Serving Asia)
McGraw-Hill Book Company
TEL +65-863-1580
FAX +65-862-3354
http://www.mcgraw-hill.com.sg
mghasia@mcgraw-hill.com

SOUTH AFRICA
McGraw-Hill South Africa
TEL +27-11-622-7512
FAX +27-11-622-9045
robyn_swanepoel@mcgraw-hill.com

**UNITED KINGDOM & EUROPE
(Excluding Southern Europe)**
McGraw-Hill Education Europe
TEL +44-1-628-502500
FAX +44-1-628-770224
http://www.mcgraw-hill.co.uk
computing_neurope@mcgraw-hill.com

ALL OTHER INQUIRIES Contact:
Osborne/McGraw-Hill
TEL +1-510-549-6600
FAX +1-510-883-7600
http://www.osborne.com
omg_international@mcgraw-hill.com